UNJUST
SEIZURE

CONFLICT, INTEREST,

AND AUTHORITY IN AN

EARLY MEDIEVAL SOCIETY

UNJUST
SEIZURE

WARREN BROWN

Cornell University Press

Ithaca and London

First published 2001 by Cornell University Press

Printed in the United States of America

Library of Congress Cataloging-in-Publication Data

Brown, Warren, 1963–
    Unjust seizure : conflict, interest, and authority in an early medieval society / by Warren Brown.
        p. cm. — (Conjunctions of religion & power in the medieval past)
    Includes bibliographical references and index.
    ISBN 0-8014-3790-3
    1. Carolingians. 2. Property—Europe—History. 3. Bavaria (Germany)—History—To 1180. 4. Power (Social sciences)—Europe—History. 5. Europe—Social conditions—To 1492. 6. Germany—Religious life and customs. 7. Germany—History—Saxon House, 919–1024. 8. Privileges and immunities—Europe—History. 9. Civilization, Medieval. I. Title. II. Series.
    DD130 .B76 2001
    940.1—dc21

                                                            00-011427

Cornell University Press strives to use environmentally responsible suppliers and materials to the fullest extent possible in the publishing of its books. Such materials include vegetable-based, low-VOC inks and acid-free papers that are recycled, totally chlorine-free, or partly composed of nonwood fibers. Books that bear the logo of the FSC (Forest Stewardship Council) use paper taken from forests that have been inspected and certified as meeting the highest standards for environmental and social responsibility. For further information, visit our website at www.cornellpress.cornell.edu.

Cloth printing   10 9 8 7 6 5 4 3 2 1

to Louise

CONTENTS

MAPS

PREFACE

This is a book about how political power functions on the ground in a society that lacks the coercive resources available to the modern state. It takes up the questions whether, how, and why people in such a society pay attention when institutions set up by a central authority claim the right to intervene in affairs. It looks in particular at what happens when one authority is replaced by another, in other words, how people react to new central institutions and on what the success or failure of those institutions depends.

I have chosen to concentrate on disputing as a point where authority and social processes meet. I am assuming that how people resolve their inevitable conflicts—whether they seek out an official forum vested with judicial powers, informally settle conflicts by negotiation or mediation, or resort to violence—has a great deal to say about how much a central authority and its institutions matter. Equally significant are the ways people record and represent disputes, that is, what information they choose to include when they describe conflict and what norms they invoke to justify their actions. As a glance at any modern newspaper shows, the struggle for control over image, representation, and moral high ground forms a crucial part of carrying on a dispute. The role that central authority plays in this struggle reflects its importance to disputants.

The early Middle Ages—specifically, the eighth and ninth centuries—provide fertile ground for such an investigation. This was a period in the history of Europe when rulers had a notoriously difficult time exercising central power and hence when people could easily choose alternatives to central institutions. At the same time, however, it saw the first serious attempt since the decline of Rome to set up an effective centralized government on a European scale. By the eighth century, the kingdom of the Franks, which had taken over the leadership of western Europe in late antiquity, was itself coming unglued. The ruling Merovingian dynasty, crippled by a series of child kings and by aristocratic competition, was gradually undermined and finally replaced in midcentury by a new family, the Carolingians. Once in power, the Carolingians consolidated and expanded their authority by eliminating their aristocratic rivals and reconquering outlying territories that had escaped Frankish control. This process culminated in the career of the greatest member of the Carolingian house, Charles the Great, or as he is more commonly known today, Charlemagne. During the last decades of the eighth century and the first decades of the ninth, Charlemagne expanded the Frankish kingdom until it stretched from the Atlantic Ocean to the river Elbe and from the Mediterranean to the North Sea. To knit the kingdom together, he tried to develop a set of administrative and judicial mechanisms that would uphold royal authority and interests across this vast area.

It is a particularly dramatic part of Charlemagne's efforts to absorb and rule new territory that has led me to my specific focus: the Duchy of Bavaria. Early medieval Bavaria, covering what is now southern Bavaria and western Austria, had by the second half of the eighth century a long history and a visible sense of itself as a political entity. It had developed in late antiquity from the fusion of Germanic migrant groups with the remnants of a romanized population. Under a line of dukes imposed on it by the Merovingian kings, it had come to form an eastern outpost of the Frankish realm. In the confusion that accompanied the rise of the Carolingians, however, the Bavarian dukes broke away from the Franks. By the early eighth century, they had established Bavaria as an essentially independent duchy, which they governed in tandem with the Bavarian aristocracy and with the principal institutional holdover from the Roman world, the Roman Church.

In the year 787, Charlemagne conquered Bavaria. Over the next few years, he removed the Bavarian ducal house from power and integrated the duchy into his kingdom. Charlemagne's conquest of Bavaria thus provides an opportunity to study the conscious and direct imposition of a new set of institutions, authority figures, and resources for handling disputes onto a geographically defined area. It allows us in particular to see how this imposition affected the ways Bavarians handled disputes and thus how well Charlemagne's attempt to create a lasting institutional structure in the region succeeded.

The disputes I look at here concern primarily (but not exclusively) property rights, especially the landed property rights of churches and monasteries. Church property plays such an important role for two reasons. First, since property formed the basis of economic and political power in the early Middle Ages, people frequently fought over it. Second, ecclesiastical property records form the bulk of the available evidence. Documents recording church and monastic property rights, including the outcome of property disputes, have tended to survive the early Middle Ages, whereas other kinds of records have not. They have endured above all because many early medieval monasteries and churches remained in being beyond the Middle Ages, and because monks and churchmen have had an ongoing interest in keeping track of their property holdings.

I have chosen to title this book *Unjust Seizure* in part because the vast majority of the conflicts I examine involve just that: allegations by a church that someone else had unjustly seized its property. The title also has a much broader significance. One of the major themes of this work is that the introduction of a new authority in Bavaria at the end of the eighth century changed what it meant for Bavarian landowners both to hold property and to hold it justly or unjustly. In other words, the very charge *unjustly seized* acquired a new set of possible meanings and a new set of uses in the wake of the Frankish conquest. Part of my purpose, therefore, is to follow the ways people wielded this charge and others as they maneuvered within the web of interest and authority, of strategies and representations, which came together in individual conflicts.

Our task, therefore, is to explore the effect of Charlemagne's conquest of Bavaria on property disputes involving churches and monasteries in order to see whether or not the authorities and institutions the conquest brought with it had any impact on the ground. Put more simply, we will look at whether or not Bavarians, in their conflicts over property, paid any attention to the "new sheriff in town" and the new political order he brought with him, and if so, why and for how long.

Twelve hundred years after Charlemagne cut the last links between Bavaria and its former dukes, in 1994, Patrick J. Geary casually mentioned to his UCLA graduate seminar on medieval conflict resolution that there were some early Bavarian charter collections with lots of disputes in them that needed to be studied. In the long process of taking his hint, I have been helped and supported by a great many people. First and foremost, I want to thank Professor Geary himself, who as my dissertation adviser helped me shape an idea into a project and whose guidance and mentoring over the years have been of incalculable professional and personal value. I also owe a great deal to Carlo Ginzburg, Ronald Mellor, Joseph F. Nagy, and David Sabean, who during my time at UCLA freely gave me the benefit of their opinions and advice and strongly influenced my intellectual development. In addition, I want to acknowledge, with the greatest respect, the late Robert L. Benson. Professor Benson died before he could read the fruits of my research, but his impact on my work continues to unfold.

Gerd Althoff, now of the University of Münster, devoted a great deal of time to me and my work during my research stay at the University of Bonn in the academic year 1995–96, a stay that was generously supported by the German Academic Exchange Service (D.A.A.D.). I must also express my gratitude to the members of Professor Althoff's graduate colloquium in Bonn that year. The opportunity to discuss my work both formally and informally with this group of scholars, especially Claudia Beinhoff, Christian Hillen, and Caspar Ehlers, turned out to be enormously important. The staff at the Bayerisches Hauptstaatsarchiv in Munich deserves my thanks for allowing me to look at Cozroh's collection of the Freising charters, as do Wilhelm Störmer, for taking time to discuss the charters with me, and Stephan Weinfurter, for inviting me to talk about my research at a meeting of his graduate seminar at the University of Munich. My time in Germany was made even more fruitful by Hanna Vollrath, who not only discussed my ideas about authority and self-interest with me over a lovely lunch in Heidelberg but has since given me both encouragement and healthy criticisms of some of my source readings.

Research became a manuscript thanks to a dissertation-writing fellowship provided me by the Department of History at UCLA. Along the way to turning the manuscript into a book, I have enjoyed the interest in my work, the advice, and the help with scholarship in other disciplines offered by my colleagues at Caltech, especially William Deverell, Philip T. Hoffman, and D. Roderick Kiewiet. I would also like to acknowledge the participants in the University of California Medieval History Seminar, held at the Huntington Library, who on two occasions read pieces of my manuscript and provided me with questions and comments. Piotr Górecki and Philippe Buc in particular not only commented on my work at the seminar meetings but also generously devoted time to reading larger segments of it and offering thorough and well-grounded critiques. Special thanks in this regard also go to my colleagues in the early medieval study group that grew out of the seminar during the academic year 1998–99: Hans Joseph Hummer, Jason Glenn, and Eric J. Goldberg. In a series of weekly meetings with them to share work in progress, I not only learned where my work was good and where it needed rethinking but also deepened one friendship and developed two new ones.

Barbara H. Rosenwein and the second anonymous reader for Cornell University Press have earned my gratitude for the repeated and close readings they have given to drafts of this book and for the time generously spent providing me with pages of detailed criticisms and suggestions for improvement. Together they helped me understand how to tell my story. Likewise I thank John G. Ackerman of Cornell University Press, who took time out from a vacation to edit parts of the manuscript and offer suggestions for making it clearer. Carolyn Patterson and Wayne Waller at the Caltech Digital Media Center did yeoman service helping me produce the maps. Finally, I thank my wife, Louise, who has patiently borne the long gestation process. To her the book is dedicated.

WARREN BROWN

Pasadena, California

ABBREVIATIONS

AQ   *Ausgewählte Quellen zur deutschen Geschichte des Mittelalters.* Freiherr vom Stein—Gedächtnisausgabe.

ARF   *Annales Regni Francorum,* ed. Reinhold Rau, *Quellen zur karolingischen Reichsgeschichte* 1, *AQ* V, 1–155.

BN   *Breves Notitiae,* in "*Notitia Arnonis* und *Breves Notitiae.* Die Salzburger Güterverzeichnisse aus der Zeit um 800: Sprachhistorische Einleitung, Text und Übersetzung," ed. Fritz Lošek, *MGSL* 130 (1990): 5–193.

HbG   Max Spindler, ed., *Handbuch der bayerischen Geschichte,* 2d ed., 1 (Munich, 1981).

HdR   A. Erler and E. Kaufmann, eds., *Handwörterbuch zur deutschen Rechtsgeschichte,* 5 vols. (Berlin, 1964–98).

Lex B   *Lex Baiwariorum,* ed. Ernst von Schwind, *MGH LL* 5, 2 (Hannover, 1926).

MGH   *Monumenta Germaniae Historica.*

           Capit   *Capitularia regum Francorum*
           Conc   *Concilia aevi Karolini*
           D Karol   *Diplomata Karolinorum*
           DrG Karol   *Diplomata regum Germaniae ex stirpe Karolinorum*
           LL   *Leges nationum Germanicarum*
           Poet   *Poetae aevi Karolini*
           SSrerMerov   *Scriptores rerum Merovingicarum*

MGSL   *Mitteilungen der Gesellschaft für Salzburger Landeskunde.*

MIÖG   *Mitteilungen des Instituts für Österreichische Geschichtsforschung.*

NA   *Notitia Arnonis,* in Lošek, *Notitia Arnonis* und *Breves Notitiae* (as above).

NCMH   Rosamond McKitterick, ed., *The New Cambridge Medieval History,* vol. 2, *c. 700–c. 900* (Cambridge, 1995).

Niermeyer   Jan Frederick Niermeyer, *Mediae Latinitatis Lexicon Minus* (Leiden, 1954–76).

TF   *Die Traditionen des Hochstifts Freising,* 2 vols., ed. Theodor Bitterauf (Munich, 1905).

TM   *Das älteste Traditionsbuch des Klosters Mondsee*, ed. Gebhard Rath
            and Erich Reiter (Linz, 1989).
TP   *Die Traditionen des Hochstifts Passau*, ed. Max Heuwieser (Munich,
            1930).
TR   *Die Traditionen des Hochstifts Regensburg und des Klosters S. Em-
            meram*, ed. Josef Widemann (Munich, 1943).

UNJUST
SEIZURE

INTRODUCTION

I n the year 834, a cleric at the cathedral church in the northwest Bavarian town of Freising, or at the nearby monastery of
Weihenstephan, wrote a poem. Titled *The Song of Count
Timo*, the poem addresses itself to the Frankish king Louis, later nicknamed
"the German," grandson of Charlemagne.[1] The poem begins as a hymn of
praise to Louis. Its unknown author did not honor the king directly, however; instead, he praised the deeds of his local representative, Count Timo.
The count appears first of all as the local source of royal justice:[2]

> Timo, your count and legate, glorious king,
> rendering justice to the good, and rightly punishing the evil,
> in Bavaria,[3] a little field in the kingdom in which it lies,
> he restored the neglected work of law.
> Hated by thieves and detested by robbers,
> he abhorred conflicts and extended justice.

1. *Carmen de Timone comite*, ed. E. Dümmler, *MGH Poet* I, 2 (Berlin, 1884),
120–24. The poem survives in an eleventh-century copy. The first four lines are
fragmentary; a note in the margin of the copy reads, "The beginning of these verses
was not lost through negligence or laziness but rather obscured by old age in the
scroll composed in ancient times, from which they are here transcribed." The poem
was most likely written on the occasion of a visit by King Louis to Freising/Weihen-
stephan; see Max Manitius, *Geschichte der lateinischen Literatur des Mittelalters*, vol. 1
(Munich, 1911), 598–99; Jakob Brummer, "Das Carmen de Timone comite," *Historische Vierteljahrschrift* 18 (1916/18): 104–5 (for a precise dating to 834); Wilhelm
Störmer, *Früher Adel: Studien zur politischen Führungsschicht im fränkisch-deutschen
Reich vom 8. bis 11. Jahrhundert*, vol. 2 (Stuttgart, 1973), 417–18, 500–502; Josef Maß,
Das Bistum Freising im Mittelalter (Munich, 1986), 79–80.

2. I thank Courtney Booker and Carl I. Hammer for sharing their translations of
the *Carmen* with me and for allowing me to compare mine with them.

3. *Noricus*, from the Roman province of Noricum, which early medieval Bavaria
partly overlapped. See the outline of early Bavarian history later in the chapter.

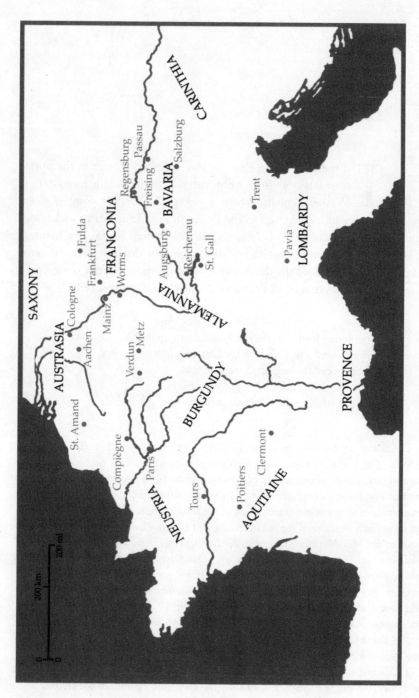

MAP 1. EUROPE IN THE EIGHTH AND NINTH CENTURIES

He knew that these things please you, most dignified king,
he therefore carried out his duties to you in a worthy fashion.
Believe me, the royal concern is to thwart criminal things,
and to lift the heavy yoke from the necks of the innocent.
Indeed, the entire royal duty is to secure the peace,
and to guide the kingdom's separate dominions with his hand.[4]

After going on to compare King Louis to the great biblical justice-bringers, such as David, Job, and Moses, the poem returns to Count Timo. It describes in detail how the count held his court on the heights at Weihenstephan:

Therefore, when the count arrives, he orders that thieves be hanged,
and that the cheeks of robbers be forever branded.
That criminals be disgracefully maimed by having their noses cut off;
this one loses a foot, and that one loses a hand.[5]

At this point, however, the poem takes a surprisingly critical tack. It represents Count Timo as also presiding over the judicial ordeal and judicial combat. In the former, the effects of various kinds of torture, such as carrying a hot iron or immersion in boiling water, reflected God's judgment of a person's guilt or innocence. In the latter, the two parties to a dispute, or their champions, fought in order to let God reveal the right by granting or withholding victory. The tumult of judicial combat in particular fills the air at Timo's court, combat that vindicates one while sending the other down in defeat:

Iron fights with iron, shield with shield,
Lead with lead, and stock with stock.
Fire, water seek hidden crimes in vain,
True reason proves them to be entirely futile.[6]

Our poet viewed these practices with indignation. In the following lines, he embarks on a lengthy diatribe against them as blasphemous attempts to command information from God and as contrary to reason. If these techniques could answer judicial questions, he declares, "reason would not be required, wisdom would not be necessary."[7]

4. *Carmen*, lines 5–16.
5. Ibid., lines 65–68.
6. Ibid., lines 71–74.
7. Ibid., line 77. On the ordeal and judicial combat, see Robert Bartlett, *Trial by Fire and Water: The Medieval Judicial Ordeal* (Oxford, 1986). On p. 73, Bartlett discusses

The poem next moves into a story that similarly undermines the praise it had lavished on Count Timo at the beginning. It tells of a holy spring on the heights at Weihenstephan which the first Bishop of Freising, Saint Corbinian, had called forth. Many sick people had found healing at this spring. When greedy men tried to sell it for their own profit, however, it dried up. Desperate to restore the spring, the clergy and people of Freising brought Saint Corbinian's staff from the cathedral church. They walked with it in solemn procession up the hill to Weihenstephan and induced the holy water to flow again. Count Timo then made a fatal mistake. While holding his court on the heights, he let his favorite dog drink from the spring. God reacted to the blasphemy swiftly:

> From that on which man thrives, the dog died.
> Tell, dog, who persuaded you to lap from the cup of life,
> who persuaded you to honor the holy waters with filth?[8]

Here the poem ends. It clearly sends us a double-edged message. On the one hand, it praises King Louis as the ultimate source of justice and order in Bavaria. The king exercised his authority through his representative, Count Timo. Any ninth-century readers of the poem would have had no problem identifying Timo. His name alone marked him as a descendant of an ancient Bavarian aristocratic kindred.[9] This Bavarian aristocrat performed his duties as the king's representative by holding judicial assemblies, at which he judged and punished criminals and directed the settling of disputes. In short, *The Song of Count Timo* exalts royal authority by describing how it flowed through a local representative who carried out the royal task of guaranteeing peace and order at the local level.

On the other hand, the poem criticizes how the count carried out this task. It also takes aim in a larger sense at his relationship and that of the authority he represented to the divine authority. The poet takes a firm stance in favor of the latter by calling the count's use of the ordeal and judicial combat blasphemous. He takes his critique one step further with the story of the holy spring and the death of Timo's dog. This story in fact gives an

---

the parallels and possible connections between the *Carmen* poet's critique of the ordeal/duel and the well-known critique by Archbishop Agobard of Lyon (816–40); see also Brummer, "Carmen," 103–4.

8. *Carmen*, lines 148–50.

9. Joachim Jahn, *Ducatus Baiuvariorum: Das bairische Herzogtum der Agilolfinger* (Stuttgart, 1991), 310–13; Störmer, *Früher Adel*, 2:419.

unmistakable warning: the representatives of the secular authority should respect the sanctity of the holy or suffer the consequences.

In its journey from King Louis to Count Timo's dog, *The Song of Count Timo* addresses in miniature the subject of this book: the relationship between royal authority and local social processes in the early Middle Ages as seen through the lens of dispute. Indeed, the poem focuses its attention squarely on dispute as an arena where authority and local processes come together. It addresses a Carolingian king, the embodiment of an empire that in 834 still claimed to exercise authority over most of Europe. It depicts the king as acting on disputes at the local level through judicial assemblies held by his representative the count. It raises questions about the assemblies' legitimacy and effectiveness, however, by presenting Count Timo's methods as potentially unjust and untrustworthy. It also questions the count's relationship to a competing authority, namely that wielded by God through his Church.

THE PLOT

In order to explore properly the questions raised by *The Song of Count Timo*, we need to see dispute resolution as a process that can include more than just formal adjudication according to prescriptive rules. In other words, a study of central authority's impact on the ground has to include not only the laws and court procedures that such authority claimed to maintain but also alternatives such as negotiation, mediation, and even violence.

Recent studies by social and legal anthropologists of conflict in modern societies, both those with formal judicial systems and those that westerners might call "stateless," have suggested that authority can mix with this wider world of disputing in different ways.[10] Many non-Western societies do not

10. See Simon Roberts, *Order and Dispute: An Introduction to Legal Anthropology* (London, 1979), and "The Study of Dispute: Anthropological Perspectives," in *Disputes and Settlements: Law and Human Relations in the West*, ed. John Bossy (Cambridge, 1983), 1–24. British and North American lawyers and legal anthropologists in particular are intensively studying disputing processes and their relationship to central authority, in reaction to growing public and governmental interest in so-called Alternative Dispute Resolution. See *Modern Law Review* 56, no. 3 (1993), a special issue titled "Dispute Resolution: Civil Justice and Its Alternatives"; Richard L. Abel, "A Comparative Theory of Dispute Institutions in Society," *Law and Society Review* 8 (winter 1973): 217–347; Marc Galanter, "Reading the Landscape of Disputes: What We Know and Don't Know (and Think We Know) about Our Allegedly Contentious and Litigious Society," *UCLA Law Review* 31, no. 4 (1983): 4–71.

have centralized mechanisms for handling disputes. These groups nevertheless manage to maintain a stable social and political order. Conflict carried
out according to commonly understood norms contributes to this order by
providing a way to effect social or political change or to adjust relationships
between individuals or kindreds. Even violent feuds, frequently seen as a
hallmark of anarchy, can provide a framework of rules that furthers stability
rather than chaos.[11] In societies that do claim to govern themselves by
means of central mechanisms, judicial institutions interact symbiotically
with extrajudicial ways of disputing. Courts and laws do not absolutely determine what people do but rather serve as resources that people can choose
to use or not depending on where their interests lie. The power such institutions have over disputes rests on their usefulness to disputants, as well as
on disputants' skill in manipulating the system to their own advantage. The
role played by judicial institutions also depends on the quality of the relationships connecting the disputants to each other and to the people man-
ning the institutions. A court system and its rules might dominate a dispute
in which the parties and the court officials had no ties to each other beyond
the matter at issue. The system might play little or no role, however, or
serve only to legitimize a settlement reached by different means, in a case in
which the parties and the officials were connected personally or politically
or had some other kind of ongoing relationship.[12]

When rules and institutions change, the reaction on the ground can be
quite complicated. Here recent studies of conquest and colonization provide a set of useful tools. In the last several decades, scholars in fields as diverse as history, anthropology, sociology, and political science have reevalu-
ated relationships between conquerors and conquered in places ranging
from Europe to America, Africa, and the Orient.[13] Rather than assume a

11. M. Gluckman, "The Peace in the Feud," *Past and Present* 7 (1955): 1–14, and
Custom and Conflict in Africa (Oxford, 1959); Jacob Black-Michaud, *Cohesive Force:
Feud in the Mediterranean and the Middle East* (Oxford, 1975).

12. See esp. John L. Comaroff and Simon Roberts, *Rules and Processes: The Cultural Logic of Dispute in an African Context* (Chicago, 1981).

13. Among the historians, see inter alia Robert Bartlett, *The Making of Europe:
Conquest, Colonization, and Cultural Change, 950–1350* (Princeton, 1993); Patrick J.
Geary, *Before France and Germany: The Creation and Transformation of the Merovingian
World* (New York, 1988); Erich Gruen, *The Hellenistic World and the Coming of Rome*,
2 vols. (Berkeley, 1988); S. R. F. Price, *Rituals and Power: The Roman Imperial Cult in
Asia Minor* (Cambridge, 1984); David J. Langum, *Law and Community on the Mexican
California Frontier: Anglo-American Expatriates and the Clash of Legal Traditions,
1821–1846* (Norman, Okla., 1987); John P. Reid, *Law for the Elephant: Property and
Social Behavior on the Overland Trail* (San Marino, Calif., 1980) and *Policing the Ele-*

fundamental antithesis between conquerors and conquered, this body of scholarship suggests that the two groups respond to each other in complex ways.[14] Faced with the imposition of a new authority, some people resist. Others take advantage of the new authority and turn it to their own purposes. How people react is shaped in part by how the conquest has changed the landscape of possibilities and incentives. In other words, the presence of the conquering authority and its institutions creates new options and opportunities. These options and opportunities influence the people who interact directly with the new authority; their behavior in turn affects others.[15] The responses of various groups among the conquered can in turn affect the conquerors as they try to fit their forms of organization and their purposes to a new and constantly changing environment. In short, conquered peoples do not simply conform or resist but rather participate as active and often interested agents in a process of conquest and transformation that they do a great deal to influence.

Simply transferring the results of such work to the study of the early medieval past has its dangers. Early medieval Europe was very unlike many modern societies. For example, it had a complex, hierarchical social structure; people at one level could behave in one way to one another but in quite another way to those at a different level.[16] Moreover, as we shall see, it possessed a powerful institutional religion with its own set of rules and interests that strongly affected the social and political landscape. Although the

---

phant: *Crime, Punishment, and Social Behavior on the Overland Trail* (San Marino, Calif., 1997).

14. See the work of the anthropologist Eric R. Wolf, esp. *Europe and the People without History* (Berkeley, 1997) and "Distinguished Lecture: Facing Power—Old Insights, New Questions," *American Anthropologist* 92, no. 3 (1990): 586–96; Jane Schneider and Rayna Rapp, eds., *Articulating Hidden Histories: Exploring the Influence of Eric R. Wolf* (Berkeley, 1995); William F. S. Miles, *Hausaland Divided: Colonialism and Independence in Nigeria and Niger* (Ithaca, N.Y., 1994).

15. This idea has been most clearly articulated in the historically grounded works of the "new institutionalist" school of political science. See, for example, Robert H. Bates, *Essays on the Political Economy of Rural Africa* (Berkeley, 1987); Kathryn Firmin-Sellers, "Institutions, Context, and Outcomes: Explaining French and British Rule in West Africa," *Comparative Politics* 32, no. 3 (2000): 253–72; Miles, *Hausaland Divided*.

16. Stephen D. White, "Feuding and Peace-Making in the Touraine around the Year 1000," *Traditio* 42 (1986): 260, observes that medieval society differed from the egalitarian ones usually posited by anthropologists for "peace in the feud" in that it was highly stratified; feuding was routinely directed at peasants rather than at lords, often with highly destructive effect.

scholarship just discussed does not, therefore, hand us a ready-made set of answers, it nevertheless offers a set of ideas that has ignited new debates about conflict and the exercise of power in the Middle Ages.[17]

Two of these debates provide the immediate backdrop for this book. The first concerns the nature of the Carolingian regime, its effectiveness, and the speed of its demise, particularly in the regions west of the Rhine.[18] One view holds that the early Carolingian rulers, especially Charlemagne, took the practices of their Merovingian predecessors and molded them into effective public institutions of government and justice. Counts appointed by the king resolved disputes in the localities at regularly held assemblies called public *malli* (sing. *mallus*) or *placita* (sing. *placitum*). The king communicated his will to the counts by compiling or revising regional law codes for them to refer to and by issuing legislation in the form of capitularies—written directives organized into discrete headings or *capitula*. He also sent out royal agents, called *missi* (sing. *missus*), on a regular basis. These agents, who were drawn from both the secular aristocracy and the church, checked up on the behavior of the counts and other officials, distributed new legislation or instructions, and served as a point of appeal for disputes.[19]

These institutions survived Charlemagne's death in 814 and continued to function throughout much of the ninth century. They were gradually undermined, however, by the weakness of Charlemagne's successors—his son Louis the Pious, his grandsons Lothar, Louis the German, and Charles the Bald, and their descendants. The civil wars that led Charlemagne's grandsons to divide the empire in 843 forced particularly the western king,

17. The most important works in this context are *The Settlement of Disputes in Early Medieval Europe*, ed. Wendy Davies and Paul Fouracre (Cambridge, 1986); *Disputes and Settlements*, ed. Bossy; Eleanor Searle, *Predatory Kinship and the Creation of Norman Power, 840–1066* (Berkeley, 1988); Emily Zack Tabuteau, *Transfers of Property in Eleventh-Century Norman Law* (Chapel Hill, N.C., 1988); Chris Wickham, *Early Medieval Italy: Central Power and Local Society, 400–1000* (Ann Arbor, Mich., 1989).

18. For an introduction to the Carolingians and the development of the Carolingian state, see *NCMH*; Roger Collins, *Charlemagne* (Toronto, 1998); Heinrich Fichtenau, *The Carolingian Empire*, trans. Peter Munz (Toronto, 1978); Rosamond McKitterick, *The Frankish Kingdoms under the Carolingians, 751–987* (London, 1983); Pierre Riché, *The Carolingians: A Family Who Forged Europe*, trans. Michael Idomir Allen (Philadelphia, 1993).

19. On the Carolingian *missi*, see Karl Ferdinand Werner, "*Missus-marchio-comes*: Entre l'administration centrale et l'administration locale de l'empire carolingien," in *Histoire comparée de l'administration*, ed. W. Paravicini and K. F. Werner, *Beiheft der Francia* 9 (Munich, 1980), 191–239; McKitterick, *Frankish Kingdoms*, 93–97.

Charles the Bald, to cede royal powers to the aristocracy in exchange for support. The Carolingian decline in the West accelerated in the tenth century, driven by competition between and among the kings and great magnates and by the catastrophic invasions of the Vikings and others. By the turn of the first millennium, the Carolingians had been replaced as kings of the West Franks by the Capetians, and Carolingian institutions in what would become France had collapsed. In their place rose highly personal lordships based solely on military power. Formal judicial assemblies no longer regulated disputes. Members of the local and regional aristocracies instead resolved conflicts either by compromises balancing the power and interests of the parties involved or by fighting. In its most radical form, this argument posits a "feudal revolution"; in the decades immediately surrounding the year 1000, warrior aristocrats based in castles swept away the remains of the Carolingian state and seized power in their immediate areas by naked force.[20]

This narrative of the Carolingian decline and fall in the West has been challenged over the last several decades, especially by scholars from England and the United States. Relying heavily on dispute studies, these scholars have questioned how effective Carolingian institutions actually were and how fast they collapsed.[21] To begin with, they argue that under Charlemagne and his immediate successors, institutions and rules interacted flexibly with

20. A good summary of this tradition can be found in Janet L. Nelson, "Dispute Settlement in Carolingian West Francia," *Settlement of Disputes*, ed. Davies and Fouracre, 46–47; it derives ultimately from the institutional view of Carolingian government represented by Heinrich Brunner, *Deutsche Rechtsgeschichte*, vol. 1 (Leipzig, 1887) and vol. 2, ed. Claudius Freiherr von Schweren, 2d ed. (Berlin, 1928), and esp. François Louis Ganshof, *Frankish Institutions under Charlemagne* trans. Bryce Lyon and Mary Lyon (Providence, R.I., 1968). The "feudal revolution" or "mutationist" position originated with Georges Duby; see *La société aux XIe et XIIe siècles dans la région mâconnaise* (Paris, 1953) and "The Evolution of Judicial Institutions," in *The Chivalrous Society*, trans. Cynthia Postan (Berkeley, 1980), 15–58. It finds its most forceful articulation in Jean-Pierre Poly and Eric Bournazel, *La mutation féodale Xe–XIIe siècles*, 2d ed. (Paris, 1991).

21. For an excellent introduction to this side of the debate, see Patrick J. Geary, "Living with Conflicts in Stateless France: A Typology of Conflict Management Mechanisms," in *Living with the Dead in the Middle Ages* (Ithaca, N.Y., 1994), 126–29, as well as the contributions to *Settlement of Disputes*, ed. Davies and Fouracre. The debate has recently been carried out vociferously in the pages of *Past and Present*; see Thomas N. Bisson, "The 'Feudal Revolution,'" *Past and Present* 142 (1994): 6–42; "Debate: The 'Feudal Revolution.' Comment 1: Dominique Barthélemy; Comment 2: Stephen D. White," *Past and Present* 152 (1996): 196–223; "Comment 3: Timothy

social processes and relationships. Charlemagne himself depended as heavily on the cooperation of the aristocracy to make his authority felt as his successors did. He had to induce the magnates to participate in his regime with grants of lands, favors, or offices and with access to the spoils of war. In individual disputes, kinship, social ties, and self-interest determined what happened as much as laws and legislation; negotiation and compromise or even the use of physical force (or spiritual force in the case of monks or clerics) contributed as much to social order as courts and judicial procedures. Within these limitations, the Carolingian kings in the West continued to rule effectively well after Charlemagne's death. Louis the Pious and Charles the Bald, for example, did as good a job of upholding royal power in their kingdoms as their immediate circumstances allowed.[22]

The Anglo-American dispute scholarship has also questioned the picture of violent anarchy that frequently characterizes discussions of early France. In the tenth and eleventh centuries, relationships of power, kinship, and self-interest among disputants and authority holders contributed to social and political order in much the same way they did in the ninth century. Even violent feuding, long viewed as a classic symptom of feudal lawlessness, acted more to balance honor and bring about negotiations than to achieve outright military victory.[23] These conclusions suggest that the disappearance in the West of the Carolingian state and its institutional structures took place gradually rather than abruptly, against a background of social processes that display continuity as well as change.

A second and similar debate concerns not the West but the East. German scholars have long sought to understand exactly why the East Frankish/German kingdom of the tenth and succeeding centuries maintained traditions of strong central government as the Romance West fell into political disarray. In an effort to shed new light on this question, a group of German medievalists has turned away from the traditional German preoc-

---

Reuter, Comment 4: Chris Wickham, Reply: Thomas N. Bisson," *Past and Present* 155 (1997): 177–225.

22. See *Charlemagne's Heir: New Perspectives on the Reign of Louis the Pious*, ed. Peter Godman and Roger Collins (Oxford, 1990); Janet L. Nelson, *Charles the Bald* (London, 1992). For the ongoing debate about Louis the Pious in particular, see the literature cited in Chapter 5, n. 4.

23. Geary, "Living with Conflicts," in *Living with the Dead*, and *Phantoms of Remembrance: Memory and Oblivion at the End of the First Millennium* (Princeton, 1994), 23–24; Stephen D. White, "*Pactum . . . legem vincit et amor judicium*: The Settlement of Disputes by Compromise in Eleventh-Century Western France," *American Journal of Legal History* 22 (1978): 281–308, and "Feuding and Peace-Making."

cupation with political institutions and institutional ideas (such as the "imperial church system" or neo-Roman ideologies of empire) in favor of research into other kinds of processes that promote social and political stability. Their work has uncovered an effective political order among the kings/emperors and great nobles of what became Germany, maintained and buttressed not only by institutional traditions but also by ties of kinship and political friendship, by commonly understood rules for waging disputes, and by a common symbolic language for ritually expressing the results of negotiated settlements.[24]

This book aims to bring these two lines of inquiry together. I explore how the Carolingian regime worked in the eighth and ninth centuries by looking in detail at its impact on disputing practices in a newly conquered area and at how this impact changed over time. In other words, I ask how Carolingian authority and institutions affected local behavior in a region where they had not previously existed, rather than in areas where they had a long history. By bringing these questions east of the Rhine, I take up the issue whether Carolingian authority worked in the East in the same ways it did in the West, or whether these parts of the Carolingian world were somehow different. In addition, I examine disputing in the East Frankish world not at the very top of the political and social hierarchy but rather at the local and regional level. This helps me find out whether the mechanisms and processes that enabled kings to function in Germany in the tenth and succeeding centuries were new or whether they perhaps stemmed from a broader and more ancient aristocratic culture.

THE STAGE

Bavaria represents an ideal laboratory for such an investigation. Early medieval Bavaria was a geographically and politically distinct entity whose population, or at least that element of it that speaks through the sources, had a

---

24. See inter alia Karl Leyser, *Rule and Conflict in an Early Medieval Society: Ottonian Saxony* (London, 1979); Gerd Althoff, *Spielregeln der Politik im Mittelalter* (Darmstadt, 1997), and "*Ira regis*: Prolegomena to a History of Royal Anger," trans. Warren Brown, in *Anger's Past: The Social Uses of an Emotion in the Middle Ages*, ed. Barbara H. Rosenwein (Ithaca, N.Y., 1998), 59–74; Timothy Reuter, "Unruhestiftung, Fehde, Rebellion, Widerstand: Gewalt und Frieden in der Politik der Salierzeit," 296–325, and Hanna Vollrath, "Konfliktwahrnehmung und Konfliktdarstellung in erzählenden Quellen des 11. Jahrhunderts," 279–96, both in in *Die Salier und das Reich*, ed. Stefan Weinfurter, vol. 3 (Sigmaringen, 1991).

perceptible sense of group identity.[25] Bavaria lay close enough to the Frankish Empire to be within the Frankish orbit and to participate directly in the flow and ebb of Frankish imperial development. At the same time, it lay far enough away from the Frankish heartlands to experience the rapid Frankish expansion of the late eighth century as an imposition of authority from the outside.[26]

The Duchy of Bavaria covered a region bordered to the south by the Alps, to the west by the river Lech, to the north by the river Danube,[27] and to the east by a fluid frontier east of the river Enns which gradually moved farther eastward according to the fortunes of war. This area corresponds roughly to the southern part of the modern German state of Bavaria and the western two-thirds of modern Austria. In late antiquity, the region fell within the Roman provinces of Noricum and Raetia. The Romans maintained a military presence there until the 480s. Over the century or so after the Roman withdrawal, the romanized population merged with Germanic migrants from Alemannia to the west and Bohemia to the east. Under pressure from the Franks to the northwest and the Gothic kingdom to the south, this mixed population gradually fused into a society that called itself the Bavarians.

In the sixth century, a Bavarian ruling family emerges from the sources. The name of this family, the Agilolfings, presumably stemmed from an ancestor-hero named Agilulf. The sources variously describe the Agilolfings as Alemannian, Frankish, and Lombard. Modern scholarship currently views them as Franks placed in control of Bavaria by the Merovingian kings of the Franks, who absorbed Bavaria in the course of the century.[28] We do

25. On the history of early medieval Bavaria, see *HbG*; Collins, *Charlemagne*, 77–88; Herwig Wolfram, *Die Geburt Mitteleuropas: Geschichte Österreichs vor seiner Entstehung, 378–907* (Vienna, 1987).

26. Alemannia and Lombardy, which the Carolingians likewise took over after they had consolidated their hold on the West, would also provide potentially fertile ground for this kind of inquiry; see Michael Borgolte, *Geschichte der Grafschaften Alemanniens in Fränkischer Zeit* (Sigmaringen, 1984); Wickham, *Early Medieval Italy*, 47–63; Karl Schmid, "Zur Ablösung der Langobardenherrschaft durch die Franken," in *Gebetsdenken und adeliges Selbstverständnis im Mittelalter: Ausgewählte Beiträge* (Sigmaringen, 1983), 268–304.

27. At various points in its early history, Bavaria's northern border extended to include the so-called Nordgau, roughly corresponding to the modern Upper Palatinate.

28. The family nonetheless possessed strong kinship ties to the ruling houses of both Lombardy and Alemannia. See Karl Ferdinand Werner, "Important Noble Families in the Kingdom of Charlemagne," in *The Medieval Nobility: Studies on the Ruling Classes of France and Germany from the Sixth to the Twelfth Century*, ed. Timothy

not know for certain what title the Agilolfings originally bore. The sources from the sixth century call them kings, whereas later sources describe them as dukes. Whatever their original status, the decay of the Merovingian dynasty and the power struggles among the Frankish aristocracy that followed left the Agilolfings considerable freedom. By the beginning of the eighth century, they had emerged as a line of hereditary Bavarian rulers who, although by this point clearly dukes rather than kings, enjoyed quasi-royal powers and independence.

The position of the Agilolfing kindred as the sole legitimate Bavarian ruling house was enshrined in the Law of the Bavarians, a body of written law codified in the course of the eighth century.[29] The Law declared that only an Agilolfing could be duke and assigned members of the kindred a blood price four times that of ordinary free men. In addition, the Law recognized the right of five other kindreds, or *genealogiae*, to claim a blood price double that of the rest of the free population.[30] Below the level of the *genealogiae*, the sources tend to classify the population not by social status or occupation but rather by legal categories, particularly freedom versus unfreedom. Immediately below the *genealogiae* and frequently intermingling with them was a broader class of free landowners. The sources characterize its members above all by their power to own and freely dispose of property, both land and people. Modern scholarship loosely describes them as the Bavarian landowning aristocracy.[31] Bavarian society below the landowning aristocrats consisted of a mixed group of free and unfree who are often very difficult to distinguish from one another. These included the adalschalks, or "noble"

Reuter (Amsterdam, 1979), 161–62; Jörg Jarnut, *Agilolfingerstudien: Untersuchungen zur Geschichte einer adligen Familie im 6. und 7. Jahrhundert* (Stuttgart, 1986); Jahn, *Ducatus*, 9.

29. *Lex B*. Other editions: *Die Gesetze des Karolingerreiches, 714–911*, vol. 2, *Alemannen und Bayern*, ed. Karl August Eckhardt (Weimar, 1934); *Laws of the Alamans and Bavarians*, trans. Theodore John Rivers (Philadelphia, 1977). On the Bavarian Law and its development, see Wilfried Hartmann, "Das Recht," in *Die Bajuwaren von Severin bis Tassilo, 488–788*, ed. Hermann Dannheimer and Heinz Dopsch (Munich, 1988), esp. 266; *HdR*, s.v. "Lex Baiuvariorum," by Harald Siems; Gerhard Köbler, "Die Begründungen der Lex Baiwariorum," in *Studien zu den germanischen Volksrechten: Gedächtnisschrift für Wilhelm Ebel*, ed. Götz Landwehr (Frankfurt, 1982), 69–85; F. Brunhölzl, "Die lateinische Literatur," in *HbG*, 583.

30. *Lex B* C. III/1: the Huosi, the Fagana, the Draozza, the Hahilinga, and the Annonia.

31. See the more detailed discussion of the landowning aristocracy later and the literature cited in n. 64.

unfree, most likely followers of the dukes;[32] the *coloni*, farmers who were technically free but actually bound to the land they cultivated; the *servi*, unfree of varying wealth and status and equally difficult to define states of dependence; and the *mancipia*, unfree agricultural laborers who, like the *coloni*, remained bound to the property they worked.

The Agilolfing dukes displayed their independence of the Frankish kings in part by trying to set up a Bavarian church structure independent of Frankish authority in cooperation with the Roman popes. In 716, Duke Theodo (d. ca. 717/718) gained papal permission to create four Bavarian dioceses, which were to correspond with a planned four-part division of the duchy among his sons. The bishops of the new dioceses were to have their seats in the north at the ducal capital Regensburg; in the west at Freising, now a northern suburb of Munich; in the east at Passau, at the confluence of the Danube and the Inn; and in the south at Salzburg, now in northwestern Austria. The four-part division of Bavaria did not materialize; neither at first did the new dioceses. The dukes instead invited wandering saints from the west to come to Bavaria and act as bishops. They included Saint Rupert (Salzburg), Saint Emmeram (Regensburg), and Saint Corbinian (Freising). It took a mission to Bavaria by the Anglo-Saxon Saint Boniface to bring about the formal creation in 739 of the four dioceses originally planned by Theodo.

The greatest threat to Agilolfing independence lay in the expansionist ambitions of the new rulers of the Frankish West, the Carolingians. After consolidating their hold on power as mayors of the Merovingian palace, the early Carolingians, beginning with Charles Martel, sought to bring outlying regions of the Merovingian realm back under Frankish control. Duke Odilo of Bavaria (736–48), who as an Agilolfing represented an aristocratic family more ancient and prestigious than the Carolingians themselves, gradually emerged as the leader of a Europe-wide resistance to Carolingian pretensions. The struggle between the Agilolfings and the Carolingians defies one-dimensional description. Periods of détente alternated with active warfare. Odilo himself married the sister of the first Carolingian king of the Franks, Pippin III. Their son, Tassilo III, became duke on the death of his father in 749. Tassilo ruled at first under the regency of his mother and his Carolingian uncle. In 757, he took over the reins of the duchy after swearing an oath of fealty to King Pippin. Within a few years, however, Tassilo had

32. On the adalschalks and their successors the barschalks, some of whom were apparently descended from the Roman population of the region, see Jahn, *Ducatus*, 147 and 244–48.

taken up his father's mantle as the quasi-royal leader of an independent Bavaria. In 763, he and his Bavarian troops refused to fight alongside Pippin and a Carolingian army in Aquitaine. In the years that followed, Tassilo summoned church councils on his own authority and conducted an independent, expansionist foreign policy, especially on his eastern frontier. For just over two decades, Tassilo managed to achieve an essentially independent Bavarian duchy, ruled by himself as all but in name a king.[33]

Tassilo's relationship with the Bavarian aristocracy at this stage of his career remains controversial. A long-standing scholarly tradition maintains that the aristocracy in western Bavaria supported the Carolingians, forcing Tassilo to build his power base in the eastern half of the duchy. A more recently articulated view, however, sees the leading members of the western Bavarian aristocracy cooperating with their ruler right up to the point disaster struck.[34]

For disaster did strike.[35] King Pippin's son Charlemagne would not tolerate his Agilolfing cousin's pretensions. In the context of a larger Frankish expansion that brought with it the absorption of Lombardy and Saxony, tensions mounted between Charles and Tassilo. In 781, Charles forced Tassilo to come to Worms and renew his oath of homage. In 787, the Frankish king invaded Bavaria. Tassilo could not muster the support to mount effective resistance. On October 3, 787, he appeared at Charlemagne's camp near Augsburg and surrendered himself and his duchy; he received Bavaria back to hold as Charlemagne's vassal. Despite Tassilo's submission, Charles summoned the duke the next year to come to a great assembly at Ingelheim

33. See Herwig Wolfram, *Intitulatio*, vol. 1, *Lateinische Königs- und Fürstentitel bis zum Ende des 8. Jahrhunderts* (Vienna, 1967), 125–84, for a survey of Agilolfing charter titulature and in particular how it began to mimic Carolingian royal titulature as Tassilo reached the height of his power.

34. See Friedrich Prinz, "Herzog und Adel im Agilulfingischen Bayern: Herzogsgut und Konsensschenkungen vor 788," *Zeitschrift für bayerische Landesgeschichte* 25 (1962): 283–311; Andreas Kraus, "Zweiteilung des Herzogtums der Agilolfinger? Die Probe aufs Exempel," *Blätter für deutsche Landesgeschichte* 112 (1976): 16–29; Jahn, *Ducatus*, 494, 585.

35. The literature on the Carolingian takeover of Bavaria includes Jahn, *Ducatus*, esp. 522–50; Wolfram, *Geburt Mitteleuropas*, 100–106 and 187–92; Wolfram, "Tassilo III. und Karl der Große—Das Ende der Agilolfinger," in *Die Bajuwaren von Severin bis Tassilo*, ed. Dannheimer and Dopsch, 160–66; Johannes Fried, "Zum Prozeß gegen Tassilo," in *794—Karl der Große in Frankfurt am Main* (Sigmaringen, 1994), 113–15; Lothar Kolmer, "Zur Kommendation und Absetzung Tassilos III.," *Zeitschrift für bayerische Landesgeschichte* 43, no. 2 (1980): 291–327.

near Mainz. There he retroactively charged Tassilo with treason for abandoning King Pippin in 763 and commuted the resulting death sentence to banishment to a monastery.

A great many Bavarian aristocrats, whatever their previous alignment, dealt opportunistically with the new situation and smoothly accepted their new master. Charlemagne nonetheless had to overcome some resistance. The Frankish king remained personally in Bavaria from 791 to 793, the longest period of time he had stayed in any one place up to that point. In 794, he brought Tassilo out of monastic exile to a great assembly held at Frankfurt. There he forced Tassilo to renounce formally all Agilolfing ducal property on behalf of himself and his family.

Despite his forceful approach to Tassilo himself, Charles took care to respect Bavarian sensibilities. Although he abolished the ducal office, he installed a member of the Agilolfing house, Gerold, as his prefect in Bavaria.[36] In cooperation with Pope Leo III, Charles also raised a member of the Bavarian aristocracy to the highest position in the Bavarian church: in 798, Bishop Arn of Salzburg became archbishop and metropolitan of Bavaria.[37] Charles moreover permitted Bavaria to continue in existence as a territorial entity, and he allowed the Law of the Bavarians to remain in force, although he added two capitularies to it.[38]

After Charlemagne's death in 814, his sole surviving son, Louis the Pious, granted Bavaria to his own eldest son, Lothar, as a sub-kingdom within the Carolingian Empire. In 817, this position fell to one of Louis's younger sons, the still minor Louis the German. In 825, Louis the German reached his majority and began ruling actively as king of the Bavarians. In 829, a rebellion against Louis the Pious erupted which involved leading

36. Gerold is seen as a member of the Alemannian branch of the Agilolfings; through his mother, Imma, he was a great-great-nephew of Duke Odilo. See Werner, "Important Noble Families," in *Medieval Nobility*, ed. Reuter, 161–66; Michael Mitterauer, *Karolingische Markgrafen im Südosten: Fränkische Reichsaristokratie und bayerischer Stammesadel im österreichischen Raum* (Vienna, 1963), 8–25; Joachim Jahn, "Urkunde und Chronik: Ein Beitrag zur historischen Glaubwürdigkeit der Benediktbeurer Überlieferung und zur Geschichte des agilolfingischen Bayerns," *MIÖG* 95 (1987): 1–51, esp. 40.

37. See the detailed treatment of Arn of Salzburg in Chapter 3.

38. *MGH Capit* I, ed. Alfred Boretius (Hannover, 1883), 157–59. In addition to these two capitularies, a new clause appeared in the Bavarian Law sometime between 788 and 794 which mandated the deposition of a Bavarian duke who refused to obey royal orders: *Lex B* C. II/8a; Kolmer, "Zur Kommendation und Absetzung," 308–18; Jahn, *Ducatus*, 539 and n. 79.

Frankish magnates and Louis's three elder sons. The rebellion inaugurated a lengthy period of civil war within the empire. In 833, after the three elder sons of Louis the Pious defeated their father at the "Field of Lies" near Colmar, a division of the empire left Louis the German with an independent kingship consisting of all Frankish territory east of the Rhine. In 838, Louis the German was again reduced to Bavaria by his father, and his other eastern territories fell away from him. His hold on the East was not cemented until after his father's death. In 843 at Verdun, the three surviving sons of Louis the Pious—Lothar, Louis the German, and Charles the Bald—divided the Frankish Empire among themselves, and Louis became once and for all king in eastern Francia.

Bavaria nonetheless retained its territorial and political integrity within the East Frankish kingdom. Louis the German's son Carloman, for example, received Bavaria as a sub-kingdom and actively ruled as king of the Bavarians after his father's death in 876 until his own in 880. In the first decades of the tenth century, however, a devastating series of invasions by the Hungarians combined with the minority reign of the last East Frankish Carolingian, Louis the Child (899–911), to unravel finally the threads of Carolingian rule in Bavaria. In the midst of disorder, a leading Bavarian family—the Liutpoldings—emerged to lead a de facto independent Bavarian duchy that consciously leaned on and exploited the traditions of both the Carolingian sub-kingdom and the older Agilolfing duchy. The creation of the Liutpolding Duchy of Bavaria in a sense closed the historical circle and opened a new period in Bavarian history.

From the last quarter of the eighth century through the end of the ninth, therefore, Bavaria experienced the imposition of Frankish authority by military conquest and then the fragmentation, transformation, and eventual decline of that authority through rebellion, civil war, and invasion. This series of political developments happily coincides with the existence of a remarkably rich set of sources for the study of disputing, namely, the surviving early medieval charter collections from the great Bavarian churches and monasteries.

The study of local and regional social history in the early Middle Ages depends heavily on the study of charters.[39] These archival documents record

---

39. I use the term *charter*, following the definition given by Davies and Fouracre, *Settlement of Disputes*, 270, to mean any document that records the transfer or confirmation of property rights or privileges, or any other kind of transaction. This definition is meant to provide an easily accessible label for all documents of this kind, whether first-person records issued at the scene of a transaction or later third-person descriptions of a transaction. A more strictly correct, but also more cumbersome,

the transfer or affirmation of rights, either to property, such as land or un-free people, or to privileges, such as immunity from royal jurisdiction. They could come either from kings, in the form of royal diplomas granting rights to a person or institution, or from lesser laymen or churchmen as they carried out transactions with one another (the so-called private charters).[40] Most of the extant early medieval charters deal with the rights of churches and monasteries; because of their institutional longevity, church and monastic archives have often survived where lay archives have not. Even ecclesiastical charters rarely survive as originals, however. They more commonly exist in collections of copies made for purposes and at times that varied from place to place.[41]

In contrast with the great narrative chronicles of the Middle Ages, which tend to focus on the deeds of the most powerful, these charter collections contain snapshots of local and regional social activity. They memorialize gifts by lay landowners of property to a church, exchanges or sale of property by the church, and, most important for our purposes, disputes over property rights between the church and its neighbors. As such, they offer priceless information about the issues that caused disputes, about the people involved, and about their methods of handling conflict.

Charters naturally have their pitfalls as sources. To begin with, they tend to use formulaic language, that is, they contain the behavior of human beings within formulaic phrases and stylized depictions of procedure. Second, since most surviving charters come from churches, the available dispute charters record only those disputes that involved a church in some fashion or that a church was interested in. Most record only disputes that turned out

definition would see charters only as the former and would describe the latter as notices. I use the term *charter collection* to refer to collected copies of these documents (as Davies and Fouracre use the term *cartulary*), including both what is called in German a *Kopialbuch*, that is, collected copies of first-person documents, and the *Traditionsbuch*, which can contain primarily third-person notices or a mixture of both first-person and third-person records. See the literature cited in n. 40.

40. On early medieval charters in general, see the introduction to *Settlement of Disputes*, ed. Davies and Fouracre, 1–5; Heinrich Fichtenau, *Das Urkundenwesen in Österreich vom 8. bis zum frühen 13. Jahrhundert* (Vienna, 1971); Rosamund McKitterick, *The Carolingians and the Written Word* (Cambridge, 1989), esp. chap. 3. See also Geary, *Phantoms*, 87–114, for the development of charter collections and in particular for the differences between western and eastern collections.

41. An important exception is the earliest archive of the monastery of Saint Gall, a great deal of which has survived in its original form; see the *Urkundenbuch der Abtei Sanct Gallen*, 4 vols., ed. Hermann Wartmann (Zürich, 1863–1931).

in a church's favor, since a church would have little interest in keeping records of property it had lost. Third, because of their very nature, dispute charters deal almost exclusively with disputes over property rights. Other kinds of disputes rarely appear in the collections; when they do, they often rate only a passing reference.[42]

Despite these flaws, charters can provide a great deal of useful information. Because the power of a person in the early Middle Ages depended on how much property he could control, people could fight intensely over property rights.[43] As Barbara Rosenwein has made clear, and as likewise emerges in the course of this book, property disputes could also serve as a backdrop for struggles over honor or for the adjustment of personal and religious relationships.[44] Central authority too took a strong interest in property rights; kings not only issued legislation about property but also tried to draw property disputes into royal forums for settlement. The impact of this interest shows up in the charters. In addition, not all property disputes developed in ways that scribes could easily constrain within preset formulas. Compromise solutions in particular forced scribes to bend their formulas to include nonstandard information or procedures. Scribes sometimes had to dispense with formulas altogether when disputes bypassed formal venues in favor of informal arrangements. Finally, and perhaps most important for this study, how scribes constructed their charters itself provides useful material. The very information that scribes decided to record, the formulas they did or did not choose to use, and how their choices changed over time can provide vital information about trends in the disputing process and about the relationship of the people recording the disputes both to the disputants and to central authority.

Bavaria boasts an outstanding collection of such charters, namely, the earliest charter collection of the cathedral church at Freising.[45] Between the years 824 and ca. 855, a Freising priest named Cozroh and his successors collected and copied the Freising cathedral archives, which contained documents dating back to the 740s. By his own testimony, Cozroh began the collection on the orders of Bishop Hitto of Freising (r. 812–35). The bishop, as

42. See Chris Wickham, "Land Disputes and Their Social Framework in Lombard-Carolingian Italy, 700–900," in *Settlement of Disputes*, ed. Davies and Fouracre, 105, for a good articulation of this problem.

43. See *Property and Power in the Early Middle Ages*, ed. Wendy Davies and Paul Fouracre (Cambridge, 1995).

44. Barbara H. Rosenwein, *To Be the Neighbor of Saint Peter: The Social Meaning of Cluny's Property, 909–1049* (Ithaca, N.Y., 1989).

45. Published edition: *TF*.

part of a general program of renewing the textual holdings of his church, ordered Cozroh to compile the collection first "so that the memory of those who had enriched this house with their property and had made it their heirs, and of whatever they had handed over and given to this house for the salvation of their souls, might endure in perpetuity."[46] Moreover, the Freising archives had suffered from loss and from the depredations of both outsiders and "false brothers" who wished to alienate the church's property. To prevent further loss and to make it easier to refer to the documents, Bishop Hitto ordered Cozroh to copy carefully "whatever he found written in each charter and confirmed by certain testimony" into a single volume.[47] The bishop further ordered the deacon to copy the originals literally, altering only obvious scribal errors.

Cozroh's work resulted in a codex, now in the Bavarian state archives in Munich, that contains some seven hundred record copies whose accuracy has never come into serious question.[48] Just under one hundred of these records concern conflicts. The collection has the additional advantage of completeness. Only one section is missing; the records it contained have nonetheless survived, albeit without witness lists, in copies made in the twelfth century.[49] Cozroh's collection covers the period from the beginning of the Freising archives in 744 through the end of the reign of Bishop Hitto's successor, Erchanbert (r. 836–54). Cozroh grouped the individual records by episcopal reign, starting with Bishop Ermbert (730?–48) and continuing through Bishops Joseph (748–64), Arbeo (764–83), Atto (783–811), Hitto, and Erchanbert. Within each reign—unlike his nineteenth-century editor Theodor Bitterauf, who tried to order the records chronologically—Cozroh apparently followed the organization of the archives themselves. He separated records of gifts written in the first person from third-person notices and placed documents with related content next to each other.[50] This structure would have made it difficult to consult the

46. Cozroh, Prologue: *TF*, 1:1–2.

47. Ibid.

48. Bayr. Hauptstaatsarchiv, Hochstift Freising Lit. 3a; labeled Codex A by Bitterauf. On Cozroh's accuracy, see Joachim Jahn, "Virgil, Arbeo und Cozroh: Verfassungsgeschichtliche Beobachtungen an bairischen Quellen des 8. und 9. Jahrhunderts," *MGSL* 130 (1990): 212; Geary, *Phantoms*, 93–96. On places in the collection where earlier documents are missing because they were superseded by later ones, see Jahn, "Virgil," 204–5, 212 and n. 29; Fichtenau, *Urkundenwesen*, 65–67.

49. By a Freising sacristan named Conrad: Bayr. Hauptstaatsarchiv, Hochstift Freising Lit. 3c; Bitterauf's Codex A'. See Bitterauf, introduction to *TF*, 1:xxii–xxv.

50. *Traditiones* (first-person) and *notitiae* (third-person); Jahn, "Virgil," 245.

codex for practical purposes; although there is a table of contents, its often imprecise titles do little to help the reader locate documents. Cozroh's codex instead functions best, as Cozroh himself stated, as a memorial collection. It not only preserves the memory of donors to the church and of the properties they gave but also acts—as Patrick Geary has recently pointed out—as a memorial to the deeds of the Freising bishops in preserving and expanding the property holdings of their church.[51]

Fragmentary charter collections have also survived from other Bavarian bishoprics and monasteries, particularly the cathedral church at Regensburg and its companion monastery of Saint Emmeram, the cathedral church at Passau, the monastery at Mondsee, and Freising itself after 850. These collections, unlike Cozroh's, have suffered drastically from loss. Nonetheless, the twenty-one conflict records they contain from the eighth and ninth centuries enable us to compare Freising disputes with others from an area covering most of early medieval Bavaria.[52]

Although we spend most of our time looking at the Bavarian charter collections, we do have other evidence from the period at our disposal. For example, I draw along the way on the Law of the Bavarians to find out how much written norms affected how Bavarians handled disputes. The Law was certainly well known by the group that produced most of the charters, namely, the Freising clerical community. The Freising scriptorium copied out a complete manuscript of the code and part of another at about the same time Cozroh began to compile his charter collection.[53] Useful legal prescriptions also appear in the acts of several church synods and councils held in Bavaria during the late eighth and early ninth centuries. These synodal acts not only deal with church affairs; those of the late-eighth-century councils of Dingolfing and Neuching in particular contain secular prescriptions that reflect the concerns of the Agilolfing duke Tassilo III.[54]

---

51. On the organization and purpose of the Cozroh Codex, see Geary, *Phantoms*, 93–96; Jahn, "Virgil," 240–77.

52. *TM*; *TP*; *TR*. Bitterauf draws his Freising material for the second half of the ninth century from a Freising "book of exchanges" (*codex commutationum*), Bayr. Hauptstaatsarchiv, Hochstift Freising Lit. 3b—Bitterauf's Codex B; see Bitterauf, introduction to *TF*, 1:xxv–xxxiii. On the Mondsee, Passau, and Regensburg collections, see Geary, *Phantoms*, 90–91.

53. Bayr. Staatsbibliothek, Clm 19415; Clm 29086 (fragment—chaps. 1–4): see B. Bischoff, *Die südostdeutschen Schreibschulen und Bibliotheken in der Karolingerzeit*, vol. 1, *Die bayerischen Diözesen* (Wiesbaden, 1974), 102–3.

54. *Concilium Baiuwaricum* (ca. 740–50), *Concilium Ascheimense* (ca. 755–60), *Concilium Dingolfingense* (770), *Concilium Neuchingense* (ca. 771), *Concilium Rispacense* (ca.

The fact that I began this introduction not with a charter or a law but rather with a poem indicates that I also use literary sources. Specifically, hagiography—the biography of religious heroes and heroines—provides a narrative alternative to charters as a source for early medieval social history. Saints' lives were generally produced by local or regional churches or monasteries. They therefore tend to depict their subjects' interaction with the rulers and inhabitants of a given locality or region. This interaction quite frequently included conflict.

Hagiography has its dangers as a source genre, the most important of which mirror those presented by the charters. Saints' lives were designed not to provide accurate historical information but rather to portray their subjects as models for either emulation or adulation by the faithful, to whom they were read aloud.[55] They therefore drew heavily on stereotypes of saintly behavior, stereotypes that frequently go back to the earliest days of Christianity. In addition, both the authors and later copyists or editors of saints' lives almost always constructed and reconstructed them as propaganda pieces in order to further their own interests or those of a particular church or aristocratic family. For example, a new or freshly revised saint's life could bolster a church's claim to the saint's relics, the bones or personal possessions of the holy man or woman through which he or she maintained a very real presence on earth. Or it could enhance the church's position in a dispute with its lay neighbors by describing the consequences of provoking the saint's anger. As a result, students of hagiography frequently face descriptions of behavior drawn from a society centuries older than that which they are actually studying or from a monk or cleric's passionately held conviction about how the world should function for the best advantage of God and his Church.

The very fact that the writers of saints' lives reached into a grab bag to find the building blocks for their stories, however, provides the saving grace for hagiography as a source. The writers or copiers of saints' lives wrote in a particular context; they had a purpose in mind and made individual choices about what building blocks to include. They aimed to teach a living audience or to persuade (or polemicize) on behalf of a specific cause. In either case, they had to choose from among elements that had meaning to the intended audience. We are therefore entitled to draw conclusions about the

---

798), *Concilia Rispacense, Frisingense, Salisburgense* (ca. 800), ed. Albert Werminghoff, *MGH Conc* I (Hannover, 1906), 51–53, 56–58, 93–97, 98–105, 196–201, 205–19.

55. On hagiography and the use scholars have made of it in recent decades, see Patrick J. Geary, "Saints, Scholars, and Society: The Elusive Goal," in *Living with the Dead*, 9–29; *Saints and Their Cults: Studies in Religious Sociology, Folklore, and History*, ed. Stephen Wilson (Cambridge, 1983).

social and cultural world in which they moved from both the combination of traditional elements they chose and passages where they elected to depart from tradition.[56]

A saint's life does more than just provide information about the social and cultural milieu of its creator at the time of its creation. Saint's lives themselves have a history, a history in which they were composed and then copied and recopied at different times and places. At each point, a copyist had to decide that the life was worth copying as it stood or that it needed changing to reflect a change in values or in purpose. If a single version of a saint's life survives in manuscripts written over a certain span of time and within a particular area—say, Bavaria in the eighth and ninth centuries—it therefore provides information about an envelope, rather than a discrete point, in time and space.[57]

Two major saints' lives from early medieval Bavaria have survived, both written by Bishop Arbeo of Freising. These lives concern the bishop/saints Corbinian of Freising and Emmeram of Regensburg.[58] The surviving manuscripts, in the versions that stand closest to Arbeo himself, fall exactly in

56. Cf. František Graus, *Volk, Herrscher und Heiliger im Reich der Merowinger: Studien zur Hagiographie der Merowingerzeit* (Prague, 1965); Friedrich Prinz, *Frühes Mönchtum im Frankenreich: Kultur und Gesellschaft in Gallien, den Rheinlanden und Bayern am Beispiel der monastischen Entwicklung (4. bis 8. Jahrhundert)*, 2d ed. (Darmstadt, 1988), 490–501, esp. 499; Thomas Head, *Hagiography and the Cult of Saints: The Diocese of Orléans, 800–1200* (Cambridge, 1990). On hagiography as a tool in conflicts, see Paul Fouracre, "'Placita' and the Settlement of Disputes in Later Merovingian Francia," in *Settlement of Disputes*, ed. Davies and Fouracre, 37–39; Patrick J. Geary, "Humiliation of the Saints," in *Living with the Dead*, 95–115; Amy G. Remensnyder, *Remembering Kings Past: Monastic Foundation Legends in Medieval Southern France* (Ithaca, N.Y., 1995).

57. See Geary, "Saints, Scholars, and Society," in *Living with the Dead*, 19–27, esp. 22.

58. Editions: Arbeo of Freising, *Vita Corbiniani*, ed. and trans. Franz Brunhölzl, in *Vita Corbiniani: Bischof Arbeo von Freising und die Lebensgeschichte des hl. Korbinian*, ed. Hubert Glaser, Franz Brunhölzl, and Sigmund Benker (Munich, 1983), 77–159; Arbeo of Freising, *Vita et passio Sancti Haimhrammi Martyris*, ed. Bernhard Bischoff (Munich, 1953). In addition to the lives of Saints Corbinian and Emmeram, two versions of a life of Saint Rupert of Salzburg from the ninth century exist, but they are so short and broadly painted that they provide no useful information on conflict: see the *Conversio Bagoariorum et Carantanorum: Das Weißbuch der Salzburger Kirche über die erfolgreiche Mission in Karantanien und Pannonien*, ed. Herwig Wolfram (Vienna, 1979), and the *Gesta sancti Hrodberti confessoris*, ed. Wilhelm Levison, *MGH SSrerMerov* VI (Hannover, 1913), 140–62. See Wilhelm Wattenbach and Wilhelm Levison, *Deutschlands Geschichtsquellen im Mittelalter: Vorzeit und Karolinger*, vol. 1

our period, the last decades of the eighth century and the first decades of the ninth. They contain a great deal of useful information about how a late-eighth-century Bavarian bishop and the clerics who later copied his work chose to represent disputes.

In addition to Arbeo's hagiography, quasi-hagiographical accounts of the see of Salzburg's early history have survived in two Salzburg property catalogs, the *Breves Notitiae* and the *Notitia Arnonis*.[59] These catalogs are rather curious mixtures of genres. Compiled shortly after the Carolingian conquest of Bavaria, they blend records of property transactions with saints' lives and other material into narrative descriptions and histories of Salzburg's property holdings. Among these narratives are dispute stories that also have something to say about clerical attitudes toward conflict.

This book is not the first to confront this rich source material. The early Bavarian charters, laws, and saints' lives have long held the attention of historians concerned with south-central Europe. German and Austrian medievalists in particular have used them to explore the region's religious, social, political, and economic development and the family relationships of its inhabitants.[60] Few of these scholars, however, have studied disputing for its own sake. When they have discussed dispute, they have generally ap-

---

(Weimar, 1952), 144n. 358, for other minor lives purporting to be of eighth- and ninth-century Bavarian ecclesiastics but written much later.

59. *NA*; *BN*. On the catalogs' dating and purpose, see Lošek's introduction to his edition, 9–10 and 19–42; Heinrich Wanderwitz, "Quellenkritische Studien zu den bayerischen Besitzlisten des 8. Jahrhunderts," *Deutsches Archiv* 39, no. 1 (1983): 27–84; Herwig Wolfram, "Libellus Virgilii: Ein quellenkritisches Problem der ältesten Salzburger Güterverzeichnisse," in *Mönchtum, Episkopat und Adel zur Gründungszeit des Klosters Reichenau*, ed. Arno Borst (Sigmaringen, 1974), 177–214; Jahn, "Virgil," 213–27, and "*Tradere ad sanctum*: Politische und gesellschaftliche Aspekte der Traditionspraxis im agilolfingischen Bayern," in *Gesellschaftsgeschichte: Festschrift für Karl Bosl zum 80. Geburtstag*, ed. Ferdinand Seibt, vol. 1 (Munich, 1988), 404–7; Geary, *Phantoms*, 88.

60. Select examples of this historiography: Prinz, *Frühes Mönchtum*; Wolfram, *Geburt Mitteleuropas* and *Salzburg, Bayern, Österreich: Die Conversio Bagoariorum et Carantanorum und die Quellen ihrer Zeit* (Vienna, 1995); Störmer, *Früher Adel*. Non-German examples include Philippe Dollinger, *L'évolution des classes rurales en Bavière, depuis la fin de l'époque carolingienne jusqu'au milieu du XIIIe siècle* (Paris, 1949), translated into German in 1982 as *Der bayerische Bauernstand vom 9. bis zum 13. Jahrhundert*, trans. Franz Irsigler (Munich, 1982); Carl I. Hammer, "Land Sales in Eighth- and Ninth-Century Bavaria: Legal, Economic, and Social Aspects," *Early Medieval Europe* 6, no. 1 (1997): 47–76, "The Handmaid's Tale: Morganatic Relationships in Early-Mediaeval Bavaria," *Continuity and Change* 10, no. 3 (1995): 345–68, and

proached it institutionally and systematically. In other words, they have drawn together charters from a broad period of time (say, the entire Carolingian period) in order to put together a static description of such things as the rules and practices governing courts, the procedural roles played by officials and assemblies, or their judicial powers.[61] Even those studying kinship and other personal relationships have tended when dealing with dispute to retreat into an institutional analysis that does not include the wider context for individual disputes that they themselves have provided.[62] This search for the typical has led most of the scholars who have worked with this material to overlook the complex variation over time in Bavarian disputing practices that is my focus and thus to miss what this variation has to say about how power functioned on the ground.

The work of the late Joachim Jahn represents an important exception. In his masterful book *Ducatus Baivariorum*, as well as in several articles, Jahn drew heavily on the Bavarian charters and other sources to study the social and constitutional development of Agilolfing Bavaria before its absorption by the Carolingians.[63] Jahn treated disputes as social and political processes that had a great deal to say about the workings of power. Nevertheless, he remained primarily concerned with the Agilolfing period. As a result, he left the door open for us to focus specifically on conflict in both Agilolfing and Carolingian Bavaria in order to explore the wider and longer-term relationship between Bavarian interests and Carolingian authority.

THE ACTORS

The Bavarian charters contain information not about a cross-section of Bavaria's early medieval population but rather about the minority that

---

"Family and Familia in Early Medieval Bavaria," in *Family Forms in Historic Europe*, ed. Richard Wall (Cambridge, 1983), 217–48.

61. See, for example, Hans K. Schulze, *Die Grafschaftsverfassung der Karolingerzeit in den Gebieten östlich des Rheins* (Berlin, 1973); Jürgen Weitzel, *Dinggenossenschaft und Recht: Untersuchungen zum Rechtsverständnis im fränkisch-deutschen Mittelalter*, vol. 1 (Cologne, 1985), esp. 575–606. Weitzel, despite an expressed desire to get away from overlegalized modern preconceptions of dispute resolution, provides here a lengthy discussion of the "bayerische Gerichtsverfassung" in which, for example, he tries to determine the exact function of the *iudex* in light of the laws and the charters.

62. See, for example, Störmer, *Früher Adel*, esp. vol. 2, chap. 9, part 2, "Graf und Grafschaft."

63. Jahn, *Ducatus*, "Virgil," "Urkunde und Chronik," "*Tradere ad sanctum*," in *Gesellschaftsgeschichte*, ed. Seibt.

could own and alienate property. This subsection—our cast of characters, so to speak—comprised the landowning aristocracy.[64] The members of this aristocracy were in general free men (but also sometimes women) who owned property outright, as either inheritance or acquisition, and could give it to, sell it to, or receive it from a church. They acted not only as individuals but also as members of nuclear families and extended kin groups. The sources sometimes tell us about these families and kin groups. When they do not, as is all too frequently the case, we can still reconstruct family and kindred relationships, at least in part, through patterns of naming and property ownership. In a society that did not use surnames, single names sufficed to give information not only about personal identity but also about kinship. Direct evidence for this practice comes from the famous *Hildebrandlied*, a poem fragment copied into a manuscript at the monastery of Fulda around the year 800. The poem, whose roots go back to the fifth and sixth centuries, concerns the tragedy of a son, Hadubrand, separated as a child from his father Hildebrand son of Heribrand, who unknowingly meets his father in battle. At the crisis of their meeting, the father asks the son

64. It is hard to define "aristocracy" precisely in this period. We have no explicit legal definition from the early Middle Ages of who was aristocratic and who was not, and the charters use titles such as "noble" (*nobilis*) inconsistently. A general picture of the early medieval aristocracy has emerged from the work done since World War II by members of the Freiburg school, particularly by Karl Schmid and his successors. It describes a socially and politically prominent group characterized by freedom and the ability to own and dispose of property and loosely organized in horizontal (cognatic) rather than patrilineal (agnatic) kin groups. Individuals drew their group identity from powerful relatives, especially those who held secular or ecclesiastical office, along maternal or paternal lines as best suited their interests. See the contributions to *Medieval Nobility*, ed. Reuter, as well as Wilhelm Störmer, *Adelsgruppen im früh- und hochmittelalterlichen Bayern* (Munich, 1972); Régine Le Jan, *Famille et pouvoir dans le monde franc (VIIe–Xe siècle): Essai d'anthropologie sociale* (Paris, 1995). Scholars still debate whether or not this aristocracy was a legally defined class. See Störmer, *Früher Adel*, 1:1–3, and Werner, "Important Noble Families," in *Medieval Nobility*, ed. Reuter, 179–80, for arguments in favor of a legal nobility; Franz Irsigler, "On the Aristocratic Character of Early Frankish Society," in the same volume, 105–36, argues for a de facto social aristocracy. Alexander C. Murray, *Germanic Kinship Structure: Studies in Law and Society in Antiquity and in the Early Middle Ages* (Toronto, 1983), offers a useful critique of older views of Germanic society as based on unilineal descent groups, or "clans," without, however, really coming to grips with the work of Schmid and his followers.

With few words, who his father was
From among the heroes of the people . . .
. . . "or of what ancestry are you?
Name but one, the others I will know,
Youth, in the kingdoms all the kindreds are known to me."[65]

Hildebrand's own name tells us how a name could reveal a person's kindred; it clearly connects him both to his son Hadubrand and to his own father, Heribrand, through the common *H* at the beginning and the common *brand* at the end.

Members of landowning kin groups in Bavaria passed on names, or pieces of names, in this fashion.[66] For example, one kin group that appears in the Freising charters in 791 (and proves to be important to our story) surrounds a priest named Tutilo. Tutilo shows up giving a church to Freising with his father, Pirhtilo, and mother, Ata; brothers named Fritilo, Cozzilo, Petilo, and Waltfrid; and nieces and nephews named Fritilo, Situli, and Swidpuruc. Here the characteristic name piece consists of the frequently repeated final name element *-ilo*; the name *Fritilo* passed complete to the next generation.[67]

Landowning kindreds also tended to cluster around property holdings in a particular place or group of places. Tutilo and his relatives appear in connection with a place called Rottbach. Another important grouping around a church in a place called Bittlbach first appears in a charter from the year 758. In that year, a man named Haholt gave the church at Bittlbach to the see of Freising and dedicated his son Arn, the future archbishop of Salzburg, to the ecclesiastical life. In 827, another Haholt, with a wife named Perhtild and a son named Arn, also gave property at Bittlbach to Freising. The

---

65. *Das Hildebrandlied*, ed. and trans. Georg Baesecke (Halle, 1945); Dieter Geuenich, "Zur althochdeutschen Literatur aus Fulda," in *Von der Klosterbibliothek zur Landesbibliothek: Beiträge zum zweihundertjährigen bestehen der Hessischen Landesbibliothek Fulda* (Stuttgart, 1978), 99–124. The English translation used here comes from *Readings in Medieval History*, ed. Patrick J. Geary, 2d ed. (Peterborough, Ontario, 1997), 111.

66. Here the prosopography done for Bavaria, particularly but by no means exclusively by Störmer and Jahn, becomes invaluable. See inter alia Störmer, *Adelsgruppen* and *Früher Adel*; Jahn, *Ducatus*; Wolfgang Hartung, "Tradition und Namengebung im frühen Mittelalter," *Regio* 1 (1988): 23–79, and "Bertolde in Baiern: Alamannisch-baierische Adelsverflechtungen im 8. und 9. Jahrhundert," *Regio* 1 (1988): 115–60; Mitterauer, *Karolingische Markgrafen*.

67. *TF* 143a.

coincidence of names and place makes it virtually certain that the latter Haholt and Arn were related to the former, although exactly how remains hidden.[68]

The charters identify a very few kindreds by a group name, such as, for example, the Mohingara—the "People from Moching."[69] The most prominent such kindred is the Huosi, one of the five *genealogiae* named by the Bavarian Law as rating a blood price, or wergeld, double that of other free men.[70] The Huosi appear in three Freising charters, over a period from the end of the eighth to the middle of the ninth century.[71] These three charters have provided enough name and property evidence for scholars to make out a network of interrelated aristocrats, with property concentrations ranging from the Alps to the Danube and kinship links reaching far outside Bavaria and upward into the Agilolfing house itself.[72]

Whether the members of this extended network regarded themselves as "Huosi" or not is another matter. Building objective pictures of kindreds based on such labels is less useful than simply relying on naming patterns and property holdings to establish a connection.[73] Such objectification tends to obscure the fact that people related to one another by naming tradition and property holdings did not necessarily form unified interest blocs but could split into subgroups depending on the needs and interests of the moment.[74] I therefore avoid the use of all-embracing labels such as *Huosi* for wide groups unless the sources explicitly permit it. Whenever possible, I base my conclusions about how kinship affected disputing on relationships identified by the charters. Nonetheless, the kind of prosopography outlined

68. *TF* 11, *TF* 540ab. Störmer, *Früher Adel*, 1:36–37, lists further examples from early Freising charters. On the prosopographical method outlined here, see Werner, "Important Noble Families," in *Medieval Nobility*, ed. Reuter, 149–53.

69. *TF* 235.

70. *Lex B*, C. III/1.

71. *TF* 142 (791); *TF* 703a (849); *TF* 736b (853).

72. On the *genealogiae* in general and the Huosi in particular, see Jahn, *Ducatus*, 232–38, 352–56, 440–48; Störmer, *Adelsgruppen*, 90–120. Murray, *Germanic Kinship Structure*, 99–108, sees the *genealogiae* as at best "shallow descent groups" of co-heirs united for inheritance purposes, with only a short-lived corporate identity that could become transmitted to territorial units. He does not, however, make use of the three Freising charters that deal with the Huosi, nor does he apply prosopography based on naming tradition and property holding, which indicate a longer-lived sense of bilateral kin-group identity.

73. Cf. Störmer, *Adelsgruppen*, 91.

74. A number of scholars have criticized the argument advanced by the Freiburg school for early medieval clans as unified interest groups; see Nelson, *Charles the Bald*, 174–75, and the literature cited therein on 175n. 72.

above proves to be of enormous value—when used carefully—for dealing with disputants' identities in cases in which names and property holdings are all we have.

The Bavarian charters capture these local and regional aristocrats as they carry out property transactions and engage in property disputes with churches and with one another. These people, it must be stressed, represented the upper reaches of Bavarian society. Many of them had connections—if not of kinship then at least social and political—to the highest level of political society in the early medieval world. To see this, we need only look at a single Freising charter from the year 843. This charter concerns a land sale carried out between Bishop Erchanbert of Freising and a nobleman named Paldricus. The sale occurred "in the place called Dungeih next to the city of Verdun, where the peace of the three brothers Lothar, Louis, and Charles and the division of their kingdom was carried out." The enormous list of witnesses to this transaction, plainly people who had come to Verdun for the assembly that officially divided the Carolingian Empire, contains names such as Reginperht, Orendil, Kepahoh, Keio, Piligrim, Erchanperht, and Tagaperht,, which will become familiar to us as typical of the Bavarian landowning aristocracy. In other words, the players in the game of dispute in the Bavarian charter collections consisted of people who were not only local and regional landowners but also powerful aristocrats whose political and social horizons covered the entire Carolingian Empire. These aristocrats still clearly felt themselves to be Bavarian, however. The Verdun charter ends by noting that the witnesses to the sale had all been authenticated by the characteristic Bavarian practice of tugging on their ears: "These are the witnesses pulled by the ears according to the law of the Bavarians."[75]

Let us now turn to the behavior of our Bavarian landowners as they carried on their disputes with one another. My aim is to help us understand disputing processes and how political events affected them. This book is not a new study of judicial institutions and procedures; in other words, I do not try to uncover rules governing how counts, judges, witnesses, or royal agents behaved in disputes. Instead, I look at conflict as a total social phenomenon from inside the world of our sources in order to see how the rhythm of social interaction, and the way the people who wrote the sources viewed that interaction, changed over time. This approach tells us how events outside this world affected what took place inside it.

75. *TF* 661.

CHAPTER ONE
CONFLICT IN AGILOLFING BAVARIA

I n order to understand disputing in Bavaria before the Carolingian conquest, we must sift through a varied mix of
sources. These sources provide a series of different images of
conflict and of how the various actors on our stage participated in it. Some
of the images connect to one another immediately and easily. Others, however, reveal connections only when they emerge again further down the
line, in the context of the changes that took place in Bavaria after the Carolingian takeover.

To begin with, we have the charters from the cathedral church at Freising. Five of the approximately one hundred twenty Freising charters surviving from this period mention conflict.[1] No charters from the other Bavarian
collections do, although some that did may have been lost. The five Freising
records tell a variety of stories. Nevertheless, they have one important fea-
ture in common: all mention conflicts tangentially, that is, as incidents that
did not involve the church directly but rather prompted someone to make or
confirm a property gift to the church. In this regard, they differ markedly
from most other early medieval dispute charters, which generally deal with
property disputes directly involving a church or a monastery as a party.[2]

Instead of showing the church as a party to conflict, the Freising charters
from this period reveal members of landholding kindreds in conflict with
one another. Some of this conflict was violent. We learn of it because two
men who were attacked and seriously wounded, as well as a third man whose

---

1. *TF* 11, 19, 23, 65, 86. The figure "approximately one hundred twenty" reflects
some confusion visible in the Freising charters about when Duke Tassilo actually
stopped ruling Bavaria. *TF* 120 (October 1, 788) is already dated to Charlemagne's
regnal years. The last charter in the collection dated to Tassilo's regnal years, however, and one that moreover refers to a transaction carried out with Tassilo's permission, is *TF* 125 (February 20, 789). See Störmer, *Adelsgruppen*, 12; Jahn, *Ducatus*,
546.

2. See *Settlement of Disputes*, ed. Davies and Fouracre.

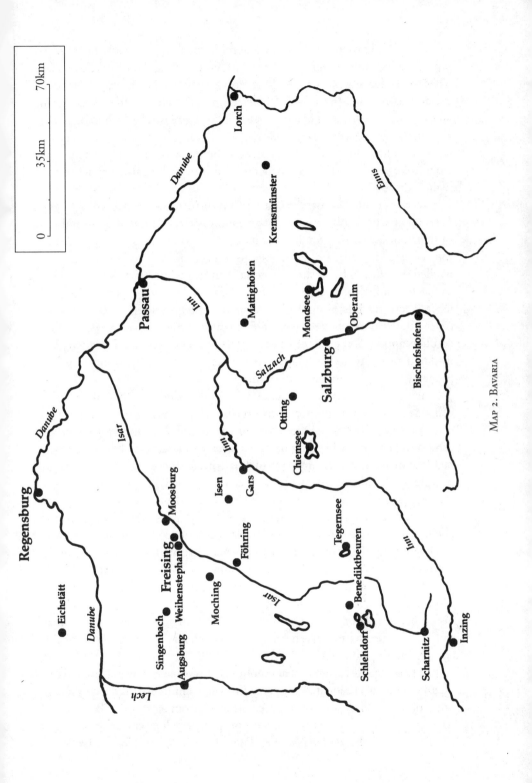

MAP 2. BAVARIA

Regensburg

Eichstätt

Danube

Lech

Singenbach

Augsburg

Freising

Weihenstephan

Moosburg

Moching

Föhring

Isen

Gars

Isar

Schlehdorf

Benediktbeuren

Tegernsee

Scharnitz

Inzing

Inn

Isar

Danube

Passau

Inn

Salzach

Otting

Chiemsee

Mattighofen

Mondsee

Oberalm

Salzburg

Bischofshofen

Kremsmünster

Lorch

Enns

0   35km   70km

son was killed, gave property to the church to benefit their souls and to support members of their families. The charters recording these gifts do not say what the violence was all about. The stories they tell, however, suggest that the attacks resulted from feuds between kindreds, and possibly even within an extended kin group. This impression is strengthened by Bishop Arbeo of Freising's *Life of Saint Emmeram*. Arbeo's biography of Regensburg's patron saint is built around a story of outraged honor and violent revenge. The story indicates that Bavarian aristocrats in this period regarded violence as a legitimate response to insult or injury.

Bavarians could also handle conflict in nonviolent ways. According to the Freising charters, some people involved in disputes appealed to assemblies of their kin for help in finding a solution. The kindreds were supported in the peacemaking process by the bishops of Freising; kindred gatherings forwarded disputes to the bishops, who in turn helped the parties involved respond to conflict or defuse it. In contrast to the charters mentioning violence, these records of nonviolent dispute settlements tell us exactly what caused the disputes they record: conflict within kindreds over property. The conflicts appear in the charters because the parties ended them by giving the disputed property to the church or by rearranging or restating disputed property rights that involved the church.

The way the bishops cooperated with the kindreds to end disputes echoed a much broader cooperative relationship between the two that was expressed in property holding. Bavarian landholders routinely gave property to the church at Freising or to a church or monastery they themselves had founded under Freising's spiritual patronage. Nevertheless, they just as routinely continued to control and use the property they had given. Such gifts created ties between the donor kindreds and the see of Freising, anchored in specific properties, churches, or monasteries, which could last for generations. These ties were sometimes strengthened by kinship; the bishops of Freising themselves appear to have been related to some of the more important donor groups. The relationship between the bishops and the donor kindreds also closely concerned the Agilolfing duke of Bavaria Tassilo III. Tassilo frequently participated in the forging of such ties by giving his explicit consent to them. Moreover, he acted in one dispute in a way that shows his interests to have been inextricably bound up with those of the church and the kindreds.

Just how strongly the social and political landscape in Bavaria favored the ongoing control of donated property by donor kindreds is reflected by another of our sources, a set of dispute narratives from Salzburg. These narratives are contained in the two Salzburg property catalogs known as the *Notitia Arnonis* and the *Breves Notitiae*. They describe what happened when a bishop who was not a native of Bavaria, in this case Bishop Virgil of Salzburg, tried to override a donor kindred's customary claims and exercise sole control of donated property: he failed completely in the face of concerted opposition by both the kindred and the Agilolfing duke.

Although the bishops of Freising seem to have avoided disputes with their landholding neighbors and kin, a second saint's life from this period, Arbeo of Freising's *Life of Saint Corbinian*, reveals that at least one Freising bishop was very concerned with conflict. Arbeo's biography of Freising's patron saint and first bishop is full of disputes that directly involve the saint as a party. These disputes concern the saint's property rights or his prestige, or both. Arbeo has the saint-bishop, who by implication personified his church, resolve the disputes bilaterally, without the intervention of any third-party authority, according to a repeated and almost formulaic script. This script provided a way for the saint and his opponent to achieve and express the balance between rights and face on the one hand and substantive concessions on the other which was necessary to restore a positive relationship between them. Thus, the dispute narratives in the *Life* offer a set of images of a bishop of Freising resolving conflict directly with his opponents without resort to any outside judicial authority.

VIOLENCE

At the beginning of the Freising charter collection, between his table of contents and his prologue, the priest Cozroh placed a copy of a charter that he titled in red ink, "The Gift of Haholt and His Son Arn." The charter was produced at the monastery of Saint Zeno at Isen, some thirty-two kilometers southeast of Freising, on May 25, 758. It most likely earned its prominent position in the collection, and certainly the attention of modern scholars, because it records among other things the dedication of Arn, the future archbishop of Salzburg and confidant of Charlemagne, to an ecclesiastical career.[3]

This record tells of a property gift that Arn's father, Haholt, made to the cathedral church at Freising. At some time in the past, we read, an unnamed person attacked Haholt and seriously wounded him, to the point that he feared for his life. On what he thought was his deathbed, Haholt gathered his relatives together and asked them how best to provide for his soul and

3. Hochstift Freising Lit. 3a, fol. 1a; *TF* 11. See Jahn, "Virgil," 243–45, on this charter's position in Cozroh's book, which most probably reflects Cozroh's intent to memorialize the recently dead archbishop (Arn died in 821; Cozroh began his book ca. 824).

for his son's future. Haholt's kinsmen advised him to summon Bishop Joseph of Freising. The bishop hurried to Haholt's bedside. On Joseph's advice, Haholt ordered a church built on property he owned near Isen, which the bishop consecrated.[4] Then, with the consent and participation of his wife, son, and relatives, Haholt gave the church and the property to Freising. He did so under the condition that his son Arn have the use of the property, that is, hold it from Freising as a benefice, for the rest of his life. After a space of time, however, Haholt recovered from his wound. In gratitude for God's mercy and for their souls' salvation, Haholt and his wife personally confirmed the gift. In addition, they formally devoted Arn to a clerical life at the Freising cathedral church.

This record tells us that an unknown person attacked Haholt. The attack, however, is not the charter's main concern, and we learn nothing about Haholt's assailant or the reason for his assault. We learn only that the attack prompted Haholt and his wife to give property to Freising for the benefit of their souls and to support their son in his new career.

We can nevertheless hazard a guess about why Haholt was wounded. Two other charters suggest that he was involved in a feud. In the year 763, a kindred headed by a man named Reginperht and his brother Irminfrid turned a church they had built at Scharnitz, in modern-day Tyrol, into a monastery.[5] Members of the kindred endowed the new foundation with generous gifts of property. One man, named Cros, had a special reason for his gift. "Compelled by the admonition of God and struck down by Count Keparoh with an incurable wound," Cros gave all his property to the monastery and entered it himself as a monk.

Here, as in the Haholt charter, an act of violence prompted its victim to make a property gift. This time we have a name for the attacker: Count Keparoh. The name Keparoh also appears in another charter, this time on the receiving end of a violent attack. In this record, from the year 774, a man named Onulf makes the statement that his favorite son, Keparoh, had been insidiously murdered.[6] Onulf responded to his son's death by giving the property his own father had left him, as well as that left his wife by her father, Keparoh, to the Freising cathedral church. The property was to support his wife and surviving son for their lifetimes.

Onulf's gift charter and the Scharnitz foundation charter together provide evidence for a feud stretching over generations. In 763, Count Keparoh

4. Außer/Inner-Bittlbach, ca. four kilometers northwest of Isen.
5. *TF* 19.
6. *TF* 65.

struck down Cros. Eleven years later, in 774, a Keparoh fell victim to an assault. This younger Keparoh had a grandfather who was also named Keparoh. It is entirely possible that the person who attacked the younger Keparoh was a partisan of Cros and that the younger Keparoh's grandfather was related to the count who attacked Cros or was even the count himself.[7] In each case, the attacks prompted property gifts to a kindred monastery or to the cathedral church at Freising.

It turns out that Cros and the Keparohs were most likely related to each other. To give a brief example of what the evidence behind such a statement looks like: Cros was the kinsman of the principal Scharnitz founders Reginperht and his brother Irminfrid.[8] Reginperht and Irminfrid had another brother named David, who witnessed the foundation at Scharnitz. David also appears with Irminfrid making another property gift sometime between 758 and 763.[9] In this latter gift, the name Keparoh stands third among the witnesses, immediately following David and Irminfrid. Given his prominent position on the witness list, it is extremely likely that this Keparoh was related to David and Irminfrid and therefore also to Reginperht and Cros. Keparoh's apparent kindred relationship to the Scharnitz founders, therefore, suggests that the feud was a violent conflict within an extended kin group.

The Cros-Keparoh feud helps explain the Haholt charter. Since the Cros and Keparoh stories are very similar to Haholt's, it makes sense to conclude that Haholt too was wounded in the course of a dispute with another aristocrat. Seen as a group, then, the three charters indicate that Bavarian landowners processed disputes at least in part through violent feud. They do not, however, give any details about the feuds or the disputes that prompted them. To add depth to our picture of feud in Agilolfing Bavaria, we must briefly leave the charters and turn to the life of a saint.

7. Jahn, *Ducatus*, 417; Störmer, *Früher Adel*, 1:190–91.

8. From this point on, I keep prosopographical analyses in the notes as much as possible. A great deal of research has been carried out on the members and property holdings of the Scharnitz founding kindred; see Jahn, *Ducatus*, 409n. 117. For further discussions of the name and property evidence linking the Keparohs to the Scharnitz founders, see Störmer, *Adelsgruppen*, 84–85; "Mammendorf an der Maisach und seine adeligen Besitzer im frühen Mittelalter," *Amperland* 3, no. 2 (1967): 39–40; and "Eine frühmittelalterliche Adelsfamilie im Dachauer Umland," *Amperland* 3, no. 4 (1967): 80–81; Jahn, *Ducatus*, 349–51.

9. *TF* 12.

As noted previously, we have at our disposal two saints' lives written by Bishop Arbeo of Freising, who succeeded Bishop Joseph in 764. One of them, the *Life of Saint Emmeram*, has violent conflict as its centerpiece. Arbeo wrote his biography of Emmeram, the patron saint of the cathedral church and monastery at Regensburg, sometime around the year 772.[10] He evidently had little direct information about Emmeram to go on; he paints his subject for the most part in broad strokes that rely heavily on older hagiographic models.[11] According to Arbeo, Emmeram was a wealthy Gallo-Frankish nobleman who was born in the Aquitanian city of Poitiers sometime in the seventh century. By virtue of his sanctity and his generosity to rich and poor alike, he quickly rose to become bishop of that city.[12] After

10. The impulse for Arbeo's *Life of Emmeram* seems to have been the construction in 772 of a church at the site of Emmeram's martyrdom in Helfendorf; Arbeo visited Regensburg the same year. See Hubert Glaser, "Bischof Arbeo von Freising als Gegenstand der neueren Forschung," in Arbeo of Friesing, *Vita Corbiniani*, ed. Glaser, Brunhölzl, and Benker, 11–76, esp. 18, 53–55; Bischoff's "Nachwort" to his translation of Arbeo of Freising's *Vita Haimhrammi*, 85–96. The single extant manuscript of Arbeo's original text, Paris. Bibl. Nat. Lat. 2990 A, stems from the first or second quarter of the ninth century. According to Bischoff, it comes from the Flemish monastery of Saint Amand. Apparently, Arbeo's text traveled first to Salzburg through Arbeo's friendship with Bishop Virgil of Salzburg; there it later became available to the archbishop of Salzburg and abbot of Saint Amand, Arn. See Bischoff, *Die südostdeutschen Schreibschulen und Bibliotheken in der Karolingerzeit*, vol. 2, *Die vorwiegend österreichischen Diözesen* (Wiesbaden, 1980), 106. The "Arbeonic" version of the *Life*, therefore, covers the heart of Bavaria in the last three decades of the eighth century and the first few decades of the ninth. In addition to the "Arbeonic" text, the *Life* appears in a second, somewhat altered ninth-century version that Bischoff argues stems from Regensburg. The substantive changes in the story do not involve dispute, with a single important exception that is discussed later.

11. Primarily patristic and Merovingian; see Bischoff, "Nachwort," in *Vita Haimhrammi*, 89–93; Glaser, "Bischof Arbeo," in *Vita Corbiniani*, ed. Glaser, Brunhölzl, and Benker, 59–60.

12. Emmeram's Frankish origins have been disputed. Some scholars see both him and Saint Corbinian as Irishmen in the tradition of the wandering Irish saints of the seventh century; Arbeo, according to this view, turned them into Franks to please the Carolingians. See Glaser, "Bischof Arbeo," in *Vita Corbiniani*, ed. Glaser, Brunhölzl, and Benker, 21–22. Others have taken Arbeo's ethnic identification at face value; see Bischoff, "Nachwort," in *Vita Haimhrammi*, 89; Karl Bosl, "Der 'Adelsheilige': Idealtypus und Wirklichkeit, Gesellschaft und Kultur im merowingerzeitlichen Bayern des 7. und 8. Jahrhunderts: Gesellschaftliche Beiträge

pouring out the gift of his preaching on the regions of Gaul, Emmeram heard that a people called the Avars, who dwelled far to the east in Pannonia, had not yet been converted to Christianity.[13] Handing over his office to a hand-picked successor, Emmeram promptly set out through Gaul and Germany with a party of retainers, aiming to win over this people for Christ or achieve martyrdom in the attempt.

Eventually, Emmeram's party reached Bavaria. In the capital city, Regensburg, Emmeram met the Agilolfing duke of the Bavarians, Theodo (d. ca. 717/718).[14] The duke, on hearing of Emmeram's mission, informed the bishop that war was currently raging between the Bavarians and the Avars; he could not permit Emmeram's party to proceed. He pleaded instead with Emmeram to remain and serve the Bavarians as bishop or at least reform the Bavarian monasteries.[15] Emmeram reluctantly agreed to stay, especially as the incomplete conversion of the Bavarians themselves offered him a fertile field for his missionary zeal and desire for an ultimate martyrdom.

This early and relatively short part of the story occasionally uses the imagery of conflict. Bavaria would serve as Emmeram's "battlefield"; he looked forward, girded with a shield like a champion on the field of battle, to the day of his final reward.[16] The narrative becomes most interesting, however, when it begins to move toward this foreshadowed martyrdom. After missionizing in Bavaria for three years, Emmeram asked permission to go on a pilgrimage to Rome. Before he could leave, however, Ota, daughter of Duke Theodo, enters the story. Driven by lust and the urging of the devil, Ota had allowed herself to be seduced by the son of one of the duke's judges. When the young woman could no longer hide the resulting pregnancy, the despairing couple threw themselves at Bishop Emmeram's feet, admitted their sin, and implored him for aid. Moved by pity, the bishop ordered the pair to do penance for the salvation of their souls. He also instructed them under an oath of secrecy to place the fault publicly for Ota's pregnancy on him so that they might more easily escape earthly death. The bishop took

zu den Viten der bayerischen Stammesheiligen Emmeram, Rupert, und Korbinian," in *Speculum Historiale: Geschichte im Spiegel von Geschichtsschreibung und Geschichtsdeutung*, ed. Clemens Bauer, Laetitia Boehm, and Max Müller (Munich, 1965), 167–87.

13. The Avars were an Asiatic people whose territory bordered Bavaria to the east; they were eventually conquered by Charlemagne. See Walter Pohl, *Die Awaren: Ein Steppenvolk in Mitteleuropa, 567–822 n. Chr.* (Munich, 1988).

14. Jahn, *Ducatus*, 25–75, esp. 29–30.

15. *Vita Haimhrammi*, 12.

16. Ibid., 16.

the blame because he knew that when this sin became known, "he would certainly be unable to obtain forgiveness for the pair from the girl's father."[17] Emmeram then set out for Rome in the company of a group of clerics. On the third day of his journey, he discovered his "battlefield"—a village with a clear flowing spring called Helfendorf. There, to the puzzlement of his followers, he stopped and waited.

Meanwhile, Duke Theodo had discovered his daughter's condition. Enraged, he would have drawn his sword to kill the baby in the womb had not his men restrained him. No such restraint hindered Ota's brother Lantperht from avenging his sister's dishonor. Filled with wild fury, he assembled his own following and set off after Emmeram's party. On reaching Helfendorf, Lantperht had the bishop brought before him and showered him with angry accusations. The bishop calmly denied the charge of seduction and asked that he, along with whatever companion Lantperht might choose, be allowed to proceed to Rome to seek a judgment from the pope according to church law. Lantperht refused; instead, he had the bishop stripped and tied to a ladder. Lantperht's men then began to cut off Emmeram's extremities and limbs piece by piece while the bishop praised God and prayed for their salvation. They finished by ripping off Emmeram's genitals and tearing out his tongue; leaving the mutilated torso to die, Lantperht and his men departed. Soon afterward, Emmeram's soul departed his body. God took care of punishing his executioner: Lantperht himself ended his days in exile, his children and his children's children were forced to leave Bavaria, and his palaces were reduced to overgrown ruins.[18]

Emmeram's death is on the one hand built of traditional elements. It turns the saint into a Christ-like figure who took on the sin of another and suffered an unjust death as a result. What is unusual about the story is the mechanism it uses to bring about the martyrdom and the stomach-turning but deliberate detail with which it describes Emmeram's death.[19] As sug-

17. Ibid., 20.

18. Ibid., 20–50.

19. Bischoff, "Nachwort," in *Vita Haimhrammi*, 90–92, notes that although accusations of unchastity appear in other hagiographic works, such as in the eighth-century life of Saint Goar (*Vita Goaris confessoris*, ed. B. Krusch, *MGH SSrerMerov* IV [Hannover, 1902], 402–23) and Arbeo's own life of Corbinian, and although graphic mutilation scenes appear both in late antique saints' lives and in the passion of the Merovingian bishop Leudegar of Autun (*Passiones Leudegarii Episcopi et Martyris Augustodunensis*, ed. B. Krusch, *MGH SSrerMerov* V [Hannover, 1910], 282–322), the Emmeram story exceeds them by having such an accusation directly result in a violent death rather than in a miracle that proves the saint's innocence. Bischoff looks

gested before, Arbeo had to construct a martyrdom story that made sense to his audience out of bits and pieces of tradition, topoi, the cultural language of his society, and his own imagination. He responded by translating the Christ story into one of martyrdom by the ethic of feud. Lantperht viewed the bishop's alleged seduction of his sister as an assault on his family's honor. He responded with an act of revenge that he and at least a majority of his followers clearly perceived as justified:[20] he exploded with rage, assembled a war band, and hunted down his sister's ravisher. Lantperht then had the bishop mutilated and tortured to death. The grisly process ended with a symbolic gesture directly related to the alleged crime, namely, Emmeram's castration.[21]

This narrative suggests what may have lain in the silences left by the Freising feud charters: an insult, rage, and a violent, symbolic response. Arbeo presents the feud ethic in a negative sense, however. Just as in the passion of Christ a negative representation reveals the imperatives driving the Jewish establishment and the Roman authorities, so too Arbeo illuminates feud in Bavaria by a scathing criticism of it. Lantperht's willingness to use violence kills the ideal saint; furthermore, it drives Lantperht, his men, and his descendants to both their worldly and their ultimate perdition. The path to their salvation, although it would have kept them from giving Emmeram his martyrdom, would have followed an entirely different normative system. It would have led to Rome, a hearing before the pope, and a judgment of the case according to canon law.

---

for a parallel not in hagiography but rather in the legal sphere. He points out that *Lex B* C. I/10 forbids the murder of a bishop on suspicion of guilt for a range of crimes (including unchastity); the clause mandates instead recourse to a court and, if the bishop is found guilty, condemnation according to canon law. Bischoff suggests that the clause reflects an actual event and that Arbeo, with only a dim memory of the violent death of his subject, reached for it to give structure to his story. See also Glaser, "Bischof Arbeo," in *Vita Corbiniani*, ed. Glaser, Brunhölzl, and Benker, 64.

20. Arbeo has two of Lantperht's men asking God for forgiveness while they slice away at Emmeram.

21. Jahn, *Ducatus*, 44–45, carries this observation to rather systematic lengths: Ota was brought to a formal judicial hearing ("wohl einem bairischen 'Pfalzgericht'") where she confessed to criminal intercourse with the bishop. Emmeram was found guilty, whereupon the feud and revenge responsibilities of her relatives took over; it became the general duty to consummate his outlawry. Lantperht, who in Jahn's view acted like a Frankish-Merovingian royal legate and, like a judge, carried a staff (*virga*), followed the usual procedure for punishing criminals who had been caught in the act. He left the dying Emmeram at a crossroads, as the Ripuarian Law coincidentally demanded.

The *Life of Saint Emmeram* helps us understand what might have caused the violence that appears in the charters. What it does not do, however, is explain why the people on the receiving end of the violence responded by giving property to a church or monastery. Jahn has suggested that the gifts were directly related to the feuds that prompted them; the donors gave their property to a church or monastery in an effort to avoid paying the blood price, or wergeld, due for killing someone. The argument runs as follows: when one free man killed another, the Bavarian Law required the killer to compensate his victim's kindred and the duke with a sum that could ruin an aristocrat. Haholt, Cros, and Onulf were all involved in feuds; they gave their property to Freising or to a family monastery to protect it from wergeld claims by their opponents. That such claims could pose a real threat to property is revealed by another Freising record produced sometime between 765 and 767. This record apparently shows two brothers named Reginolt and Egino, who were connected to the Onulf/Keparoh kin group and possibly also to the Scharnitz founders, having to sell a church they had endowed to raise money for wergeld.[22]

This theory has some problems. First, protecting property from wergeld claims in this way would seem to be counterproductive. If in fact Haholt, Cros, and Onulf had killed someone and then sheltered their property by giving it to a church or monastery, it seems likely that the families of their victims, robbed of compensation, would resort to further violence. Second, the tactic does not seem to have worked very well. If Jahn is correct that Reginolt and Egino sold their property in response to a wergeld claim, then they had completely failed to protect it by endowing a church. Instead, they were forced to sell the church and their property to come up with the necessary cash.

Third, it seems unnecessary to blame matters on wergeld. The property

22. *TF* 24b has Reginolt and his brother the monk Egino selling family property along with a church they had endowed earlier (*TF* 22) to Bishop Arbeo of Freising for "plus or minus" 200 solidi. This sum matches the wergeld mandated by the Bavarian Law for the death of a freeman plus the accompanying fine due the duke. See *Lex B* C. IV/29; Jahn, *Ducatus*, 417–19 and nn. 155–57; Brunner, *Deutsche Rechtsgeschichte* 1:334. The four leading witnesses to this sale—Hato, Chuno, Sullo, and Popo—also appear as witnesses to Onulf's property gift in response to his son's death, and the name Reginolt provides at least circumstantial evidence of a relationship to the Scharnitz founders. See Jahn, *Ducatus*, 314–19, 323–24; Störmer, *Adelsgruppen*, 98n. 51.

gifts all came after attacks on the grantors themselves or their families. There is nothing wrong with taking the charters at face value and seeing the gifts as responses to death or to impending death. Another Freising charter from the year 772 shows a Bavarian aristocrat responding similarly to a mortal injury in a situation that had nothing to do with feud or wergeld. A kinsman of Duke Tassilo's named Hiltiprant fell off his horse because of "incautious riding" and injured his head to the point that his doctors despaired of his life. On his deathbed, Hiltiprant gave property he was holding as a benefice from Duke Tassilo to Freising with the duke's permission.[23]

To understand the property gifts in our feud charters, we need to look at what they accomplished. Haholt took care of his son Arn and his upkeep and provided for his own soul and those of his family. He had Arn's rights over the family property secured by Freising's formal ownership and by a written document in Freising's archives. Onulf too provided for his wife and son both memorially and with the family property and had the use and inheritance rights to this property specified in writing.[24] Cros placed himself in a doubly tight relationship with the new monastery at Scharnitz as donor and as monk. Along the way, he took part in the process by which the Scharnitz founding kindred concentrated its property in the monastery's endowment.

We must therefore see these property gifts, and by extension the conflicts that prompted them, as embedded within the larger world of property-giving visible in the Agilolfing-era charters. In this world, landowning

23. *TF* 49. This charter explicitly states that Hiltiprant was Tassilo's kinsman; see Störmer, *Adelsgruppen*, 26–27. Hiltiprant was also firmly connected to the kindreds involved in the feud charters. Haholt's son Arn appears as a deacon on the witness list to *TF* 49; he is accompanied by three of the leading witnesses to Onulf's gift in *TF* 65: Chuno, Sullo, and Popo. Jahn, *Ducatus*, 418, tries to fit this charter into his wergeld argument by suggesting that Hiltiprant may have been deliberately knocked off his horse and that *TF* 49 may therefore also reflect a feud in progress, despite the explicit *incaute aequitante* and the fact that all our other grantors explicitly say they had been attacked.

24. The scholarship has frequently pointed out that giving property to a church has the effect of nailing down formal title and use rights to the property in writing and in front of important witnesses and thus rendering them immune from challenge; see Wolfgang Hartung, "Adel, Erbrecht, und Schenkung: Die strukturellen Ursachen der frühmittelalterlichen Besitzübertragungen an die Kirche," 417–38; Jahn, *"Tradere ad sanctum,"* esp. 415, both in *Gesellschaftsgeschichte*, ed. Seibt. See the more extensive discussion of these articles at the beginning of Chapter 2. See also Ian Wood, "Disputes in Late Fifth- and Sixth-Century Gaul: Some Problems," in *Settlement of Disputes*, ed. Davies and Fouracre, 22, for a related argument that church archives in the early Middle Ages replaced vanishing late-Roman land registers.

aristocrats, the bishops, and the Agilolfing duke all cooperated with one another to achieve their own ends.[25] At one level, property gifts could simply involve the mutual interests of bishop and landowner in property and salvation. A Freising charter from the year 778 provides a good and typical example. According to this record, a priest named Arperht and a deacon named Maginrat built a church and invited Bishop Arbeo of Freising to consecrate it. Once the bishop had done so, Arperht and Maginrat gave property to the church and then gave the church and its endowment to the see of Freising. They did so under the condition that they would continue to hold the property for their lifetimes.[26] In other words, Bishop Arbeo asserted his control over churches in his diocese by consecrating the new church; moreover, he received formal title to the church and its endowment. Arperht and Maginrat for their part continued to enjoy the use of the church and its property and had a document placed in the Freising archives protecting that use from challenge. This arrangement bound the donors and the bishop in a mutually beneficial relationship that would last as long as the donors lived.

This kind of cooperation between the kindreds and the bishops appears on a much larger scale in the foundation of the monastery at Scharnitz. As we saw above, Reginperht and his kin converted the church at Scharnitz into a monastery and endowed it with their property. The connections forged by this act, however, reached beyond the founding kindred. The foundation and endowment of the new monastery took place in the presence of Bishop Joseph of Freising and the Freising archpriest Arbeo, who would later succeed Joseph as bishop. Duke Tassilo too expressed his interest in the new monastery and its huge endowment by giving his consent.[27]

25. The best exploration of this kind of phenomenon in the early Middle Ages remains Rosenwein, *To Be the Neighbor*.

26. *TF* 92. See the similar arrangement between Arbeo and the founders of a church in Kronacker recorded in *TF* 28, in which Bishop Arbeo dedicated the church and then agreed to let the founders keep control of it subject to episcopal oversight.

27. Reginperht alone gave the monastery an endowment of properties in eleven locations, stretching in an enormous semicircle from the Inn valley west of Innsbruck, north to the western suburbs of modern Munich, and northeast of Munich to the Rott River: Polling, Flauerling, Imst, Schlehdorf, Hofheim, Sindelsdorf, Schöngeising, Pasing, Gräfelfing, *in villa quae dicitur Curtana iuxta Fruen flumine* (possibly Kurthambach or Gurten), and Wallgau am Barmsee. On the locations, see Jahn, *Ducatus*, 410–11, and n. 125.

The founders gave the spiritual direction of the new foundation to Arbeo.[28] Arbeo, it turns out, was himself connected to the founding group and possibly belonged to it.[29] Nevertheless, chief founder Reginperht continued to exercise control over the monastery, even after it was moved north from Scharnitz to the village of Schlehdorf.[30] Reginperht not only controlled the monastery's properties but also influenced its spiritual direction. When Arbeo became bishop of Freising in 764, for example, he needed Reginperht's consent to install the future Freising bishop Atto as the monastery's new abbot. Reginperht and Atto, who was likewise connected to the founding kindred, continued to cooperate.[31] In 772, for instance, the two men

28. The foundation was carried out *in praesentia Joseph episcopi ortatoris rei et Arbionis archipresbiteri qui ecclesiam cum donatione tradendi studio commendavimus ad regendum.*

29. Arbeo has long been seen as connected to the greater Huosi kindred, which seems to have included the Scharnitz-Schlehdorfer. The conclusion that Arbeo was directly related to the Scharnitz-Schlehdorfer rests on the following prosopographical chain: in *TF* 44 (772), Arbeo stresses his blood relationship with a nun named Alpunia and her son Karolus. The pair had property in Langenpettenbach, where, according to *TF* 177 (799), an Odilo—apparently the Otilo [*sic*] who appears in the Scharnitz foundation charter *TF* 19—also had property. Alpunia's father was named Erchanfrid; an Erchanfrid was the leading witness to *TF* 19. Several scholars have also raised the possibility that Arbeo was connected to the Fagana, another of the *genealogiae* mentioned by the Bavarian Law. Hubert Glaser has recently concluded from this discussion that Arbeo had close family ties to the innermost circles of the aristocracy propertied between the Lech and the Inn. See Glaser, "Bischof Arbeo," in *Vita Corbiniani*, ed. Glaser, Brunhölz, and Benker, 28–32; Jahn, *Ducatus*, 414; Störmer, *Adelsgruppen*, 104, and *Früher Adel*, 2:331; Josef Sturm, "Bischof Arbeos von Freising bayerische Verwandte," *Zeitschrift für bayerische Landesgeschichte* 19 (1956): 568–72; Hubert Strzewitzek, *Die Sippenbeziehungen der Freisinger Bischöfe im Mittelalter* (Munich, 1938), 252.

30. *TF* 53.

31. Atto's connections to the Scharnitz-Schlehdorfer rest on his early and close relationship to the monastery and on prosopographical evidence for connections to the Huosi. Jahn, *Ducatus*, 422, argues from *TF* 53, where Arbeo refers to himself, Atto, and the Scharnitz monks as *fratres*, that both Atto and Arbeo entered into the new monastery's community at its foundation; he sees this as the strongest evidence that both men were members of the founding kindred. Störmer, *Früher Adel*, 2:331 and 361, referring back to Sturm and Strzewitzek (as n. 29), likewise places Atto among the Huosi and inclines strongly toward seeing him as a Scharnitz-Schlehdorfer.

traveled together to Rome to obtain the relics of Saint Tertullian for their monastery.[32]

In the years that followed, a series of aristocrats made further gifts to the monastery at Schlehdorf with Duke Tassilo's permission; their names and the properties concerned all anchor them firmly to the kinship network of the original founders. Most of these donations were either gifts designed to revert to Schlehdorf after the death of the grantors—that is, gifts *post obitum*—or gifts that contained explicit provisions for the return of the property as a benefice to the donor and/or his son.[33] One such gift from the year 776 makes clear the workings of the relationship of the founding kindred, their dependents, and Freising's ecclesiastical authority.[34] Two men named Hroadinc and Nendinc gave property to Schlehdorf. They asked Abbot Atto and a man they called "our lord Isanhard" for permission to make this gift with Duke Tassilo's consent, under the condition that after their deaths their sons Ellanod and Kaganhart could receive the property as a benefice from Abbot Atto and the monk Reginperht. The "lord" Isanhard was himself closely connected to the foundation and its founders; in the same year, he also gave property to Schlehdorf with Tassilo's permission.[35] His dependents Hroadinc and Nendinc made their gift with the explicit intention of passing it down to their sons; they regarded not only Abbot Atto but also the founder Reginperht as the authorities on whom the benefice arrangement depended.[36]

32. Jahn, *Ducatus*, 420–22, 427–29.

33. *TF* 45ab (772): Abbot Atto gives property in Kienberg, given to him with Tassilo's permission by Oadalker and his father, Anulo, to Schlehdorf *post obitum*; *TF* 75 (776): Isanhart gives property at Herrsching, Holzhausen, Raisting, and Erding to the church at Schlehdorf with Tassilo's consent; *TF* 76a (776): Reginhart, son of Isanhart, gives property at Dürrnhausen and Raisting to Schlehdorf *post obitum* with Tassilo's consent; *TF* 77 (776): Hroadinc and Nendinc give property at Vorder/Mitterfischen to Schlehdorf with a benefice arrangement for their sons Ellanod and Kaganhart; *TF* 171 (794): Hrimcrim gives property at Dettenhofen to Schlehdorf, arranging that his son Tozi accept the property as a benefice from Bishop Atto; *TF* 177 (799): Gaio gives all his paternal inheritance in three villas *in pago* Poapintal, namely, Oberhofen, Zirl, and Langen/Amperpettenbach, to Schlehdorf and receives as a benefice property in Langen/Amperpettenbach originally given by Otilo (presumably uniting it with the property there he had just given).

34. *TF* 77.

35. *TF* 75: among the witnesses are a Reginhart as well as Kaganhart and Nendinc. See Jahn, *Ducatus*, 432.

36. See Jahn, *Ducatus*, 431–33.

Property arrangements of this kind gave something to everyone. The bishop of Freising, by consecrating new foundations and by receiving them and their properties as gifts, had his right to control all churches and monasteries within his diocese respected.[37] Moreover, since he held formal title to the foundations and their properties, he could expect this right to translate into actual power when the donor or his heirs died. The donor kindreds, for

37. This right had its basis in canon law. As early as late antiquity, popes and church councils had asserted that because bishops had the right to consecrate churches, they had legal control over all churches within their dioceses—including those founded by aristocrats. During the early Merovingian period, the Frankish bishops developed this doctrine to include all churches, monasteries, and their properties. From the seventh century, however, diocesan rights in the Frankish world underwent a process of negotiation. First members of the Merovingian royal house, then members of aristocratic kindreds began patronizing religious foundations that were exempt from diocesan control as a way to forge personal and political connections transcending diocesan boundaries and as focal points for family identity and power. The Carolingians adapted such exemptions, as well as grants of immunity from royal jurisdiction, as part of an effort to make themselves the patrons and protectors of important churches and monasteries throughout their realm. They did not rigidly oppose the bishops, however; instead, they flexibly supported abbots, lay founders, or bishops as it suited their needs.

In Bavaria, in contrast, no canonical church organization existed before the mid-eighth century. When Saint Boniface set up the four Bavarian bishoprics in 739, he created the basis for one but did not give the new bishoprics defined geographical dioceses. The Bavarian bishops were left to create them on their own by asserting their canonical rights to consecrate individual churches and monasteries. The bishops, however, faced a society that considered the rights of founders over their foundations to be self-evident—indeed, as we have seen, the bishops of Freising came from this society. The Agilolfing dukes also strongly supported founders' rights. When Duke Tassilo reached his majority, the Bavarian bishops had to warn him to respect their control over all ecclesiastical affairs and properties (*Concilium Ascheimense*, c. III, 57). What resulted were the cooperative arrangements already discussed; the bishops had their rights honored but nonetheless participated in the continuing de facto control of churches, monasteries, and their endowments by their founders. See Geary, *Before France and Germany*, 169–78; Wilfried Hartmann, "Der rechtliche Zustand der Kirchen auf dem Lande: Die Eigenkirche in der fränkischen Gesetzgebung des 7. bis 9. Jahrhunderts," in *Cristianizzazione ed organizzazione ecclesiastica delle campagne nell'alto medioevo: Espansione e resistenze* (Spoleto, 1982), 397–441; Jahn, *Ducatus*, 291–300; Barbara H. Rosenwein, *Negotiating Space: Power, Restraint, and Privileges of Immunity in Early Medieval Europe* (Ithaca, N.Y., 1999).

their part, continued to control both the churches and monasteries they had built and the property they had endowed them with. In many cases, they could expect to pass these prerogatives down to the next generation. Duke Tassilo too had an interest in promoting such arrangements. By giving his consent to the creation of kindred monasteries, he ensured himself of the kindreds' loyalty and exercised at least nominal oversight of important foundations with a great deal of religious and economic power.[38]

The weight of custom and ducal authority in Agilolfing Bavaria strongly favored the ongoing control of donated property by the donor kindreds. This fact emerges most clearly in accounts of what happened when a churchman who was not a native of Bavaria violated this tradition. In late 745 or early 746, the Irishman Virgil arrived from the Frankish court to take up the direction of the see of Salzburg.[39] After his arrival, Virgil tried to take control of property that had been donated to Salzburg a half-century before, in the face of claims raised by a descendant of the original donor kindred. He failed because the claimant enjoyed the firm support of the Agilolfing duke Odilo, father of Tassilo III.

38. The exact nature of Tassilo's interest in foundations of this kind remains unclear. Jahn, *Ducatus*, 409–11, 416, 424–25, elevates it to an Agilolfing program to use monasteries controlled by loyal kindreds as tools of lordship and as sources of support against the Carolingians. According to his argument, both Tassilo and his father, Odilo, promoted monasteries to avoid having to rely on the Bavarian episcopate, which represented a power structure independent of ducal authority that had its own legal basis in canon law. The duke's formal consent to new monastic foundations reflected a claim to lordship over them. Tassilo's modus vivendi with the Bavarian episcopate allowed him to make this claim while still respecting the bishops' formal rights. How monasteries benefited the Agilolfings is made apparent by the Scharnitz-Schlehdorf foundation. The monastery at Scharnitz was founded in 763, the year Tassilo broke away from the political control of his Carolingian uncle Pippin. Along with a daughter house at Innichen, it provided Tassilo with a band of properties controlled by a kin group related to and loyal to him in the west and south of Bavaria, covering a strategic area fronting Alemannia and controlling the entire traffic from Bavaria to South Tyrol, Upper Italy, Lombardy, and Rome—that is, directly opposite the threat from the Carolingians.

39. After arriving on the continent from Ireland, Virgil spent two years at the court of Pippin III at Quierzy. In 745, Pippin sent him to Bavaria to take up the post of bishop of Salzburg; he arrived in late 745 or 746. Duke Odilo's cooperation reflects his dependence on Pippin at this stage in his career. Virgil seems to have served first as abbot of Saint Peter's in Salzburg. In June 749, he accepted ordination as bishop. See Jahn, *Ducatus*, 141–44; Wolfram, *Salzburg, Bayern, Österreich*, 252–75.

This incident is described in the two property catalogs from the see of Salzburg, the *Notitia Arnonis* and the *Breves Notitiae*.[40] The accounts stem from a now lost text apparently written by Virgil himself.[41] The story they tell fits in with the evidence we have seen thus far in the charters. During the reign of Salzburg's first bishop, Saint Rupert (d. ca. 716),[42] two men witnessed a miracle in the Pongau south of Salzburg at the site of what is now Bischofshofen.[43] The men, named Ledi and Tonazan, were unfree; Ledi is described as a *servus* of the duke and Tonazan as a *servus* of Bishop Rupert.[44] The event prompted Rupert to ask Duke Theodo (the same Theodo as in the *Life of Emmeram*) for permission to build a small monastery dedicated to Saint Maximilian on the site, which lay on property belonging to the ducal fisc. Theodo gave his permission but died shortly afterward. His son Theotbert continued his father's support for the new foundation; he also gave it property from his forest, which stretched for three miles around it.[45] He then gave the monastery and its property to the see of Salzburg.[46]

At least one of the men who first witnessed the miracle also gave property to the new foundation or had it given for him. Here the different versions of

40. See the Introduction, n. 59.

41. Now called by scholars the *Libellus Virgilii*. The *Notitia Arnonis* only briefly summarizes the *Libellus*: *NA* c. 8.1–8.7, 94–96, c. 24–25, 88–90. Herwig Wolfram argues that the compiler of the *NA* most likely used an early set of notes put together by Virgil shortly after his arrival in Bavaria. The compiler of the *Breves Notitiae*, however, reproduced a virtually intact text of the *Libellus* in its final form: *BN* c. 3.1—3.15, 104–18; c. 8.1–8.11, 112–14; c. 13.1–13.10, 120–22. See Wolfram, "Libellus Virgilii," in *Mönchtum, Episkopat und Adel*, ed. Borst, esp. 185–86 and 201. My discussion relies mainly on the text of the *Libellus* as contained in the *BN* with references to the version of the narrative contained in the *NA* as it becomes relevant.

42. Rupert arrived in Bavaria at the latest in 696; he died, in Worms, at the earliest in 716. See Wolfram, *Salzburg, Bayern, Österreich*, 227–51, esp. 244–45; Jahn, *Ducatus*, 48–64.

43. The miracle consisted of burning lights and a sweet smell. See Wolfram, *Salzburg, Bayern, Österreich*, 132–35; Jahn, *Ducatus*, 48–69, 203–11.

44. *BN* c. 3.1, 104. The *NA* calls them two brothers named Tonzano and Ursus, with no mention of their status: c. 8.1, 94.

45. *BN* 3.10, 106.

46. The *BN* gives this last piece of information not here but rather later, in the form of a comment that Duke Odilo did not know that his predecessor Theotbert had given the monastery and its property to the see of Salzburg: c. 8.3, 112. The *NA* in contrast openly states at this point in the story that Duke Theodo (who did not die in this version) made the gift not to the see of Salzburg itself but to the monastery of Saint Peter's: c. 8.4, 94.

the story in the two catalogs become important. According to the *Breves Notitiae*, Duke Theotbert granted the monastery property held by the ducal unfree Ledi and Ledi's brother Urso at "Albin"—now Oberalm, south of Salzburg.[47] In the *Notitia Arnonis*, however, both the original witnesses (called the brothers Tonzano and Ursus) themselves give all their property at Oberalm to the monastery with ducal permission.[48] As the discrepancies in the two versions suggest, we are not dealing here with simple serfs. These men came from a distinct and powerful kindred centered on Oberalm called the *genealogia de Albina*. The members of this kindred, who were most likely descended from the Roman population of the region, appear to have belonged to the elevated group of unfree in direct ducal service.[49]

Whether the men from Oberalm were able to give the property themselves or had it given for them by the duke, the property itself plainly came from the ducal fisc. The gift of the property to the Saint Maximilian monastery did not, however, sever the link between the property and the kindred. Instead, the brothers sent two younger relatives (either their nephews or their sons—the texts are unclear) to be trained as clerics at Salzburg. The younger pair then asked for and received the property, or at least half of it, from Salzburg as a benefice.[50] These two then passed the property down in a similar fashion to the next generation. This part of the story comes surrounded by the rhetoric of bad faith and ultimate betrayal. The first pair "with evil intentions" asked Bishop Rupert to grant them half their forebears' property as a benefice; Rupert complied, "in the hopes that they would faithfully serve his see."[51] The next generation held the prop-

47. *BN* 3.10. 106. On Oberalm, see Wolfram, "Libellus Virgilii," 192.

48. *NA* c. 8.4, 94.

49. The Albina served the Agilolfings in a military capacity in this Alpine region. This function, the prominent and powerful role they play in this dispute narrative, and the high offices some obtained (one served as a ducal *cancellarius* and one, as we see later, as a ducal *capellanus*) have led some scholars to identify them as belonging to the elevated group of ducal unfree known as the *servi principis* or adalschalks. See Wolfram, *Salzburg, Bayern, Österreich*, 132–35; Jahn, *Ducatus*, 234, 244–48, 559. Störmer, *Früher Adel*, 1:212–14, prefers to see them as ducal vassals and their identification here as *servi* as a deliberate construction by Salzburg to advance its property claims.

50. *BN* c. 3.11, 106; *NA* c. 8.4–8.5, 94. Lošek translates the terms used here, *nepotes* and *parentes*, as "descendants" and "forebears"; Jahn, "*Tradere ad sanctum*," in *Gesellschaftsgeschichte*, ed. Seibt, 404–5, reads them to mean "uncles" and "nephews." The *Libellus* names the pair that first received the property in benefice Wernharius and Dulcissimus; the *NA* calls them Uurmhari and Cissimo.

51. *BN* c. 3.12, 106.

erty for a long time, although it too "served the see [of Salzburg] with intent to betray it."[52] The hostile rhetoric notwithstanding, it is clear that Bishop Rupert understood and participated in a classic Agilolfing-era arrangement in which a kindred that had given its property (or had it given by the duke) to a new foundation could expect to continue to hold the property for generations. The relationship between the kindred and its property ended only when neighboring Slavs overran the site and the foundation was left abandoned.[53]

The story next jumps to the early 740s, to the time of Duke Odilo. During a rebellion against his rule, Odilo was forced to take refuge in the Frankish kingdom with the Carolingian mayor Pippin III.[54] With Odilo as his chaplain was a priest named Ursus, who belonged to the kindred from Oberalm.[55] Ursus went to the duke and asked for the abandoned foundation as a benefice. Odilo granted his request.[56] Here we learn that both Ursus and Odilo still regarded the foundation and its property as the duke's to dispose of and that both men saw Ursus's expectation of using the land his forebears had held as justified.

The bishop of Salzburg at the time, John (d. 745), did nothing to stop this arrangement.[57] Things changed, however, when Virgil arrived on the scene. Learning about the Saint Maximilian monastery, Virgil went to Odilo, told him the foundation's story, and asked that the monastery be returned to Salzburg. The monastery and its property, in his opinion, belonged to Salzburg de facto as well as de jure. The bishop ran into a stone wall with the duke, however; Odilo refused to relinquish his ultimate rights over the property. Neither would he disappoint his chaplain's expectation of continued use of his kindred's land, despite all Virgil's threats and appeals to the circumstances of the monastery's foundation. Odilo recognized Virgil's claims only to the point of offering a compromise exchange.[58]

52. *BN* c. 3.14, 106.

53. *BN* c. 3.15, 106–8.

54. *BN* c. 7.5, 112. On Odilo's exile 740/741, see Jahn, *Ducatus*, 172–73.

55. *BN* c. 8.1, 112.

56. The *Libellus* treats Odilo gently by commenting that he did not know that his predecessor Theotbert had given the foundation and its property to Salzburg: *BN* c. 8.3, 112. The *NA* sternly states that Odilo took the property from Salzburg by force: c. 8.6, 94.

57. Jahn, *Ducatus*, 142; Wolfram, *Salzburg, Bayern, Österreich*, 133.

58. The *NA* states simply that Odilo offered to give Virgil equivalent property somewhere else but that Virgil turned the offer down; Odilo therefore continued to hold the property: c. 8.7, 94–96. The *BN* puts things much more pointedly. Based on Bishop Rupert's rights as master of the Oberalmer *servus* Tonazon, one of the pair

The narrative continues in very colorful fashion. Odilo at last agreed to give Virgil half the disputed property. Virgil proceeded to build a church on that half and continued to demand the rest of the property. He ordered priests to service the new church continuously, "and therefore there was often great conflict."[59] Ursus fired back by building his own new church near Virgil's and summoning a seeless bishop named Liuti to consecrate it.[60] Virgil responded by excommunicating the bishop and forbidding anyone to carry on divine services at Ursus's church. There the matter rested; the church "remained banned, as long as Bishop Virgil lived."[61] This exchange gives us more evidence that as far as Ursus was concerned, the dispute hinged on his rights to his kindred's land at Oberalm rather than to the property belonging to the Saint Maximilian foundation as a whole. It hardly seems likely that the two parties would have built new churches at the place where the actual monastery and its church lay. Nevertheless, competing churches make a great deal of sense in a struggle over rights to the Oberalmer property.[62]

We learn two important things from this story. First, late in the reign of Duke Odilo, a conflict flared up between two ways of understanding property ownership. On the one hand, a descendant of a landholding kindred in ducal service expected to be able to hold family property given to a monastery, whereas the duke expected to retain ultimate control over what had belonged to the ducal fisc. On the other hand, Virgil claimed to exercise real control over property belonging to a foundation he regarded as having been given to his see. Second, at the time Virgil wrote his account of the dispute, his efforts to uphold what he regarded as his rights had failed utterly. The balance of power lay with the traditional Bavarian interpretation of such property arrangements; Virgil's story trails off with a stream of invective but no real concession from Odilo.[63]

---

that had witnessed the original miracle, Virgil demanded half the property. Odilo instead offered to exchange the property for other property. Virgil indignantly refused: c. 8.6–8.8, 112–14.

59. *BN* c. 8.9, 114.

60. *BN* c. 8.10, 114.

61. *BN* c. 8.11, 114.

62. The story of the competing churches makes the identification of "Albin" as modern Oberalm more certain. According to Wolfram, "Libellus Virgilii," 197, nowhere in the Salzach valley above Salzburg are there two churches so close together as at the paired villages of Oberalm and Puch—still regarded today as a "double-village" (*Doppelort*).

63. There are indications that Virgil and Odilo agreed to let the matter of the Oberalmer property quietly drop. According to the available evidence, relations be-

A second and much briefer conflict story contained in the two property catalogs shows Virgil later trying and failing to stop a similar situation from ever arising. Early in the reign of Odilo's son Tassilo, a certain Count Gunthar built a small monastery and a church on his own inherited property at Otting, near the Chiemsee.[64] Gunthar summoned Bishop Virgil to the site and declared his intent to provide the foundation with monks and an abbot, along with sufficient property to support them. Virgil insisted on asserting his rights over the churches and monasteries in his diocese. He asked under whose control the abbot and his monks would be; the count "at first did not want to tell him."[65] Virgil then stated baldly that he would not consecrate the church, the monastery, or the abbot until he knew "according to the laws of the church" under whose authority the foundation would fall.[66] Gunthar's reluctance indicates that he had probably hoped to keep the foundation under his own control. Virgil's threat, however, had its intended effect. Gunthar capitulated; he gave Virgil not only the monastery itself but also the right to provide it with monks and an abbot and to direct the community "just as he did the other churches of his diocese."[67]

It appears, however, that Virgil's assertion of control was short-lived. The *Notitia Arnonis* states that at some future and unspecified time, the monastery was unjustly taken away (*iniuste abstractam*) from Salzburg. King Charlemagne, "to the increase of his heavenly grace," had it returned.[68] The text does not identify the guilty party, but the other evidence discussed so far suggests that a relative or descendant of Gunthar had continued to control the monastery and its endowment. This unknown person would therefore have interpreted the original arrangement in the same way as the arrangements found in the Freising charters: the bishop of Salzburg enjoyed de jure rights over the foundation, but members of the founding kindred still had de facto control. In any case, Salzburg could apparently do little to

tween Virgil and Odilo were in general quite good. Nor did the dispute surface again during the reign of Odilo's son Tassilo. Even the wandering bishop Liuti, whom Ursus engaged to consecrate his "church of discord," found a place in the confraternity book of the monastery of Saint Peter's at Salzburg, in marked contrast to the pointed absence of some of Virgil's opponents such as Saint Boniface. See Wolfram, "Libellus Virgilii," 203.

64. Ibid., 186; Jahn, "Virgil," 216, and *Ducatus*, 288–90.
65. *BN* c. 13.2, 120.
66. *BN* c. 13.3, 120.
67. *BN* c. 13.4, 120; c. 13.7, 120.
68. *NA* c. 6.25, 88–90.

enforce its rights while Tassilo reigned. As we shall see, only after Charlemagne arrived on the scene could Salzburg exploit a new political landscape to make good its claims.

The cooperative relationship between the bishops and the kindreds visible in the Freising charters extended further than property. Two final Freising records tell us that the bishops of Freising could also help aristocrats find nonviolent solutions to conflict. Both these records add to our picture of how dispute was intertwined with land gifts and with aristocratic and episcopal interests in Agilolfing Bavaria. Moreover, they provide another very important piece of information. In contrast to the charters recording violence, these charters say what caused the conflicts they record: competition within a kindred for property.

The first of these records, produced in Freising in 765, tells how a nobleman named Poapo gave inherited property to the cathedral church at Freising.[69] Poapo began by calling together a large number of his relatives to get their advice concerning a "certain difficulty among my sons." Poapo's kinsmen advised him to give his inheritance to the church at Freising. Poapo duly appeared with his relatives and followers at a synod being held at Freising and suggested this course of action to Bishop Arbeo. The bishop, in the words of the charter, "consoled us and graciously accepted this counsel, and promised to confirm our memory in that house of God forever." Poapo then gave his property, for the salvation of his soul and the absolution of his sins, to Freising in the presence of the clergy and with the confirmation of his relatives. In return, he received the lifetime use of the property for himself and his sons. Poapo added the condition that "no one be able to take my inheritance from the church of Saint Mary [i.e., at Freising] because of any dispute among my sons, if such should occur."

The Poapo charter tells us about some alternatives to violence. Faced with an inheritance dispute among his sons, Poapo called a kindred council, which advised him to give his property to Freising in order to stop the dispute. Although the family continued to enjoy use rights, the church's formal ownership acted to dampen the conflict. Bishop Arbeo did his part by graciously accepting Poapo's offer (to which he could not have been averse in any case) and by promising to preserve the memory of the kindred in Freising's prayers. The prominent role played by the family council here matches that played by a

69. *TF* 23. The record explicitly calls Poapo a *vir nobilis*.

similar council in the Haholt charter we looked at earlier. There Haholt called the council not to mediate a dispute but rather to help him decide how to react to one that had put him on his deathbed. Haholt's kindred, like Poapo's, acted in tandem with the bishop of Freising to determine Haholt's actions.

The second dispute likewise stemmed directly from conflict over property within a kindred. It reveals another possible alternative to violence: resort to the Agilolfing duke himself. This dispute forms the climax of a sequence of events, recorded in separate charters, surrounding a man named Toto. In 775, Toto made a gift to Freising of the property left him after he had divided the family patrimony with his sons as the Bavarian Law required.[70] A year later, one of Toto's sons, Scrot, fell mortally ill. For the salvation of his soul and with his father's consent, Scrot gave his share of the family property to Bishop Arbeo of Freising. Soon afterward, Scrot died. After his death, "seven days of masses having been celebrated as was customary," Toto confirmed his son's gift on the altar of the church at Freising in the presence of a large number of relatives and of the entire Freising clergy.[71] At this point, we learn that Toto had another son, named Wago, who was apparently much affected by his brother's death. On the same day, Wago gave his share of the patrimony to Freising for the souls of himself, his father, and his ancestors. The gift was to take effect after his death. His father, Toto, and his two other brothers, as well as all his neighbors, consented to the gift.[72]

In the following year, evidence for a dispute within Toto's family emerges, a dispute that seems to have been connected to the death of Toto's first wife and his subsequent remarriage. On November 16, 777, the kindred met at Duke Tassilo's palace at Freising. The duke and his "senate"—meaning his closest circle of advisers—ordered Toto and his sons to agree on and confirm an adjustment to their property arrangements.[73] Two of Toto's sons each received an unfree dependent over and above the portions they had received earlier.[74] In addition, Toto was required to honor his dead son Scrot's earlier gift to Freising by dividing his own share of the family patrimony as well as some property on the river Isen in half and giving the

---

70. *TF* 70; *Lex B* C. I/1. Here I differ with Jahn (*Ducatus*, 488), who regards the property division in *TF* 70 as resulting from an inheritance dispute (*Erbauseinandersetzung*).

71. *TF* 72a.

72. *TF* 72b.

73. *TF* 86. On the meaning of "senate" in this context, see Jahn, *Ducatus*, 490.

74. One, Cundhart, received a *colonus* whereas the other, Ratolt, received a *servus* and his wife and son.

resulting portion to Freising for Scrot "as had been given earlier." It appears that Toto, despite his earlier confirmation of Scrot's gift, had not given up some of Scrot's property and had to cede it to Freising with some of his own. Given the fluid nature of property gifts, however, this clause may simply have been intended to record Freising's de jure rights among the tangle of actual possessions. Particularly interesting is an explicit declaration that the new arrangement could not be violated in favor of Toto's new wife. The record stipulates that no further divisions were to take place among Toto's sons, or with respect to their stepmother, Ospurga, or with respect to Toto himself, or with respect to the see of Freising. This suggests that the arrangement must have been intended primarily to nail down the original sons' rights with respect to possible offspring of their father's second marriage.[75] Duke Tassilo and the other nobles present consented to the arrangement in the presence of witnesses from both Toto's kindred and the Freising clergy. Two judges also consented and decreed that the arrangement should remain in force forever.

The most striking thing about this arrangement among Toto, his sons, his new wife, and the bishop of Freising is that it took place in the presence and with the participation of Duke Tassilo. The scribe who wrote the record represented Tassilo as acting with all the coercive public authority inherent in his office. The duke appears in full ducal array with his panoply of judges and his "senate" in the ducal palace at Freising. The notice states that the agreement between Toto and his sons was worked out at the order of the duke and with the participation of the senate; it was, moreover, affirmed by the decree of the two judges. To modern eyes, it looks as if the Toto kindred's property and inheritance arrangements were an affair of state.

Toto and his family in fact belonged to the highest ranks of the circle surrounding Tassilo. One need only look at the requiem masses held by Bishop Arbeo and the entire Freising cathedral clergy for Scrot to get an idea of the family's status.[76] Moreover, a great deal of circumstantial evidence points to a kindred relationship between Toto and the Agilolfings.[77]

75. Jahn, *Ducatus*, 488–89.

76. This impression of the Toto kindred's status is reinforced by the impressive list of witnesses to *TF* 86, which included some of the most prominent aristocrats in Bavaria and Bishop Virgil of Salzburg, who with several others had rushed all the way across Bavaria from Kremsmünster to Freising to be present; see Jahn, *Ducatus*, 490.

77. On the Toto group's connections, see Jahn, *Ducatus*, 488–89, 490–94. Jahn lays out the following evidence for a kindred relationship between the Toto group and the Agilolfings: in the witness list to *TF* 86, right behind Toto's sons Cundhart

When seen against this background, Toto's inheritance arrangements in the wake of his second marriage and the nature of his relationship with the see of Freising are clearly "matters of state." Duke Tassilo acted as a mediator, both in his capacity as duke and in his capacity as head of an interlocking network of kin groups, to ensure stability among close relatives and his closest followers. The stability of the duchy and the stability of a family group flowed one from the other, explaining the blending here of family inheritance arrangements with the full display of public power on the part of the duke. It becomes in this case so difficult to distinguish "family" from "state" matters that the (in any case modern) categories have no meaning. The participants themselves may well have not understood the distinction.

CONFLICT, MERCY, AND THE SAINT

Up to this point, we have seen that the bishops of Freising during the Agilolfing period avoided direct conflict with their aristocratic neighbors. Instead, they helped the aristocratic kindreds settle disputes within their own ranks and worked with them as they made their inheritance arrangements or founded and endowed churches and monasteries. Nevertheless, at least one Freising bishop, Arbeo, was very concerned with how a bishop should act when he was a party to conflict. Arbeo expressed this concern in his second saint's life, the *Life of Saint Corbinian*. Corbinian was Freising's first bishop and the see's patron saint. His life as Arbeo tells it is full of conflict, much of it over property, which involves the saint himself as a party.[78] The

---

and Ratolt, appears the Hiltiprant who is explicitly labeled a relative of Duke Tassilo's in *TF* 49. The Toto group's property was concentrated on the Isen, to the north of Freising on the Amper, around Airischwand, and at Holzen by Zolling. In a later Freising charter, *TF* 198 (804), Wago, who by this point had entered on a clerical career, appears acting as the head of the Zolling church and receiving property gifts (see the further discussion of Wago in Chapter 2). Zolling also appears in the very first Freising charter, *TF* 1, in which Duke Odilo confirmed a gift made by a Moatbert and his wife Totana of property at Zolling to Freising. The connection of property and Totana's name leads Jahn to suspect that Moatbert and his wife were related both to Toto, possibly as his parents, and to Duke Odilo. Toto itself represents a contraction of the Agilolfing name Theodo. The Toto clan, like the Agilolfings, also had kin connections to Alemannia and to the Lombard royal house: see Hans Jänichen, "Warin, Rudhard, and Scrot: Besitzgeschichtliche Betrachtungen zur Frühgeschichte des Stiftes Buchau," *Zeitschrift für württembergische Landesgeschichte* 14 (1955): 372–84; Hartung, "Bertolde in Baiern," 115–60.

78. This is in marked contrast to the peacemaking or other third-party interventions in conflict by clerics, saints, or their relics described by Edward James,

Life of Corbinian thus offers us a chance to see how a bishop of Freising viewed the proper way to resolve conflict when the patron of his see was directly involved.

Arbeo most likely composed the *Life of Corbinian* sometime around 769 to coincide with the translation of Corbinian's relics to Freising.[79] He evidently had a great deal more to go on than he did when he composed the *Life of Emmeram*. Arbeo was himself only a generation removed from the saint.[80] He could therefore draw on eyewitness accounts of others who had known Corbinian, in particular his own mentor at Freising, Bishop

---

"*Beati pacifici*: Bishops and the Law in Sixth-Century Gaul," in *Disputes and Settlements*, ed. Bossy, 25–46, and Geoffrey Koziol, "Monks, Feuds, and the Making of Peace in Eleventh-Century Flanders," in *The Peace of God: Social Violence and Religious Response in France around the Year 1000*, ed. Thomas Head and Richard Landes (Ithaca, N.Y., 1992), 239–58, as well as in the Bavarian charters from the Agilolfing period. The single exception fits well with the evidence presented by James: see n. 90.

79. See Brunhölzl, introduction to his translation of the *Vita Corbiniani*, 77–81, and Glaser, "Bischof Arbeo," 11–76, esp. 18, both in *Vita Corbiniani*, ed. Glaser, Brunhölzl, and Benker; Bischoff, *Südostdeutschen Schreibschulen*, 1:98, 207. The life exists in two versions. One, which survives only in two ninth-century manuscripts, has been identified as essentially Arbeo's primarily because of its retention of the bishop's rough and idiosyncratic Latin style. The second, a linguistically polished and substantively altered version, is generally held to stem from the early tenth century, thus taking it out of our purview. Of the two "Arbeonic" manuscripts, one consists of a fragmentary text copied in the early part of the ninth century at the monastery at Reichenau contained in the "Legendary of Reginbert" (Karlsruhe Codex XXXII). The second, part of a collection of saints' lives (Brit. Lib. Addidamenta 11880), has been more precisely dated to Regensburg during the reign of Bishop Baturic (818–47). Both these manuscripts apparently originate from a common ancestor produced at Freising, but whether this ancestor was Arbeo's original production remains debated. The latest opinion, based on the observation of interpolations in the Regensburg and Reichenau texts that postdate Arbeo (none of which concerns conflict), holds that their common ancestor was written at Freising sometime after Arbeo's death in 783 and possibly as late as the 830s. With the exception of this added material, then, the text of Arbeo's *Life of Corbinian* contained in the Regensburg and Reichenau manuscripts covers the period from Arbeo's original composition in 769 through at least the first decades of the ninth century and possibly as late as 847.

80. Arbeo himself as a young boy, according to his own testimony in *Vita Corbiniani*, c. 32, 148–50, was saved from death shortly after Corbinian's burial by the saint's intervention.

Ermbert.[81] As a result, the *Life of Corbinian* paints its subject with an immediacy and individuality that separates it markedly from other contemporary saints' lives.[82] This portrayal includes a number of highly individual descriptions of conflict.

Corbinian was a Frankish nobleman of the period around the turn of the eighth century who felt an early call to the monastic life.[83] After abandoning his home for a small cell at the entrance to his village's deserted church, the young saint began manifesting his holy power through a series of miracles. The second of them gives us our first glimpse of Corbinian in conflict. Seduced "by the whisperings of the ancient enemy," that is, by the devil, a thief dared to steal the saint's mule.[84] Hearing this, Corbinian prayed the night through and had a vision that the thief would return. The following morning the mule indeed returned, carrying the thief in a helpless trance. Corbinian had the man laid on the ground and began to berate him with accusations and admonitions. The thief awoke terrified and swore he would never do anything evil again, even if he should be ruined through poverty. At this, the saint ordered him to get up, which he was suddenly able to do. After relating how the mule had become uncontrollable and had dragged him through the forest the entire night, the thief accepted his penance from the saint. Corbinian responded by giving the thief three silver pieces so that he would not have to resort to thievery again and joyfully sent him on his way.

This short story can be reduced to the following building blocks. A man committed a crime against the saint. Divine power, summoned by the saint's prayers, prevented him from enjoying the fruits of his crime and instead compelled him to return what he had taken. The saint angrily rebuked the thief, prompting repentance. He then forgave the criminal and went so far as to act mercifully: he gave him money to keep him from having to resort

81. A direct reference to Ermbert appears in *Vita Corbiniani*, c. 30, 140, as we see later.

82. For the identifiable hagiographic models in the *Life of Corbinian*, which include the *Dialogues* of Gregory the Great, Jerome's *Vita Antonii et Pauli* and *Vita Hilarionis*, and the *Vita Columbani* of Jonas of Bobbio, see Brunhölzl's introduction to the *Vita Corbiniani*, 80–83, and Glaser, "Bischof Arbeo," 21–25, 64 and n. 167, both in *Vita Corbiniani*, ed. Glaser, Brunhölzl, and Benker. Brunhölzl has very helpfully noted the appearance of the pertinent models in his apparatus; they are discussed later in the (few) cases in which they bear on conflict narratives.

83. On the "historical" Corbinian, see Jahn, *Ducatus*, 69–73, 98–118; Wolfram, *Geburt Mitteleuropas*, 118–22, 125, 146–47.

84. *Vita Corbiniani*, c. 4, 88–94.

to further crime. In short, divine intervention and his own anger allowed Corbinian to uphold his property rights. The thief's humiliation and repentance then set the stage for reconciliation and a gracious act of mercy.[85]

Somewhat later in the *Life*, we find a curious pair of nested tales concerning the theft of horses. They follow the same pattern but add the plot device of a third-party intercession that triggers the act of mercy.[86] After fourteen years, saddened by the attention and riches showered on his tiny community, Corbinian left his homeland for Rome to ask the pope for a place where he and his followers might find solitude. The pope responded by making Corbinian a bishop and ordering him back to Gaul to preach. Corbinian reluctantly obeyed. Deeply disturbed by the fame that an impressive and growing array of miracles was bringing him, however, he set out again for Rome. This time he took a different route: he passed through Alemannia and ended up in Bavaria. After refusing princely gifts offered him by the Agilolfing duke Theodo,[87] Corbinian traveled to the seat of Theodo's son Grimoald at Freising. Grimoald pleaded with the bishop to stay with him. The saint likewise refused and headed across the Alps into northern Italy.

When Corbinian and his party reached Trent, the count of the city, Count Husing, saw that the saint had an especially noble stallion and decided he absolutely had to have it. On finding that he could not buy it, Husing ordered that it be quietly stolen. The story of how the count was punished for his misdeed by divine intervention, however, is put off until "we reach the appropriate place in the narrative."[88]

---

85. A similar story appears in Jonas of Bobbio's *Vita Columbani*: late in Book I, when Saint Columbanus and his companions are in Tours, the saint returns from praying at the tomb of Saint Martin to his ship moored on the Loire. There he finds his companions saddened by the theft of all their property. Columbanus does not pray to God, however; he returns to the grave of Saint Martin and berates the saint, saying he had not spent all night praying at Martin's grave only to have his property stolen. Thereupon terrible pain strikes the thief, and his companions hurriedly return the property and beg for forgiveness. There is no mention of reconciliation or an act of mercy; Jonas simply notes that from then on, everyone regarded Columbanus's property as sacrosanct. *Ionae Vitae Columbani I*, ed. and trans. Herbert Haupt, *Quellen zur Geschichte des 7. und 8. Jahrhunderts*, AQ IVa (Darmstadt, 1982), c. 22, 468–70.

86. *Vita Corbiniani*, c. 16, 112–14; c. 21, 122–24; c. 22, 126–28.

87. Again, the same Duke Theodo as in the *Life of Emmeram* and the *Notitia Arnonis/Breves Notitiae*.

88. *Vita Corbiniani*, c. 16, 112.

Corbinian's party next reached the Lombard capital, Pavia. The king of the Lombards, after showering the saint with gifts, ordered a leading citizen of the city to make sure Corbinian and his party crossed the river Po safely. At the harbor on the river, the nameless citizen noticed that Corbinian had a pretty Spanish horse. He offered to buy it, but the saint declined, saying he planned to give it to the pope. The stubbornness of the "ancient enemy" filled the citizen with such desire for the horse that he ordered it held back at the end of the train and secretly gave instructions to one of his men to steal it. This man, as soon as Corbinian had crossed the river, sprang onto the horse and rode it into the woods. The citizen played dumb and ran about looking for the man and horse. Not finding them, he threw himself at the feet of the saint and begged him not to report him to the king for his carelessness. Corbinian did nothing, knowing full well that God would punish the citizen. Again, the end of the story is saved for later.

The endings of these two virtually identical tales unfold in reverse order. When Corbinian reached Pavia on his way back from Rome, he met a party bringing a corpse on a bier out the city gate. The corpse turned out to be that of the citizen who had ordered the theft of the Spanish horse. At an audience with the Lombard king, the wife of the dead man threw herself grief-stricken at Corbinian's feet. She had brought the Spanish horse with her and moreover two hundred gold solidi. The woman reported that on the day he had stolen the horse, her husband had had a stroke. After the doctors had given up on him, he had called his wife to him. He had asked her to care for the horse, to admit what he had done, and to give Corbinian the horse and the money so that he might pray God to forgive him. The Lombard king, full of sympathy, sprang from his throne, likewise threw himself at the saint's feet, and begged him not to reject what the woman offered. Everyone else present also pleaded with the saint on the woman's behalf. Corbinian reluctantly gave way; as the king arose, Corbinian spoke to him mildly, saying no one should be punished twice—if a man had been punished in body and had admitted his sin, God would not thrust him into eternal damnation. Further, he promised to support the man as best he could with prayer.

The end of the story involving Count Husing follows the same pattern. After leaving Pavia, Corbinian neared Trent. Several of his people saw the stallion that had been stolen running behind a mare but in such bad condition that it was hardly recognizable. As the party reached the city gates, Husing came out and threw himself at Corbinian's feet. He freely admitted what he had done and told how God had punished him. The count had led the stallion to his mares, which all fell prey to the "elephant sickness" (*elefantino morbo*) and died, with the exception of the one animal the stallion now followed. The stallion itself was in terrible shape; not only was it emaciated, but its male member, which hung bare and limp, was so battered by the hooves of the mare that it could no longer fulfill its natural function.[89] After making this confession, the count offered the saint two of his best Spanish horses and two hundred solidi. He further asked the saint humbly not to reject this compensation and to forgive him his sin, for which he had already paid. Corbinian laughed out loud; he then forgave the man and went on his way.

These two stories follow an expanded version of the pattern we saw in the case of the mule thief. A person committed a crime against the saint. Divine intervention both punished the evildoer and prompted repentance and total surrender. Once he had achieved these goals, the saint responded with mercy: he accepted compensation and agreed to pray for the men who had hurt him. In the case of the citizen from Pavia, we are told that the saint was forced to display clemency by the pleas of the assembled, including the king of the Lombards himself. This "begging group" provided the saint with the opportunity to accept the return of his horse and the compensation, and to forgive and pray for the dead man, without showing weakness.

Six of the eight conflict stories in the *Life* follow this narrative pattern.[90] The pattern describes bilateral, and in some cases negotiated, settlements in a way that allows the saint to forgive his opponents, to act mercifully, and to meet community expectations about the proper resolution of the disputes without surrendering any of his authority or rights. In none of the disputes does Corbinian reach for an outside judicial authority or mediator. Indeed,

---

89. A point amended in the Arbeonic texts by the interpolated qualification "which the tongue for shame is reluctant to say." Ibid., c. 22, 126.

90. One of the two exceptions, the conflict between Corbinian and the duchess Pilitrud, is discussed later. The other is a typical Merovingian-era "gallows miracle" that is unusual in this *Life* for its adherence to hagiographic tradition. Corbinian, on his way to an audience with the Frankish mayor Pippin, found a robber named Adalpert about to be hanged. Unable to persuade the executioners to release him, Corbinian made the sign of the cross on Adalpert's neck and went to Pippin to ask for the robber's body. Messengers sent to the scene found that Adalpert had miraculously survived the hanging (*Vita Corbiniani*, c. 10–12, 100–106). This story is part of a larger tradition, recently explored by Edward James, of depicting the saint/bishop as duty bound to intervene in the machinery of secular justice on behalf of mercy; see James, "*Beati pacifici*," in *Disputes and Settlements*, ed. Bossy, 33–38; František Graus, "Die Gewalt bei den Anfängen des Feudalismus und die 'Gefangenenbefreiung' der merowingischen Hagiographie," *Jahrbuch für Wirtschaftsgeschichte* (1961): 61–156; Brunner/v. Schwerin, *Deutsche Rechtsgeschichte* 2:602.

there is no higher authority than the saint save God, who intervenes on Corbinian's behalf to force his opponents' surrender. Instead, Corbinian stands as the equal or superior of his adversaries, whether commoners, counts, dukes, or even kings, and resolves the disputes directly with them.

The script applies regardless of the social or political position of the saint's opponent, with the caveat that in the case of opponents of lower status the required surrender is involuntary. The mule thief, for example, was forced to surrender by the divine intervention that rendered him helpless. Similarly, another conflict story in the *Life* pits Corbinian against a group of fishermen who tried to take a giant fish caught by one of his men on the journey to Rome. After the fish had been recovered, Corbinian ordered the fishermen lashed feet first to a stake and whipped, while he reproached them for stealing the gift of God to his pilgrims. The saint then had the fishermen released and given money so they would not have to return empty-handed from their day's work.[91]

On three occasions, Corbinian has a run-in with someone of very high status indeed, namely, the ducal son Grimoald at Freising and his wife Pilitrud.[92] In the first two cases, the pair surrenders voluntarily. In the third, however, Pilitrud refuses to surrender and instead chooses to escalate the conflict. It is from this story that we learn the terrible consequences of refusing to go along with what we can begin to call in shorthand the "act of mercy" script.

When Corbinian arrived back at Freising, he sent messengers to Grimoald saying he would not see him until the duke separated himself from the "lover" he had taken to wife: Pilitrud, the ex-wife of his dead brother, Theodald. By entering into what the church saw as an incestuous marriage, the ducal couple had committed a crime not against the saint but rather

91. *Vita Corbiniani*, c. 18–19, 116–20. At least two of these stories seem to have enjoyed a particular importance to Bishop Arbeo and his community at Freising. Two passages in the "Arbeonic" text, noted by Brunhölzl as interpolations, mention a silver tablet showing scenes from the saint's life set up at Corbinian's grave after the translation of his relics to Freising. The first passage (ibid., c. 19, 120) notes that the tablet contained a representation of the whipping of the fishermen. The second (ibid., c. 22, 128) notes that it depicted, in explicit detail, the ravaged Spanish stallion stolen by Count Husing as it followed the sole surviving mare from the count's herd. Apparently, scenes representing the divine or human punishment consequent on stealing the saint's property merited a position of particular and graphic visibility at the saint's shrine.

92. On Pilitrud, see Jahn, *Ducatus*, 98–107; K. Reindel, "Das Zeitalter der Agilolfinger," in *HbG*, 159–60, 162–64.

against God. In response, Corbinian withdrew his presence. For forty days, he refused to see Grimoald; he instead sent daily messengers with alternating threats of hell and appeals to the pleasures of heaven. Finally, the pair agreed to separate. They enacted their surrender ritually; they came before the saint, threw themselves at his feet, and admitted their sin. Corbinian laid his hands on their heads and strengthened them with the sign of the cross. Then he raised them up, directed them to do penance and to give alms, and ordered them to sin no more. Thereupon everyone went indoors and took a common meal, namely, "food for the body and the sacrament for the soul."[93]

Corbinian's second run-in with Grimoald and Pilitrud likewise involves the saint in a defense of God's rights. One day the three were sitting at table, and the bishop blessed the table and food. Then Grimoald took a piece of bread—not from any special supply but from the table—and without thinking threw it to his favorite dog. Corbinian exploded with rage; he kicked the table over with his right foot, sprang up, and cried out that he who was not ashamed to throw blessed things to the dogs was not worth the blessing.[94] Again, he withdrew his presence; he stormed out of the house and threatened no longer to concern himself with the duke or to eat with him. Pilitrud reacted with a decision to poison Corbinian, which we examine later. Grimoald, however, with much more restraint, ordered the entry to the palace blocked so that Corbinian could not leave. Then he went out from the palace with his nobles, threw himself at Corbinian's feet, offered satisfaction, and calmed the angry saint with presents. Although Arbeo does not make this point explicit, the presence of Grimoald's nobles at the tableaux would seem to imply the presence of a "begging" group similar to the one that had put pressure on Corbinian in Pavia. Faced with Grimoald's surrender, Corbinian told the duke to get up and offered him the kiss of peace before once again taking a common meal with him.

The last conflict story in the *Life* tells of the final showdown between Corbinian and Pilitrud.[95] On the way to the Freising church, Corbinian met

---

93. *Vita Corbiniani*, c. 24, 130–32. On the common meal in the early Middle Ages as a way to symbolize the restoration of peace, see the work of Gerd Althoff cited in the Introduction, n. 24, as well as "*Amicitiae* as Relationships between States and People," in *Debating the Middle Ages: Issues and Readings*, ed. Lester K. Little and Barbara H. Rosenwein (London, 1998), 191–210.

94. This appears to be a model for, or at least a parallel to, Count Timo's crime in the *Carmen de Timone comite* of allowing his dog to drink from the holy spring; see the Introduction.

95. *Vita Corbiniani*, c. 29–31, 138–42.

a peasant woman, whom he knew to be a witch, loaded down with gifts. When the saint challenged her, the witch explained that she had just freed Grimoald's favorite son from demons. Corbinian flew into a violent rage. He leaped off his horse, beat the woman personally, and distributed her gifts to the poor. He then left Freising and returned to his house; raging at Pilitrud's duplicity in engaging a witch to heal her son, he refused to reenter the city. Pilitrud, on hearing the witch's story, herself flew into a rage. The duchess then prepared in secret, without telling her husband, a plot to get rid of Corbinian. She commissioned a man to wait for the court to leave Freising and then take a few men and kill the bishop.

When the court left the city, a man named Ermbert (whom Arbeo identifies as the future bishop of Freising and his own spiritual mentor) got wind of the plot and warned Corbinian. The bishop hastily abandoned Freising for Mais, in the South Tyrol. From there he sent a warning message to Pilitrud, saying she would soon lose her position and end her life in poverty. Grimoald, hearing of the attempted assassination, sent messengers to Corbinian asking him to return. The bishop refused, saying he had to protect himself from the attacks of "a Jezabel."[96] The rest of the story concerns what happened to Pilitrud, her family, and her accomplices. The ducal child the witch had healed died; Grimoald himself fell to an assassin. The man who had actually carried out the attack died from a lance blow he received while at the latrine. The duchess herself indeed ended her life in poverty. Taken by the Frankish mayor Charles Martel after his invasion of Bavaria in 725, she lost fame, power, and possessions. She ended up possessing only the donkey cart on which she traveled to Italy, where she died. The rest of her children never reached positions of rulership and lost their lives under unhappy circumstances.[97]

Some have interpreted the tale of the demise of Pilitrud and her family, like that of Lantperht in the *Life of Emmeram*, as representing Arbeo's antipathy for the Agilolfing house.[98] The evidence that supports this conclusion is ambiguous at best. The story remains carefully focused on Pilitrud; it even represents the death of Grimoald as stemming from her crime. It does

96. Ibid., c. 30, 140; "Jezabel" refers to the wife of King Ahab of Israel in the Old Testament Book of Kings.

97. On the respective ends of Grimoald and Pilitrud and the invasion of Bavaria by Charles Martel in 725, see Jahn, *Ducatus*, 101–7.

98. See, for example, Prinz, *Frühes Mönchtum*, 500; Maß, *Bistum Freising*, 68; in opposition, Bosl, "Der 'Adelsheilige,'" in *Speculum Historiale*, ed. Bauer, Boehm, and Müller, 177; Glaser, "Bischof Arbeo," in *Vita Corbiniani*, ed. Glaser, Brunhölzl, and Benker, 57.

not provide a blanket condemnation of the Agilolfings; not only does it not touch on Grimoald's father, Duke Theodo, but it represents a nephew of Grimoald's, Hucbert, as winning the favor of Bishop Corbinian by behaving toward him with all honor and submission.[99]

When looked at from the perspective of conflict imagery, the Pilitrud narrative would seem to serve as a warning rather than a political statement. If the previous stories present a model for how the holy hero had to behave in order to uphold his own and God's rights and prestige, the Pilitrud story tells us what would happen when an opponent refused to go along. By her refusal to surrender in the face of the saint's anger, Pilitrud sealed her fate; dishonoring God and his saint led to the destruction of her hopes and the withering of her house.[100]

In the Freising charters from the Agilolfing period, we have seen sparse and indirect but nonetheless tangible evidence for conflict within the Bavar-

---

99. *Vita Corbiniani*, c. 32, 143. The same holds true for the *Life of Emmeram*; the consequences of Emmeram's martyrdom remain confined to Lantperht, his off-spring, and the men who carried out the execution. Only the tenth-century revision of the *Life* broadens the story to encompass the downfall of the entire Agilolfing house in 794: see Bischoff, "Nachwort," in *Vita Haimhrammi*, 95–96.

100. In Jonas of Bobbio's *Vita Columbani*, the conflict concerning Saint Colum-banus and Queen Brunchildis and her grandson King Theuderich of Burgundy is in many ways similar to that involving Corbinian, Pilitrud, and Grimoald. The conflict began when Columbanus, like Corbinian, attacked Brunchildis's grandson King Theuderich for keeping concubines instead of a proper wife. Brunchildis, like Pil-itrud, became angry at the saint at the prompting of "the ancient serpent" and is de-scribed as a "Jezabel." When she exploded with rage at Columbanus's refusal to bless Theuderich's illegitimate children, the saint left the court (accompanied by a mirac-ulous earthquake). As the conflict escalated, Columbanus approached Theuderich but refused to enter his palace; the king tried to mollify him with a sumptuous ban-quet. Columbanus dashed the meal to the ground, prompting a terrified Theuderich to beg for forgiveness. Jonas's account, however, never quite settles down into the narrative pattern of conflict, surrender, and peacemaking that so regularly character-izes Arbeo's conflict stories. Columbanus's withdrawal from the Burgundian court did not prompt surrender and an overt reconciliation; at Theuderich's terrified plea for forgiveness, Columbanus simply "was pacified" and went back to his monastery at Luxeuil. When Theuderich returned to his libertine lifestyle and the saint once more reproached him, the young king allied himself with his grandmother and ex-iled the saint. The consequences of escalating the conflict were the same as in the

ian landholding kindreds. Some of this conflict was violent; brief reports of violent assault appear in the charters because their victims responded by giving property to the see of Freising. Two of these reports indicate that the violence could stem from a feud within an extended kin group. Unfortunately, the records do not reveal what the feud was all about. Bishop Arbeo's critique of feud in the *Life of Saint Emmeram*, however, suggests that at least part of the Bavarian aristocracy regarded killings such as those that claimed Cros and the younger Keparoh as a legitimate way to respond to a grievance.

Violence was not the only way landholders in Agilolfing Bavaria handled disputes. Both kindred councils and the bishops of Freising played important advisory or mediating roles in resolving conflict. When Haholt had to devise a response to his apparently impending death, he summoned his kin, who urged him to turn to Bishop Joseph. Similarly, Poapo's kin not only advised Poapo to go to Bishop Arbeo but also suggested that he give the property his sons were fighting over to the see of Freising as a way to end the conflict. Arbeo in turn blended self-interest with his role as a peacemaker by accepting the disputed property as a gift.

Duke Tassilo himself could get involved in dispute settlement as well. The duke, who appears at one and the same time as the ruler of Bavaria and the head of a large interconnected network of aristocrats, acted as the mediator and enforcer of the settlement of the Toto kindred's property arrangements. The quality of Tassilo's involvement in this case makes it very difficult to separate "state" from "family" matters, showing that the distinction is here less than useful.

In the examples of nonviolent dispute settlement, property emerges as one of the flashpoints for conflict within the kindreds. Poapo ended a dispute among his sons over his family's property by giving the property to Freising; the Toto family was summoned by Duke Tassilo to resolve the tension over property created by Toto's remarriage. It is important to repeat that the bishops of Freising do not appear as direct parties to these property disputes; during this period, there is no sign of conflict over property between Freising and its landholding neighbors. Property disputes appear in the Freising charters only when a settlement resulted in a gift of property to Freising or touched on Freising's property rights. The way these disputes appear in the Freising collection suggests that they represent

---

Life of Corbinian: when Theuderich threatened to violate the sacred inner rooms of Columbanus's monastery, the saint prophesied that he, his offspring, and his kingdom would perish, a curse that was later fulfilled. *Ionae Vitae Columbani I*, c. 18–20, 448–64.

only the tip of a much larger iceberg of conflicts over property within the kindreds, conflicts that do not show up in the charters because the parties resolved them without involving the church.

The cooperative role played by the bishops of Freising in disputes reflects the larger symbiotic relationship among the bishops, the landholding kindreds, and the Agilolfing duke which was anchored in property holding. This relationship finds its expression in the charters in gifts by landholders to the see of Freising or in the foundation and endowment by landholders of churches or monasteries with Duke Tassilo's permission, arrangements in which the donors and frequently their heirs maintained substantial rights in their properties and foundations. The bishops of Freising, by consecrating new foundations and accepting them and their endowments as gifts, or by placing one of their own in a new monastery as abbot, exercised their rights as bishops over churches, monasteries, and properties within their dioceses. Nevertheless, they acquiesced in arrangements whereby the donor or founding kindreds continued to control their gifts, either as benefices from Freising or as members of a new monastery with substantial powers over the monastery and its properties.

Arrangements of this kind represented a particular way of understanding what property ownership meant; both the giving and the receiving parties enjoyed and exercised rights in the property. It is possible that the Freising bishops participated in such arrangements because of their own connections to Bavarian aristocratic society. As we saw in the case of the Scharnitz-Schlehdorf monastery, the participants in a foundation cannot be strictly categorized by the hats they wore. The principal founder, Reginperht, led the founding kindred and continued to wield power over the new foundation; he also entered his own monastery as a monk. The first two abbots of the monastery, Arbeo and Atto, both came from Freising and would later become bishops of Freising; nevertheless, both had kinship ties to the founding kindred. It could very well be, therefore, that all the parties involved had a common understanding of how such relationships were supposed to work.

It is also very clear that the bishops of Freising had little choice but to go along with the traditional Bavarian interpretation of aristocratic property gifts and ecclesiastical foundations. This interpretation was firmly grounded both in property donors' expectations and in ducal authority. As we saw in the Salzburg property catalogs, Bishop Virgil of Salzburg tried to assert his control over property donated to a monastery by a kindred that had participated along with an Agilolfing duke in the monastery's foundation. He failed completely in the face of Agilolfing support for the kindred's expectations.

Despite the vision offered by the charters of a Freising church that avoided conflict with the kindreds and the Agilolfings, we have a contemporary image of Freising as a party to dispute. In Bishop Arbeo's *Life of Saint Corbinian*, a bishop of Freising portrays his see's patron and first bishop as a frequent party to conflict, both over property rights and over his own rights and prestige as the representative of God. Arbeo has Corbinian resolve his disputes without resort to any third-party authority, according to an almost formulaic script. This "act of mercy" script, which balanced the defeat and surrender of the saint's opponents with a merciful countergesture from the saint, allowed the saint to make peace and even meet some of his opponents' needs in a way that saved face and preserved his rights intact. This manner of representing negotiated dispute settlement becomes important when it surfaces again, not in the hagiography but rather in the charters, after the Carolingian conquest.

INTERLUDE
THE TRANSITION TO
CAROLINGIAN BAVARIA

I n the fall of 787, ten years after Duke Tassilo had helped settle the Toto kindred's property arrangements, Charlemagne
invaded Bavaria. By 794, his conquest of the duchy was complete. All resistance to Frankish rule had been stifled, and Duke Tassilo had
formally renounced the Agilolfings' right to rule Bavaria. The duke himself,
his wife, Liutpirg, and his sons and daughters had disappeared into monastic exile.

At almost the exact midpoint of this transition from Agilolfing to Carolingian rule in Bavaria, an unknown Freising scribe wrote a dispute charter
that, for our purposes at least, stands out as perhaps the most important
record in the Freising collection.[1] Titled by Cozroh "Concerning the
Church at Haushausen,"[2] this record miraculously captures a moment of
transition in Bavarian disputing. It describes an effort to handle an old kind
of dispute, namely, a property dispute within a kindred, first in an old way
and then in a new one. The course the dispute followed, and the way it was
eventually resolved, point to the methods of handling and resolving conflict
that would prevail under the Carolingians.

Dated to September 20, 791, the charter records a dispute over inheritance rights to the church of Saint Martin at Haushausen, about twenty
kilometers northwest of Freising, among members of the Huosi kindred.[3] It

---

1. *TF* 142. Cozroh also thought this charter was important; it is the only other
charter in his collection besides the Haholt charter, *TF* 11, to be titled in red ink.
Cozroh may have intended the red ink to draw attention to Bishop Arn of Salzburg;
if *TF* 11 records Arn's dedication to a clerical career at Freising, *TF* 142 records his
first appearance as a *missus*.

2. "Awicozeshusir," identified by Bitterauf and by Störmer as Haushausen near
Pfaffenhofen; see Bitterauf's notes to *TF* 142 and Störmer, *Adelsgruppen*, 92. Jahn,
Ducatus, 486, suggests Aufkirchen near Fürstenfeldbruck as an alternative.

3. See the discussion of the Huosi in the Introduction.

begins by describing how two men, Hiltiport and Egilolf, desired "without reason" to take possession of the church. The two men had seized the church from their co-heirs, the priest Eio and his brothers. The statement that Hiltiport and Egilolf acted "without reason" represents a bias on the part of the scribe in favor of Eio and his party; Hiltiport and Egilolf plainly felt they had good reasons for their actions.

Predictably, the seizure provoked a crisis among all the co-heirs to the church. In response, the Huosi took a step familiar to us from the previous chapter: they convened a kindred council.[4] The council could not, however, end the dispute. Finally, three leading members of the kindred proposed an equally familiar step: they urged the priest Eio to take the matter to his bishop.[5] Eio's bishop was none other than Atto of Freising, the abbot of Schlehdorf who had become bishop of Freising after the death of Arbeo in 783.

In view of our previous cases, one would have next expected a recommendation from the kindred council or from Bishop Atto that the group simply end the dispute by giving the disputed church to Freising. Instead, the disputing process suddenly becomes fluid. Atto, rather than handle the matter himself, sent Eio with his co-heirs to the legates of the Frankish king, that is, to the royal *missi*, who were at Lorch on the Enns taking part in Charlemagne's campaign of that year against the Avars.[6] The *missi* were led by Haholt's son Arn, now bishop of Salzburg, and Gerold, Charlemagne's prefect for Bavaria. Lorch lies about two hundred fifty kilometers east of Freising. Either Bishop Atto's suggestion entailed an enormous journey to catch up with the *missi* or, as Wilhelm Störmer has suggested, the principal members of the Huosi were already there with Charlemagne's army.[7]

Atto's action provokes a question: Why did the bishop choose not to handle the dispute himself? Evidently, Atto felt some sort of interest in passing the Huosi along to the *missi*, but the record does not tell us what this interest was. Equally intriguing is the fact that the Huosi did not seek out the royal legates on their own. They did not start by taking their dispute to the representatives of Carolingian authority, as one might have expected had they been politically pro-Frankish to begin with, nor did they obey any summons to appear. Instead, despite the forcefulness of the Carolingian takeover, the presence of Charlemagne himself in Bavaria, and their own

4. *Et tunc congregati fuerunt Hosi [sic] et fecerunt concilium inter illos.*
5. The men were named Oadalker, Reginhart, and Nibelunc.
6. *ARF* a. 791, 58–61.
7. Störmer, *Früher Adel*, 1:221.

participation in Charlemagne's campaign, the Huosi tried first to resolve the dispute in old and familiar ways.

Once Bishop Atto suggested the resort to royal authority, however, the Huosi apparently accepted the new venue without question. Eio and his party duly appeared before the *missi*. The dispute went on, in the *missi*'s presence, for another three days. One would gladly know exactly what took place during those three days. The record reveals only two things. First, the wrangling produced some kind of determination that Egilolf and Hiltiport had seized the church and its properties unjustly; the charter says the two men were "legally defeated." Second, the judgment led to a settlement. Egilolf and Hiltiport "returned that church into the hands of the priest Eio and of his other co-heirs obtaining justice with him, as well as two parts of all the things pertaining to that church. The other joint owners did similarly with the remaining part, and they all confirmed this among themselves with concord."[8] Sometime later, the parties returned to the disputed church itself. There Egilolf and Hiltiport took up the cloth from the church's altar and ritually returned two-thirds of the church's property. Then "for the third part they accepted Eio as the priest."[9] The bearers of royal authority had succeeded, where the Huosi council had failed, in providing the combination of trust and threat of sanction necessary to end the dispute.

This record, like a prism taking in light from one direction and spreading it out in its component parts in the other, illuminates some of the themes of the following chapters. To begin with, it tells us that the Carolingian conquest added a new set of players to the game of dispute in Bavaria. Men

8. *Reddiderunt ipsam ecclesiam in manus Eioni presbiteri et suorum coheredum evindicantium cum eo ipsam ecclesiam duas partes pertinentes in omnibus rebus ipsius ecclesiae et alii conmarcani de alia parte similiter fecerunt et cum concordia inter se hoc confirmaverunt.*

9. *Egilolf et Hiltiport adprehensum pallium altaris et reddiderunt duas partes rebus ipsius ecclesiae cum altare, ad tertiam partem ipsius ecclesiae Eionem ad presbiterum receperunt.* It is hard to say exactly what happened to the church's property. As the excerpt quoted in n. 8 indicates, Hiltiport and Egilolf returned their two-thirds of the property to Eio along with the church itself; other unspecified "joint owners" did the same with the remaining third (see Niermeyer, s.v. *commarcanus*). The investiture clause quoted here repeats that Hiltiport and Egilolf returned two-thirds of the property; the last part of the clause, however, could be read to mean either that they accepted Eio as priest in his capacity as owner of the third part or that they did so in exchange for the third part. Reading the passage in the latter sense suggests a compromise, an impression strengthened by the phrase *cum concordia*. Thanks to Carl I. Hammer, Theo Kölzer, and Hanna Vollrath for their input on the translation; cf. Jahn, *Ducatus*, 486.

holding a Carolingian office and wielding authority in Charlemagne's name—the royal *missi*—appear here in the charters for the first time. These Carolingian officials had judicial powers; they could hear a property dispute among Bavarian aristocrats, issue a judgment, and oversee a settlement. They carried out these functions at a formal judicial hearing—likewise a new phenomenon in the charters.[10]

The Huosi dispute also points to some of the ways Bavarians responded to Carolingian authority. First, the men serving as *missi* were no strangers to Bavaria. On the contrary, they came from the regional aristocracy and from the Bavarian church. Plainly, they felt it was in their interest to participate in the new regime. Bishop Atto of Freising too decided to support royal authority, in his case by sending the dispute on to the *missi*. The Huosi in their turn agreed to follow Atto's recommendation; they accepted the *missi* court as a forum for resolving an internal dispute they had been unable to settle themselves.

To explain why Bishop Atto decided to send the Huosi to the *missi*, I ex-

---

10. Although formal judicial assemblies show up in the charters only after the Carolingian conquest, two Agilolfing-era normative texts refer to them. First, *Lex B* C. II/14 stipulates that judicial assemblies (*placita*) attended by all free men be held monthly, or after fifteen days if necessary. The count heading the assembly was to be accompanied by a judge and have a law book with him. *Lex B* also mentions judges in several other places (C. I/13; II/15–18; VII/2, 5; VIII/7, 21; IX/17–18; XIII/1–2; XVI/4; XVII/5; XIX/8) and describes them holding judicial hearings on their own (for example, C. IX/17–18). Without evidence that such hearings were actually held, however, it is impossible to say whether these references to courts and judges reflect actual practice or Frankish (or other) influence on the law code itself (see the literature cited in the Introduction, n. 29). Second, at the Synod of Ascheim, the Bavarian bishops enjoined the young Duke Tassilo III to hold a judicial assembly (*iudicium puplicum et clamor pauperorum*) at regular intervals and to have ecclesiastics present to watch over the judges (*Concilium Ascheimense*, c. XV, 58). The acts of this synod, however, most likely represent a program urged on Tassilo by the bishops, not a description of practice; see Jahn, *Ducatus*, 344–45. The only other hints of a formal judicial system in the Agilolfing period come in the form of references to judges. Arbeo of Freising's *Life of Saint Emmeram* identifies the son of a judge as the seducer of Duke Theodo's daughter (*Vita Haimhrammi*, 20). The Freising dispute charter *TF* 86 (777) has two judges consenting to and affirming the settlement of the Toto family dispute that took place before Tassilo and his "senate." These references indicate that judges existed in Agilolfing Bavaria but say little about what they did. The fact remains that only after the Carolingian conquest do formal judicial assemblies headed by officeholding authority figures appear in the church charters as venues for resolving property disputes.

plore the complicated and symbiotic relationship among the Bavarian aristocracy, its property, the church, and the holders of Carolingian office. This relationship changed after the Carolingian conquest in ways that both produced conflicts and altered how they were handled. To help us understand why the Huosi accepted the *missi*'s mediation, I discuss who these authority figures were and what kind of authority they represented. I also examine the possible "hows" of dispute processing revealed by this record, both the new phenomenon of formal hearings before officeholding authority figures and such things as compromise settlements, pressure tactics, and ritual peacemaking. Finally, I investigate biased reporting by the institutions producing the records in order to shed some light on the manipulation of information as a disputing tactic in postconquest Bavaria and on the role played by the dispute records themselves in the conflicts they record.

CHAPTER TWO
DISPUTING UNDER THE
CAROLINGIANS, 791–811

I n the first two decades after Charlemagne's takeover of
Bavaria, the number of conflicts recorded by the see of Freising rose dramatically. In sharp contrast to the five dispute
records we have from the half-century before the Carolingian conquest,
Cozroh's collection contains thirty-seven records of disputes from the years
between 791 and 811.[1] The choice of these dates as markers has a reason. In
791, the first Freising dispute records appear for the period after the conquest. In 811, two people who play a leading role in these records, Bishop
Atto of Freising and Archbishop Arn of Salzburg, disappear. Atto died in
that year, and Arn withdrew from judicial activity.[2] The records after 811
change correspondingly in ways that warrant a separate discussion.

In addition to being more numerous, the conflict records for the period
791–811 look very different from those produced under the Agilolfings.
First, they deal with disputes directly; rather than mention conflict periph-
erally as the motivation for other actions such as property gifts, they place
disputes and their resolution at center stage. Second, they do not contain
any references to violence; instead, they uniformly record the settlement of
disputes by peaceful means. Third, many refer to the new phenomenon of
formal judicial assemblies, convened for the express purpose of handling

---

1. *TF* 142, 143ab, 145, 147, 166ab, 169, 176, 181, 183, 184ab, 185, 186, 187, 189,
193ab, 197, 223, 227, 231, 232ab, 235, 237, 239, 240, 242, 245, 247, 248, 251ab, 258,
259, 268ab, 275, 277, 284, 288, 299 (note that records existing in doubled versions
have been counted as single disputes). The proportion of dispute charters to the
total number of charters contained in the collection also rises sharply; for the period
791–811, there are thirty-seven disputes in ca. 180 charters, as compared with five
disputes in ca. 120 charters for the Agilolfing period. The other Bavarian collections
together offer only five dispute charters from this period: *TM* 10; *TP* 13, 50, 54, and
TR 11.

2. See Chapter 3.

disputes and held under the aegis of officeholding authority figures. Finally and perhaps most important, the institution that produced and preserved the records, the church, no longer stands at the sidelines of disputes involving others. With rare exceptions, the conflicts recorded in these documents directly involve the church itself as a party.

Several historians have tried to explain why Freising produced so many dispute charters after the Carolingian conquest. One prominent argument refers to developments within the early medieval aristocracy. As this argument goes, some aristocrats in Bavaria (and elsewhere) took advantage of the creation of a canonical church organization in the region in the mid-eighth century to concentrate property in the hands of specific heirs. They did so by giving property to a church and having the heirs receive it back as a benefice or by founding a church or monastery that remained in the de facto control of the heirs and endowing it with their property. In this way, they avoided the danger posed to their property by Germanic inheritance custom, which required an equal division of property among all heirs and guaranteed one line of heirs the property necessary to maintain its social status. The burst of property disputes in Bavaria after the Carolingian conquest thus had little to do with political events; it simply coincides with the first generation of disgruntled co-heirs who would have protested such arrangements.[3]

Another explanation has focused on the political context of these disputes. According to this view, the downfall of the Agilolfings in Bavaria upset the comfortable compromise arrangement among the aristocracy, the bishops, and the dukes under which aristocrats had continued to hold property they had given to churches or monasteries. With the Agilolfing dukes gone, the Bavarian bishops, in particular Atto of Freising, suddenly called in de jure church rights to property. This action violated time-honored expectations on the part of the original donors and their heirs and therefore touched off a rash of disputes.[4] Jahn has extended this argument by calling attention to the number of such disputes in which the aristocratic kindreds involved can be tied, either personally or via their property, to the Agilolfings. This finding has led him to argue for a large-scale effort by Bishop

3. Hartung, "Adel, Erbrecht und Schenkung," in *Gesellschaftsgeschichte*, ed. Seibt; Hartung's evidence for this kind of long-term thinking is much more persuasive for Alemannia than for Bavaria. Cf. Jahn, "*Tradere ad sanctum*," in *Gesellschaftsgeschichte*, ed. Seibt, 410–15.

4. Jahn, "*Tradere ad sanctum*," in *Gesellschaftsgeschichte*, ed. Seibt, 400–410; Störmer, *Früher Adel*, 2:374–81.

Atto to enrich himself and his diocese with the property holdings of the deposed ducal dynasty and its allies.[5]

In this chapter, I argue for a more complicated picture in which all these factors play a role. The central element of this picture turns out to be competition for property within the landholding kindreds. Both lay and clerical members of the kindreds took part; the bishop and his clergy were likewise active and interested players. We caught glimpses of this competition during the Agilolfing period. The Carolingian takeover of Bavaria, however, substantively changed the playing field on which this game was carried out. The conquest removed one tactical resource, the Agilolfing duke, and added others, the canonical rights of the Bavarian episcopate upheld to a new and more literal degree and the Carolingian judicial assembly and its officials. Accordingly, the uses to which inheritance claims, church rights, and central authority could be put in the accumulation and protection of property changed in ways that brought the church itself into such competition as a direct participant, thus moving the game and its players into the purview of the church charters.

A CLASH OF EXPECTATIONS

Most of the surviving dispute records from the period 791–811 describe disputes between laymen and/or clerics on the one hand and the see of Freising, in the person of the bishop, his lay advocate,[6] or some other representa-

---

5. Jahn, *Ducatus*, 236.

6. Lay advocates represented churches, monasteries, or individual clerics/monks/nuns in secular matters, esp. judicial processes and other legal transactions. Their purpose stemmed ultimately from injunctions in Scripture, patristic writings, and canon law against the involvement of churches and churchmen in worldly affairs and from an early recognition that churches needed legal and political protection by lay authority or lay patrons (*defensores* or *advocati*). Although lay advocates are attested in the Frankish kingdom from the seventh century on, they do not appear in the Bavarian sources until after 800. Their first appearances in the Bavarian charters roughly coincide with a mandate from Charlemagne in his *Capitulare missorum generale* of 802 (*MGH Capit* I, 33, c. 13, 93) that bishops and heads of monasteries appoint advocates who were just and well qualified. This timing has led some scholars to speculate that Charlemagne introduced advocates into Bavaria. But the fact that the judicial processes in which the advocates appear show up only after the Carolingian conquest makes this suggestion difficult to support—the sudden onset of advocates in the charters after 800 could simply reflect the sudden onset of disputes involving the churches as parties. See Störmer, *Früher Adel*, 2:424–56, esp. 424–34.

tive, on the other.[7] These disputes hinged on a conflict between two different views of property ownership. Descendants or relatives of someone who had given property to Freising expected that they would continue to control that property. Freising, in contrast, asserted its formal rights to the property as the recipient church. In many of these cases, the records are so brief that one can only infer from names and properties that Freising's opponent was basing his claim on kinship.[8] Some, however, contain enough information to tell us more, even a great deal more, about the motives of the parties involved.

Two such records concern a single dispute that took place in the summer of 802 over property belonging to the Scharnitz-Schlehdorf monastery. As we saw in Chapter 1, this monastery was founded in the wilderness at Scharnitz in 763 by Reginperht, his brother Irminfrid, and several of their relatives. Shortly after its foundation, the monastery was moved north to Schlehdorf. The early relationship between the founders and Freising was uniformly cooperative. Freising supplied the foundation with abbots, first Arbeo and then Atto, who were themselves connected to the founding kindred. The founders nonetheless continued to have a say both in the monastery's spiritual direction and in the disposition of its property. That was especially true of the chief founder, Reginperht; it also applied to other kindred members who gave property to the monastery in the course of the eighth century and continued to use it or arranged to pass it on to their descendants.

The dispute that erupted over some of the monastery's property in 802, however, shows clearly that Freising's attitude toward the monastery and its property had changed in the wake of the Carolingian conquest.[9] The dispute pitted Bishop Atto of Freising against a man named Lantfrid, son of Reginperht's brother Irminfrid. It concerned the property Irminfrid had given the monastery at the time of its foundation. The dispute was aired at a formal judicial assembly held at Freising, headed by the imperial *missi* Archbishop Arn of Salzburg and Bishop Adalwin of Regensburg. Two descrip-

7. Twenty-three of the thirty-seven Freising dispute records deal with disputes of this kind: *TF* 145, 147, 169, 176, 183, 184, 185, 186, 187, 189, 223, 231, 235, 240, 242, 245, 251ab, 258, 268ab, 277, 284, 288, 299.

8. See, for example, *TF* 245 (Frauenvils, 806–11): Herirach and Perhtwic give up their claims to property originally donated by Wicperht. The naming pattern leads to the strong suspicion that these were sons with expectations of holding on to property given by the father. See also *TF* 169 (793–811); *TF* 223 (806); *TF* 239 (806–9); TF 288 (809).

9. *TF* 184ab.

tions of the hearing have survived in Cozroh's charter collection.[10] The first was written by a notary attached to Arn;[11] the second was produced by a Freising scribe.[12] These two accounts differ from each other in significant and sometimes dramatic ways. Putting them together, we get three different takes on the dispute: Lantfrid's, Bishop Atto's, and the *missi*'s.

According to the account written by Arn's notary, Bishop Atto's advocate (who was also named Lantfrid—a fact that becomes important later) charged the defendant Lantfrid with unjustly usurping properties that the defendant's father, Irminfrid, had given the church at Scharnitz with Duke Tassilo's permission.[13] The *missi* then carried out an inquiry. They found that Irminfrid, who by then was apparently dead, had made his original gift under the condition that if he should have any sons, they should receive a

10. Cozroh does not say why he copied two versions of the same dispute into his collection. He placed *TF* 184a (in the manuscript fol. 164', nr. 198) among a block of documents concerning Schlehdorf. The second, *TF* 184b (fol. 140, nr. 138), appears much earlier in the collection next to two other major dispute records (*TF* 197 and 193a). See Jahn, "Virgil," 260–64. It is possible that one record (most likely the relatively neutral *TF* 184b; see below) was contained in the Schlehdorf archives until the monastery's absorption by Freising. The aggressively pro-Freising *TF* 184a may well have been in the Freising archives from the beginning.

11. *TF* 184b. The *notarius*, named Bertharius, shows up five times between 802 and 804, four times in the Freising collection and once in a notice from Passau. Each time he appears with Arn. See the more extensive discussion of Bertharius in Chapter 3, n. 54.

12. *TF* 184a. The scribe, named Horskeo, wrote a total of twelve Freising charters in the period 772–802; he appears in other Freising charters as priest, cleric, or deacon up to 808. Glaser, "Bischof Arbeo," in *Vita Corbiniarni*, ed. Glaser, Brunhölzl, and Benker, 44, describes Horskeo as belonging to an inner circle of clerics who carried out the main work of the episcopal chancery. Horskeo wrote *TF* 184a at the orders of another cleric, "the unworthy Adalperht," whose affiliation is a bit harder to determine. Adalperht was connected to the production of only two Freising records, *TF* 184a and its companion *TF* 186, produced on the same day at the same place. He appears, therefore, like the notary Bertharius, only in connection with Archbishop Arn. Unlike Bertharius, however, Adalperht shows up only when Arn is dealing with Freising. He may well have been a Freising cleric; an Adalperht priest and an Adalperht cleric are attested at Freising from 769. The pro-Freising nature of *TF* 184a strongly inclines me to see him as a member of the Freising clergy.

13. At Flaurling, Polling, Schlehdorf, Hofheim, Sindelsdorf, Schöngeising, Pasing, and Gräfelfing. Cf. the property list in the Scharnitz foundation charter, *TF* 19: Chapter 1, n. 27.

share of his property.[14] They also found, however, that Lantfrid had taken not only the part of his father's property he was due but also the rest of his father's property, which should have gone, according to the strict terms of Irminfrid's gift, to the church at Scharnitz.[15] In other words, Lantfrid apparently assumed not only that he had a right to inherit a share of his father's property but also that he still had a right to hold the rest of the property his father had given to the church at Scharnitz.

Bishop Atto, despite his longstanding cooperative relationship with the Scharnitz-Schlehdorf kindred and his own connections to it, saw things differently. Atto based his claim not on customary assumptions about property holding but rather on the letter of Irminfrid's original gift. All of Irminfrid's gift, in its entirety, formed the target of his advocate's suit. Once Irminfrid had died, the property belonged to the church at Scharnitz, which itself now belonged to the monastery at Schlehdorf. Atto controlled the monastery at Schlehdorf both as abbot and as bishop of Freising. The property therefore lay under his direct jurisdiction; Lantfrid held it unjustly.[16]

The whole matter thus hinged for Bishop Atto on defining the dispute in terms of his legal rights over the Schlehdorf foundation. This fact emerges clearly from Freising's account of the dispute. Freising's version shifts our attention away from the original kindred foundation; it states that the disputed properties belonged not to the church at Scharnitz but rather to the monastery at Schlehdorf.[17] To further strengthen its case, Freising's version casts Lantfrid as a quarrelsome and greedy usurper rather than someone who had any justification on his side. It admits that Irminfrid had made his original gift with a provision for possible sons. Lantfrid, however, "acting contentiously," had exceeded his rights by trying to take more than his share.

Atto also tried to capitalize on the presence of Carolingian authority by having a Carolingian involved in the original transaction. Freising's account states that both Duke Tassilo and the Carolingian king Pippin gave their

14. As required by the Bavarian Law: Lex B C. I/1.

15. Lantfrid is described as taking a portion from the "altar of Saint Peter," meaning here a portion of the property that pertained to the church at Scharnitz, which was dedicated to Saint Peter; Jahn, Ducatus, 441.

16. See ibid., 446–48, for Schlehdorf's gradual absorption by Freising, a drawn-out process that continued past 802.

17. TF 184b: Lantfrid had "unjustly usurped property of the church of Saint Peter in the place called Scharnitz . . . which his father Irminfrid had given." TF 184a: Lantfrid "unjustly possessed property of Saint Peter from the monastery called Schlehdorf which the above-mentioned Irminfrid . . . had given to that monastery."

consent to Irminfrid's gift.[18] In the Scharnitz foundation charter, the endowments took place with the permission of Duke Tassilo only; there is no mention of any participation or consent by King Pippin. It is highly unlikely that Pippin would have been involved in the original Scharnitz foundation in 763, since by then the young Duke Tassilo had reached his majority and had begun to distance himself from the Carolingians. It is also unlikely that Atto, as abbot of Schlehdorf, would not have known this. The insertion here of Pippin's permission reflects an attempt to rewrite the past in order to make Lantfrid's usurpation of Schlehdorf property a crime not only against the church and its rights but also against Carolingian authority.[19]

The *missi* supported Bishop Atto, but only up to a point. After carrying out their inquiry, the *missi* arranged a settlement between the two parties. According to Arn of Salzburg's notary, Lantfrid agreed to return his father's share of the property while keeping his own just share, on the condition that he would pay no fines for his actions. If he raised the issue again, however, he would have to pay every fine that applied. Arn and his colleagues thus recognized Irminfrid's provision for possible sons and prevented Bishop Atto from extending his grasp over all Irminfrid's original holdings. This part of the story is confirmed by a brief notice in the Freising collection recording Lantfrid's formal return of the property after the hearing; the notice shows that Lantfrid returned only a part of what Freising had originally demanded.[20] Nevertheless, the *missi* agreed with Bishop Atto on a basic level. They upheld the exact terms of Irminfrid's original gift, and thus Atto's assertion of control over the property Irminfrid had legitimately given the monastery, over Lantfrid's customary expectations.

In Bishop Atto's view, however, the settlement placed Freising in the embarrassing position of having to accept less than it set out to win. Accordingly, Freising's description of events casts the settlement in a very different light. The *missi*,

> together with those who were present at the court, considering [Lantfrid's] stupidity and so that he might escape without heavy penalty into the mercy of the holy church of God and of the lord emperor, asked the venerable bishop

18. *TF* 184b: "which his father Irminfrid had given in the time of Bishop Joseph with Duke Tassilo's permission." *TF* 184a: "which his father Irminfrid had given to God and Saint Peter at that above-mentioned monastery in the time of the lord King Pippin and Duke Tassilo and with their consent."

19. Jahn, *Ducatus*, 438–41.

20. *TF* 185 has Lantfrid handing over properties at Holzhausen, Schöngeising, "Situlinesstetim," Gräfelfing, and Pasing; see Jahn, *Ducatus*, 440.

Atto and made an arrangement with him, that he [Lantfrid] might offer to return to him, without the required compensation, the above-mentioned properties of the holy church without harm and also without the penalty required by the royal immunity and without a royal fine. This was done under the condition that he would claim nothing further from the above-named church and that he would try to claim nothing further for himself from the above-mentioned properties.

This account, with its aggressive pro-Freising and pro-Carolingian slant, saves face for Freising. The court allowed Lantfrid to return the disputed property to Bishop Atto without paying any fines not because he had some justice on his side but because it recognized his foolishness and wanted to keep him in the good graces of the church and of the emperor Charlemagne. The *missi* did not mediate the agreement between the two parties but rather presented it to Bishop Atto in the form of a request, which the bishop graciously agreed to because of his duty to be merciful. Moreover, the outcome of the hearing is depicted as a Freising victory. No distinction is made in the final settlement between the property that Lantfrid could legitimately keep and that which he had to return: Lantfrid is represented as giving up his claims to all the properties under discussion. This last is patently not true, as the record mentioned earlier of Lantfrid's actual return of property shows.[21]

In the two versions of the Lantfrid case, therefore, we see the two different ways of understanding property gifts pitted against each other. Irminfrid's son Lantfrid assumed that as his father's heir, he still had the right to hold property his father had given a kindred foundation. Bishop Atto based his claim on the contrary assumption that property given to a church became church property de facto, not just de jure. Atto hoped to buttress his case and extend his grasp over all of Irminfrid's original gift by appealing to Carolingian sensibilities. The *missi* for their part took a middle course in

21. Jahn, *Ducatus*, 438, has sought to explain the differences in the two versions by calling TF 184b the "official" record of the proceedings produced by Arn's archiepiscopal scribe and TF 184a a "bill of indictment" (*Anklageschrift*) prepared by Freising to strengthen its case before a Carolingian court. The pro-Freising version TF 184a, however, since it presents a finished case rather than a list of charges, appears instead to represent an effort to control the record of events after the fact. Not only does TF 184a save face for Freising in a way that the mediated compromise described in TF 184b does not, it also leaves the door open for future Freising claims on that part of the Scharnitz property that the compromise in TF 184b allowed Lantfrid to keep. Cf. the discussion in Chapter 3 of the similar case TF 193ab.

one respect by recognizing Lantfrid's rights as heir to inherit some of the property. To this degree, they did not entirely ally themselves with Bishop Atto, nor did they pursue a course of indiscriminately disinheriting the heirs of former Agilolfing allies.[22] Nevertheless, the *missi* supported Atto's position in a fundamental way. By upholding a strict rather than a customary interpretation of the original gift charter, they upheld the bishop's claim that properties given to the church became the church's to control in a real way.

When he called in his formal rights to property gifts in this fashion, Bishop Atto charged people who held disputed property with unjustly usurping it. Atto's opponents, however, often seem to have been intent not on taking control of property away from Freising altogether but rather on maintaining their rights within the customary relationship that had bound landowners to the church under the Agilolfings. Sometime between the years 806 and 808, for example, a kindred called the Mohingara, or "the people from Moching," contended with Atto for control of a church they had founded.[23] At the time of the dispute, the church was being run by the archpriest Ellanod, a member of the Scharnitz-Schlehdorf kindred who had taken up a clerical career.[24] The record describing the dispute explicitly casts matters in a way that pits the Mohingara's expectations against the formal rights of the see of Freising. On the one hand, it makes no effort to hide the fact that the Mohingara stood in a hereditary relationship to the church; it states that "they who had inherited" the church sought to take control of it from Bishop Atto and the archpriest Ellanod.[25] On the other, it twice stresses Atto's rights as bishop over the church. The challengers "wished to remove the church from the power of the bishop and sought to bring it into their own power." They failed to uphold their claim, in what venue the record does not say, but the course of events strongly suggests some kind of formal hearing. The Mohingara accordingly went to the cathedral church at Freising and pledged that they would return the church

22. Jahn, *Ducatus*, 440.

23. *TF* 235; the dispute concerned the church of Saint Martin at Biberbach, ca. four kilometers north of modern Ampermoching. The term *Mohingara* is in Cozroh's title. On the "people from Moching," see Jahn, *Ducatus*, 151; Störmer, *Früher Adel*, 1:49–50 and 2:391.

24. Ellanod appears in the Schlehdorf gift charter *TF* 77 discussed in Chapter 1. Jahn, *Ducatus*, 435–36 and esp. n. 221, describes Ellanod's career and the development of his relationship with Bishop Atto.

25. The phrase *qui eam hereditaverunt* can also be translated "they who endowed" the church: see Niermeyer, s.v. *hereditare*.

to Atto "to rule and dispose of just as he had the episcopal power to do with other churches."

As the last act in the proceedings, however, Atto took the church away from the archpriest Ellanod and gave it as a benefice to a priest named Rihpert. This priest, it turns out, almost certainly belonged to the Mohingara; he appears in other Freising charters in connection with property near Moching and with people who witnessed this dispute.[26] In other words, the dispute ended in an agreement. Bishop Atto had his formal rights over the church proclaimed. The plaintiffs did not get full legal control of the church; they probably did not even want to. What they did get was a kin group member in charge of "their" church.[27] Although the term *agreement* does not appear in the record, Cozroh later recognized the affair as such; he

26. At about the same time as the dispute over the church at Biberbach, Rihperht witnessed a gift by a priest named Ratolt of property at Feldmoching, just to the south of Ampermoching (*TF* 220). One kilometer west of Ampermoching lies Reipertshofen, which derives its name from the personal name Rihperht. The first two names that appear on the witness list to *TF* 235 after the clergy and lay office-holders, Heriperht and Heimperht, also appear to represent Mohingara. Hebertshausen near Ampermoching derives its name from the name Heriperht, and the coincidence of the *H* beginning and the *perht* ending and their pairing on the witness list makes it probable that Heriperht and Heimperht were kinsmen. See Jahn, *Ducatus*, 149–50, and esp. Störmer, *Früher Adel*, 1:49–50.

27. Both Jahn and Störmer (as n. 26) see the Mohingara as striving to obtain full legal control of the church from the beginning. Cozroh attached another document to this record, however, *TF* 234a, which strengthens the conclusion that the Mohingara were outraged not by Freising's formal ownership of the church but rather by Atto's attempt to realize that ownership by placing Ellanod in charge. This document, most likely prepared by Freising in advance of the Mohingara dispute, gives a brief history of the church at Biberbach from Freising's point of view. It states that Bishop Ermbert of Freising initially had the church, which comprised two *tituli* in Biberbach and one in "Muniperteshofen." Bishop Joseph later combined the *tituli* into one church; from that time on, the church belonged to the see of Freising. The record goes on to say that afterward one Oato gave inherited property belonging to himself, his brother Immo, and his only son to the church at Biberbach; he also gave a priest named Tutilo to Bishop Arbeo. It is difficult to see what purpose giving Tutilo to Arbeo would serve other than to fill the priest's position at the Biberbach church (see Jahn, *Ducatus*, 149–51 and n. 113). Thus, it seems that these men had wielded de facto influence over the church in a typical Agilolfing-era relationship with the bishops of Freising. When Bishop Atto placed Ellanod in charge of the church, however, he met with resistance. The resistance was strong enough, or good relations with the Mohingara important enough, that Atto agreed to restore the previous status quo.

gave the record the title "Atto's agreement with the men who are called the Mohingara."[28]

One could argue at this point that Freising's dispute with the Mohingara in fact represents a planned confirmation of a long-standing relationship. In other words, despite the rhetoric of conflict, the two sides really came together to renew the arrangement by which the founding kin group held de facto control of the church while recognizing Freising's titular rights.[29] This interpretation is not out of the question. Although the language of the record is full of the bishop of Freising's titular rights, and the resolution of the dispute is represented as a surrender followed by a concession, the agreement ultimately upheld the previous status quo. In this case, however, the explicit mention of the archpriest Ellanod as the head of the disputed church and the change of priests at the end of the dispute speak against the idea. It hardly seems necessary to mention these things if the affair was in fact a mutual renewal of rights disguised as a dispute. The overt substitution of Rihpert for Ellanod instead strongly suggests a real conflict.

SALZBURG REVISITED

The sudden appearance of disputes pitting a church's formal rights to property against the customary expectations of a donor kindred was not just a Freising phenomenon. The same change in ecclesiastical attitudes took place in Salzburg, where it is evident in two property catalogs we have looked at before, the *Notitia Arnonis* and the *Breves Notitiae*.

Although they contain a great deal of material from the Agilolfing period, these catalogs were put together after the Carolingian conquest. The earliest, the *Notitia Arnonis*, was compiled ca. 788/790 at the orders of Arn of Salzburg to provide Charlemagne with an overview of the Salzburg property that had come from the Agilolfings directly or had been given with Ag-

---

28. *Convenientia Attonis cum viris qui vocantur Mohingara*. On *convenientia* as a term referring throughout the early Middle Ages to voluntary, bilaterally arranged settlements of disputes, as well as to agreements in a more general sense, see Patrick J. Geary, "Extra-Judicial Means of Conflict Resolution," in *La giustizia nell'alto medioevo (secoli V–VIII)*, vol. 1 (Spoleto, 1995), 575–85.

29. This issue has been raised for the Merovingian period by Ian Wood and by Paul Fouracre. Wood, "Disputes," in *Settlement of Disputes*, ed. Davies and Fouracre, 22, notes that disputes could be staged for the purpose of getting a written record; Fouracre, "Placita," in *Settlement of Disputes*, ed. Davies and Fouracre, 26 and n. 13, likewise points to strong evidence for fictitious disputes held to get court documentation of property ownership. See also Rosenwein, *To Be the Neighbor*, 134–35.

ilolfing permission. The second, the *Breves Notitiae*, was assembled ca. 798/800 to give Salzburg a firmer grasp of its property holdings in the wake of a grant of royal immunity by Charlemagne and to buttress Salzburg's newly preeminent position in Bavaria after Arn's elevation to archbishop in 798.[30]

As discussed in Chapter 1, both catalogs recorded two earlier property disputes involving Salzburg. These disputes hinged on the same clash of norms that is visible in the postconquest charters from Freising. The first pitted Bishop Virgil against the Agilolfing duke Odilo over the Saint Maximilian monastery in the Pongau. The monastery had been founded in a cooperative effort by Salzburg's first bishop, Rupert, who consecrated it; by the Agilolfing duke Theodo (or his son Theotbert), who endowed it with ducal property; and by the duke's dependents, the brothers from Oberalm. These last likewise gave their property to the monastery (or had it given for them by the duke) but nevertheless kept the use of it in their kindred through a series of benefice arrangements with Salzburg. After Virgil arrived in Bavaria, he tried to assert Salzburg's rights to the monastery in the face of a claim by a descendant of the Oberalmer kindred, Duke Odilo's chaplain Ursus, to control the property his ancestors had given. Virgil failed completely in the face of determined opposition by both Ursus and Duke Odilo.

The second dispute concerned the monastery and church at Otting founded by Count Gunthar. In an effort to prevent a situation like that in the Pongau from ever arising, Bishop Virgil forced the reluctant Gunthar to recognize Salzburg's canonical rights over the foundation at Otting before he would consecrate it.[31] Nevertheless, the monastery soon slipped out of Salzburg's control again. According to the *Notitia Arnonis*, it was "unjustly taken away" (*iniuste abstractam*) from Salzburg by an unspecified party.[32] The catchphrase "unjustly taken away"—paralleling as it does the similar phrases used in the postconquest Freising charters to tarnish Bishop Atto's opponents—strongly suggests that a relative or descendant of Count Gunthar had refused to relinquish the monastery and its endowment.

30. See the literature cited in the Introduction, n. 59.

31. Gunthar formally gave his new foundation to Bishop Virgil and ceded him the right to direct its community according to the canons "just as he did the other churches of his diocese." Note the similarity of this language to that used in the Mohingara charter *TF* 235 to recognize Bishop Atto of Freising's titular rights "to rule and dispose of [the church at Biberbach] just as he had the episcopal power to do with other churches."

32. *NA* c. 6.25, 88–90.

The important thing about these dispute narratives in the context of this chapter is the way they have come down to us. Both derive from the same source, an account written by Bishop Virgil and now called the *Libellus Virgilii*.[33] The *Libellus* does not exist in an Agilolfing-era manuscript, however. It has survived only in the versions written into the two Salzburg property catalogs, both of which postdate the Carolingian conquest. The compilers of the *Notitia Arnonis* and the *Breves Notitiae* had an interest in including the dispute stories from the *Libellus* in their records of Salzburg's property holdings. That interest was bound up with the reasons for compiling the catalogs in the first place, namely, to secure Salzburg's property claims in the wake of the changes that took place after the Carolingian takeover. These claims plainly included those that Bishop Virgil had asserted but had been unable to realize under the Agilolfings. In short, the text of the *Libellus Virgilii* with its two dispute narratives owes its very survival to the fact that Arn of Salzburg and his cathedral clergy felt they could make Virgil's original claims stick in the new political climate of Carolingian Bavaria. A polemic narrative that might well have been lost and forgotten had the conquest of Bavaria not occurred was revived and copied because the see of Salzburg, like the see of Freising, felt it could now press its de jure rights to donated property with some expectation of success. That this expectation was justified is shown by the conclusion in the *Notitia Arnonis* to the story of the dispute over the foundation at Otting. Salzburg regained control of the monastery only after the conquest; it was Charlemagne himself, "to the increase of his heavenly grace," who had it returned.[34]

<hr/>

33. See Chapter 1, n. 41.

34. *NA* c. 6.25, 88–90; Wolfram, "Libellus Virgilii," 203–4. The Freising and Mondsee records *TF* 145 (791–802) and *TM* 131 (811 or 812–17) suggest that the monastery at Mondsee was caught up in a similar conflict. *TF* 145 records a dispute pitting Irminheri, Hrodlant, Deotmar, and Regino against Atto of Freising over the church at Forchant, with the prominent Huosi Reginhart, Nibulunc, and Oadalker (cf. *TF* 142) in the witness list. *TM* 131 consists of a letter from the monks at Mondsee, which Charlemagne had given ca. 800 to Archbishop Hiltipald of Cologne. The monks told their lord the archbishop that Regino had seized a villa at Forchant that Duke Tassilo had once given them and that Bishop Hitto of Freising was helping them recover it. Together these records indicate that some members of the Huosi had been holding property in Forchant, some of which had been used to endow the church there and some of which Tassilo must have given to Mondsee in an arrangement like that which had originally governed the Saint Maximilian monastery. After the conquest, however, Freising and Mondsee (with Freising's help) felt able to assert their claims. Cf. Jahn, "Virgil," 249–50, and *Ducatus*, 236–37.

It would be a serious mistake, however, to see the disputes of this sort that appear after the Carolingian conquest as one-dimensional conflicts pitting the Bavarian churches against landholding kindreds. The Freising charters show us that the kindreds were in fact internally divided. Some members allied themselves with Freising and its interests in opposition to other members of the same kindreds. The Lantfrid case that began this chapter provides a good example. Bishop Atto's advocate, named Lantfrid, bears the same name as the defendant, indicating that he too was connected to the Scharnitz-Schlehdorf founding kindred. Also belonging to the kindred were Atto's second advocate, named Kaganhart, and the Freising archpriest Ellanod, who swore in the witnesses according to Bavarian custom by pulling on their ears. They appeared back in 776 receiving property their fathers had given as a benefice from Schlehdorf with the consent of Atto and the founder Reginperht.[35] Members of the Scharnitz-Schlehdorf kindred continued to cooperate with Freising and to use the monastery at Schlehdorf for their own purposes throughout the first decades of the ninth century. For example, the archpriest Ellanod himself succeeded Atto as abbot of Schlehdorf.[36] In 809, Ellanod gave property of his own to Schlehdorf under the condition that it come to his nephew Hericco (who appears in the Lantfrid case as a witness) as a benefice.[37] Ellanod carried out the arrangement with the advice and consent of Bishop Atto and with the participation of the monastery's advocate Reginhart—apparently, a branch of the kindred was still providing Schlehdorf with an advocate.[38]

If the Lantfrid dispute implicitly reveals divisions within the Scharnitz-Schlehdorf kindred, a second dispute over Schlehdorf property makes these divisions, and the ways they could intersect with Bishop Atto's interests, explicit. Here kindred members competed directly with one another for prop-

35. *TF* 77; see Chapter 1 and Jahn, *Ducatus*, 435–36. Kaganhart appears as Atto's second advocate in the witness lists to *TF* 184ab.

36. *TF* 199 (804): Ellanod is referred to as *archipresbitero et vocitato abbate*.

37. The property was in the same place, Vorder/Mittelfischen, as the property Ellanod was to receive as a benefice in 776 (*TF* 77).

38. *TF* 295. See also *TF* 435a (820), in which Kaganhart does the same thing. On his deathbed, Kaganhart gave property at Vorder/Mitterfischen to Freising; after Kaganhart's death, his nephew Reginhelm carried out the gift and received it back in benefice in exchange for a census. Relationships between descendants of the Scharnitz-Schlehdorf founders and the monastery continued deep into the ninth century; see Störmer, *Früher Adel*, 2:362.

erty, with the bishop serving as an active and interested participant in the competition. This dispute took place before the same judicial assembly that heard Lantfrid's case. On the face of it, the affair pitted Bishop Atto against the Scharnitz-Schlehdorfer Reginperht (not the original founder, but a relative).[39] In the presence of the *missi*, Atto's advocate Lantfrid charged Reginperht with having unjustly usurped properties given to the monastery at Schlehdorf by his cousin Keio. Reginperht in response stood up and "tried to retain the properties in his own possession." As in the Lantfrid case, the *missi* summoned men prepared to testify against Reginperht and ordered them to tell all they knew about the matter. The witnesses responded:

> We know that there were three brothers, and that one having died there were two surviving, and that they, Scatto and Poapo, should have divided that inheritance equally among themselves, but before this division was carried out, Poapo died and left his portion to his son Keio. And that Keio, with goodwill, gave the portion that ought to have come to him vis-à-vis his uncle to God and Saint Tertullian at Schlehdorf; but Scatto, against Keio's will, kept everything and left it to his son Reginperht.

This testimony tells us that the dispute represented in reality not a conflict between Reginperht and Bishop Atto but rather one between Reginperht and his cousin Keio. Reginperht had apparently tried to exploit a normative technicality. According to the witnesses, he based his claim on an assertion that Keio's gift to Freising had never really taken place because Keio's father, Poapo, had not managed formally to carry out his division of the family property with Reginperht's father, Scatto. Keio had nevertheless gone ahead and given what was to have been his share to the monastery at Schlehdorf. This gift turned what started as a conflict between Keio and his uncle Scatto, and after Scatto's death between Keio and his cousin Reginperht, into a conflict between Reginperht and Bishop Atto. One is tempted to surmise that Keio made his gift deliberately, although his father had not

39. *TF* 186. The fact of Reginperht's name and the disputed gift to Schlehdorf alone suffice to establish his kindred identity. This conclusion is strengthened by the locations of the disputed properties and by the characteristic Scharnitz-Schlehdorf name material in the witness list. One of the locations, Schöngeising, directly overlaps with the Scharnitz foundation charter, *TF* 19, as well as with the Lantfrid dispute, *TF* 184. The witness list for *TF* 186 includes the names Reginhart and Kaganhart. Despite the identity of the defendant's name with that of the principal Scharnitz-Schlehdorf founder Reginperht, the two are not the same; see Jahn, "Virgil," 263.

gone through all the steps necessary to ensure his rights, in order to get Bishop Atto's help in protecting the property from his uncle and cousin.[40] Atto, who naturally stood to gain from the whole affair, acted once more within the framework of his titular rights over the monastery at Schlehdorf. This point comes out clearly in a short notice recording Reginperht's actual return of property. The record casts Keio's gift not as Schlehdorf's property but as Freising's. Consisting of only one sentence and a witness list, it gives the witnesses "concerning the properties *of the churches of Freising* [italics added] from the tradition of Keio which Reginperht son of Scatto returned."[41] As this notice indicates, things did not turn out well for Reginperht; after some discussion, the *missi* Arn of Salzburg and Adalwin of Regensburg forced him to return the disputed properties to Atto—who again was represented by his advocate Lantfrid and by the archpriest Ellanod.

The competition for property within kindreds is most apparent in several disputes involving not the bishop but rather someone holding property as a benefice from the bishop. In these disputes, competition among heirs or potential heirs to property caused the conflicts; the church and its canonical rights provided one of the parties with a defensive resource. Among the best examples of this kind of competition in the Freising collection is a dispute that took place in the year 806.[42] This case involved people we have already seen settling a dispute in the presence of Duke Tassilo: Toto and his sons Scrot, Wago, and their brothers.[43] It thus illuminates the ongoing develop-

---

40. Bitterauf refers to *TF* 177 (799) as "Keio's gift." This charter does not, however, concern the properties under dispute here, which were at Alling, Garmisch, and Schöngeising. In all other respects, it would fit very nicely. It has one Gaio [*sic*] giving his inherited property "in the pagus which is called Poapintal"—namely, in Oberhofen, Zirl, and Langen/Amperpettenbach—to the monastery at Schlehdorf where "Bishop Atto governs" (*Atto episcopus ibi praeesse videtur*). In exchange, he got his property back as a benefice from Atto, together with property held by Freising in Pettenbach "from the portion of Otilo" (*de parte Otiloni*—cf. the Scharnitz-Schlehdorf founder Otilo in *TF* 19). If it were not for the fact that the property is different, this could very easily be seen as a gift made by Keio to protect his property from his cousin. See Jahn, *Ducatus*, 443, for the speculative suggestion that the defendant Reginperht in *TF* 186, after having lost the case, could have compensated Freising with property other than that which Keio originally gave.

41. *TF* 187. This notice also hints at a possible behind-the-scenes compromise in that it has Reginperht returning only part of the disputed property.

42. *TF* 227. See Hartung, "Adel, Erbrecht und Schenkung," in *Gesellschaftsgeschichte*, ed. Seibt, 431–32; Jahn, "Virgil," 265–67, and *Ducatus*, 488–94; Störmer, *Adelsgruppen*, 28, 58.

43. See Chapter 1.

ment of one kindred's property arrangements and the way these arrangements could lead again to conflict in the new political climate of Carolingian Bavaria.

As discussed previously, in 775 Toto divided his patrimony among his sons and gave his remaining portion to the see of Freising. The following year, his son Scrot, brought by illness to his deathbed, gave his portion to Freising. Scrot's brother Wago did the same, under the condition that he keep the use of the property until his death. In 777, the family reappeared before Duke Tassilo and his "senate" at the ducal residence at Freising. There its members changed their inheritance arrangements in the wake of Toto's second marriage and confirmed their gifts to Freising by ducal order.

By 806, the properties given to Freising by Toto, his second wife, and his sons Scrot and Wago had been united into a single bloc held by Wago. Wago had taken up a clerical career and had received the properties as a benefice from Freising after his father and his stepmother had died.[44] We know this because Wago successfully used Freising's rights as the recipient institution to protect his own possession of the properties from challenge by two of his relatives. At a judicial assembly headed by five imperial *missi*,[45] two kinsmen (*duo viri propinqui*) named Engilhard and Hroccolf charged Wago with holding their inheritance unjustly. Wago and his advocate responded that the property Wago held as a benefice from Freising ought not by law to pertain to Engilhard and Hroccolf because Wago's father had given his portion and those of his wife and sons to Freising with his own hand and had confirmed the gift in perpetuity. Wago and his advocate produced the original gift charters and displayed the witness lists written in them to back up their defense.[46] After seeing this evidence, the judicial assembly decided that the disputed inheritance should not go to Engilhard and Hroccolf but rather should remain Freising's property "just as Toto had confirmed it there and just as he had done in the time of Duke Tassilo." Engilhard and Hroccolf gave way and pledged not to disturb Wago any further about the property.

Engilhard and Hroccolf explicitly based their challenge to Wago's possession of the property on inheritance claims. There is thus little doubt that they were related to Wago. The most likely reconstruction of events (and it

44. See *TF* 465 (822): Wago, by then an old man, prefaced a renewal of his family's gifts to Freising with the statement that after the deaths of Scrot, Toto, and Ospurga, he himself had received all four portions from Freising as a benefice.

45. Archbishop Arn of Salzburg, Bishop Adalwin of Regensburg, and Counts Audulf, Werinharius, and Cotefred.

46. *Et testes veraces in eas scriptas ostenderunt.*

must remain only a plausible reconstruction) is that the two challengers were Toto's sons by his second marriage and that they had been sharing in the use of Toto's property. After the deaths of Toto and his wife, which must have occurred shortly before the dispute erupted, the property reverted to Freising. It then went to Wago as a benefice, prompting the disinherited men to challenge. In any case, the causes of the conflict are unmistakable: the concentration of the Toto family's property in Wago's hands prompted a challenge from two of Wago's kinsmen. Wago easily warded off the challenge by displaying the original gift charters, which indisputably gave Freising ownership of the property. Freising's rights over the gifts, in other words, protected Wago's control of the family property and prevented two men with inheritance expectations from realizing their claim.

It is hard to say whether Wago's family arranged things this way on purpose, that is, whether the concentration of family property in the hands of one family member in ecclesiastical service, under the protective umbrella of a gift/benefice arrangement with Freising, was a deliberate attempt to pass property down along one particular line.[47] We have no way of knowing whether Toto, his wife, and his son Scrot intended their gifts to Freising to end up in Wago's hands; we know only that after their deaths the property did. Nor is there evidence for any effort by Wago to continue the arrangement in the following generation. Starting in 804, Wago appears as the head of the church of Saint Mary and Saint Peter in Zolling on the Amper, which coincides with some of Toto's original property holdings.[48] As head of this church, he accepted gifts from relatives, who used what appears to have originally been a kindred foundation to make their own *post obitum* gift arrangements.[49] Wago ultimately rose to a position of considerable importance both within his larger kin group and at the Freising cathedral church. In several charters recording gifts to Freising by relatives, Wago appears as the first witness.[50] In others, he is described as being first among the Freising *familia* and as having a close relationship to Bishop Atto.[51] In only one case, however, do we see any further property arrangement between Wago

47. Jahn, "Virgil," 265–67, argues that this case illuminates typical Agilolfing inheritance practice in that it shows Toto consciously aiming to concentrate the family property in Wago's hands via a benefice arrangement with the church; likewise Hartung, "Adel, Erbrecht und Schenkung," in *Gesellschaftsgeschichte*, ed. Seibt, 431–32.

48. Jahn, *Ducatus*, 491.

49. *TF* 198, 280, and 520.

50. For example, *TF* 189, 208, 226.

51. *TF* 315, 520.

himself and a relative. In 815, Wago's *fratruelis* Toto (either cousin or nephew) gave a *colonia* to Wago under the condition that Wago be allowed to give the property to Freising.[52] Wago immediately did so. The *colonia* in question adjoined two other *coloniae* that Wago's forebears had previously given Freising. Wago and Toto carried out the gift on the condition that both receive all three *coloniae* together in benefice for both their lifetimes, after which time the united property would revert to Freising.[53] This gift is the only sign of any attempt to extend Wago's property arrangements to anyone beyond Wago himself; it covers only a fraction of the kindred property and extends things at most another generation (if Toto were a nephew and not a cousin).

Wago revisited his family's gift arrangements en bloc twice. The first time, in 822, he renewed all the original gifts to Freising by the members of his immediate family, with the addition of what he had been able since to acquire on his own.[54] The second time, in 825, the now elderly Wago (it had been forty-nine years since his first appearance in the Freising charters) likewise renewed the gift of "whatever my parents left me as my inheritance and whatever I Wago have gained by my own acquisition" to Freising.[55] Wago then specified that the property should be passed on after his death, but not to a relative; it was to go to the community of Benedictine monks at Freising. Wago died sometime within the following decade; he appears for the last time as a witness to a Freising charter in 830.[56]

Following Wago's death, the career of his family's property becomes lost in a sea of uncertainties. Men with names similar to or the same as those of the Toto/Wago group appear later in connection with the locations of the original Toto properties.[57] Thus, it is possible, perhaps probable, that descendants of Toto's larger kindred still had property in those areas. There is no way to tell, however, if one line of the kindred was basing its position on the property Wago had originally assembled. In the same period, the bishops of Freising were freely disposing of properties in the locations of Toto's original gifts,[58] suggesting that at least some of the kindred property had

---

52. According to Niermeyer, *fratruelis* can mean either a first cousin (specifically, the son of a father's brother or of a mother's sister) or a nephew.

53. *TF* 333ab.

54. *TF* 465.

55. *TF* 523a.

56. *TF* 594.

57. For example, *TF* 662 (843), *TF* 753 (855–60), *TF* 855ab (860).

58. For example, *TF* 868 (860–75), *TF* 960 (883–87), *TF* 1021 (895–99).

slipped out of de facto kindred control and into that of the Freising cathedral church.

It is therefore unlikely that Toto and his family planned from the beginning to channel their property along a particular line headed by Wago. It is much more likely that the conflict pitting Wago against Engilhard and Hroccolf resulted from Wago's opportunistic response to the arrival of Carolingian authority and especially to that authority's interpretation of property gifts. Wago's arrangement staved off a challenge to his property rights by relatives; a judicial assembly headed by Carolingian *missi* upheld the original terms of the gift charters and thus Wago's benefice holdings. This tactic would not have worked prior to 787, however. Before the Carolingian conquest, Wago's father, Toto, could not have predicted the arrival of the Carolingian judicial assemblies that would make such an arrangement useful.

Disputes such as the one that pitted Wago against his kinsmen Engilhard and Hroccolf also tell us a great deal about Bishop Atto. Atto did not act in a one-dimensional fashion to block members of donor kindreds from ever exercising any control over donated property. He seems rather to have weighed his interests situationally and to have cooperated with members of the kindreds, such as Wago, when it was in his interest to do so.

This held true even when the kindred concerned was related to the fallen Agilolfings. In the fall of 791, Atto entered into a property relationship with a priest named Tutilo, his brother Cozzilo, and their kinsman Oazo.[59] These three men had strong ties to the Agilolfings. Their names contain the element -*ilo* likewise borne by Duke Tassilo and his father, Odilo, and they held property in places with a high concentration of Agilolfing ducal property.[60] Moreover, Oazo was married to a woman named Cotania.[61] Cotania was the name of Duke Tassilo's daughter. Oazo's wife, therefore, if she was

59. *TF* 143a.

60. The -*ilo* name piece appears across three generations in the list of Tutilo's relatives helpfully provided by *TF* 143a: Tutilo's father, Pirthilo, and his mother, Ata, and his brothers Fritilo, Cozzilo, Petilo, and Waltfrid with their children Fritilo, Situli, and Swidpuruc. The link to the Agilolfings also appears in the group's property holdings. *TF* 143, 144, 157, and 432 show the Tutilo group holding property in Rottbach, Jesenwang, and Schweinbach. According to the Benediktbeuern Chronicle, Tassilo gave property in Rottbach to Benediktbeuern shortly after its foundation, and *TF* 63 (773) shows someone holding a ducal benefice in Schweinbach. See Jahn, "Urkunde und Chronik," 22–23, for more detailed evidence and passim for the reliability of the Benediktbeuern material.

61. *TF* 144.

not the ducal daughter herself, was related to her at the very least by an adoption of Agilolfing naming tradition.[62]

The arrangement Bishop Atto made with this group was designed from the beginning to concentrate kindred property in the hands of a kindred member in church service. The dispute that erupted almost immediately afterward shows just how well the umbrella of church rights backed by Carolingian authority served to protect such property holdings from challenge. The three kinsmen Tutilo, Cozzilo, and Oazo built a church on part of their inherited property.[63] After the church was finished, they went to Bishop Atto of Freising to have it consecrated.[64] Next, the three endowed the church with property.[65] Tutilo then ceremonially gave the church and its endowment to the see of Freising, whereupon he received it back from Bishop Atto as a lifetime benefice.[66] Within a year or two—the dating is uncertain—conflict erupted.[67] "Certain people" (eos quidam) wished to expel the priest Tutilo from his church. They were unsuccessful because the arrangement had been "confirmed and ordained by canonical authority and by the consent of the nearest relatives." Nonetheless, the dispute went all the way to the court of Charlemagne in the form of a written report. Charlemagne sent the dispute on to a pair of his missi,[68] who confirmed Tutilo in all his rights over the disputed church.

This record, hiding Tutilo's opponents as it does behind the faceless label eos quidam, does not tell us anything about the reasons underlying the dispute. There is, however, some room for speculation. The timing of the dispute between 791 and 793 suggests a direct link to the fall of the Agilolfings. It appears that Tutilo and his relatives, related to the Agilolfings and

62. Störmer, *Adelsgruppen*, 32–33; see also Jahn, "Urkunde und Chronik," 22–25, 44n. 223, for detailed investigations of the Tutilo group's kinship to both the Agilolfings and the Huosi.

63. *In loco qui dicitur Rotinpach*: either Rettenbach by Scrobenhausen or Rottbach by Fürstenfeldbruck; Jahn, *Ducatus*, 484n. 80, leans toward the latter.

64. The record stresses Atto's sacerdotal rights over all churches in his dioceses: *cui ordo sacerdotalis erat consecrandi ecclesias per parrochia sua.*

65. Jahn, *Ducatus*, 484, states that Tutilo gave all his property. Tutilo had more to give later, however: see *TF* 144.

66. According to *TF* 143a, the arrangement was finalized at Lorch on the Enns in September 791. The members of the Tutilo group were therefore—like the Huosi in *TF* 142 (see the Interlude)—with Charlemagne on his campaign of that year against the Avars.

67. *TF* 143b, dated by Bitterauf to between 791 and 793.

68. Gerold, the Bavarian prefect, and Meginfrid.

holding property in the same places as Duke Tassilo, may have been trying to protect their property from attempts to cash in on the wreck of Agilolfing fortunes.[69] There may well have been good cause to worry. Charlemagne himself, after his conquest of Bavaria, made it very clear that he did not consider property holdings secure just because they had come from the Agilolfings. The Frankish king declared his position on this matter in a famous diploma issued to Abbot Fater of Kremsmünster, a monastery in the easternmost part of Bavaria founded and endowed by Duke Tassilo in 777. As Charlemagne prepared for his Avar campaign in the winter of 790, Abbot Fater appeared at the royal camp in Worms. Apparently concerned that his monastery lay directly on Charles's line of march, Abbot Fater produced Kremsmünster's foundation charter and asked that it be confirmed. Charles responded that no gifts of property could be considered secure on the basis of a Tassilonian charter. Instead, he had a new royal charter produced based on the wording of the Tassilonian original that confirmed Kremsmünster in the possession of its properties.[70]

Knowledge of this diploma, and of the legal uncertainty surrounding Agilolfing property holdings that it created, might have prompted some Bavarian holders of such grants to do as Abbot Fater did, that is, look to the king for confirmation of their property rights. Others might have tried to secure their property holdings from challenge by getting another kind of written title to it, such as that provided by a gift/benefice arrangement with a church.[71]

If the church foundation that came back to Tutilo as a benefice was designed to protect his and his kindred's property from the king, however, it would necessarily entail the approval of Bishop Atto of Freising. Given Atto's highly visible positive attitude toward the Carolingians, that seems unlikely. Moreover, it is hard to imagine a dispute record hiding Charlemagne behind the anonymous label *eos quidam*. Finally, Charlemagne's *missi* upheld Tutilo and Oazo's arrangement with Freising without reservation. More plausible is the suggestion that some unknown third party felt that Tutilo and Oazo were vulnerable because they were holding Agilolfing property. In this scenario, holders of Agilolfing property, as Tutilo and his kindred almost certainly were, would have felt insecure vis-à-vis other

69. See Jahn, *Ducatus*, 299–300.

70. Engelbert Mühlbacher, ed., *Die Urkunden Pippins, Karlmanns und Karls des Grossen, MGH D Karol* I, no. 169 (Hannover, 1906), 226–28; Wolfram, *Geburt*, 188.

71. Precisely this appears to be the case in the Freising record *TF* 166a; see Chapter 4.

landowners because Charlemagne's position as stated in the Kremsmünster diploma placed their property rights in doubt. They would then have needed to renegotiate their property arrangements somehow in order to get them written down in a post-Tassilonian record. A gift/benefice arrangement with a church such as that carried out by Tutilo and Oazo fits the bill admirably. The fact that conflict indeed erupted shortly after the arrangement was made shows that there was a real danger.

It explains the evidence equally well, however, and fits with the evidence from the other dispute records much better, to argue that the unnamed *eos quidam* were related to Tutilo and felt they had rights in the property Tutilo and his kinsmen gave to their new foundation. The conflict arose in response to the foundation of the church, its endowment, and its grant to Tutilo as a Freising benefice. The dispute would then have been triggered by Tassilo's fall insofar as Tutilo and Oazo, like Wago, saw an opportunity to exploit the new political climate to assert their own property claims against a wider inheritance group. They did so by sheltering their property under the umbrella of Freising's rights as the recipient church.

Regardless of the story we tell to explain the dispute, the strategy adopted by Tutilo and his kin plainly worked. The *missi*, rather than support the unnamed challengers' attempt to take the property, acted consistent with their behavior in the other conflicts discussed here: they upheld Freising's rights as laid down in the terms of the original gift charter. Bishop Atto knew how to profit from the situation. He cooperated completely with the Tutilo group; as a result, he got ultimate title to their property. It cannot be said, therefore, that Atto exploited the Carolingian takeover unconditionally to obtain property previously held by relatives of the former ducal family. The bishop instead weighed his interests situationally and cooperated with people connected to the Agilolfings when it was in his interest to do so.[72]

The divisions occurring within kindreds appear not only in the ways some people allied themselves with the church against their kin but also in the composition of the Carolingian courts that upheld such arrangements.

72. The cooperative relationship between the see of Freising and this part of the Tutilo kindred continued through at least two more generations in the persons of Oazo's daughter Engilsnota and Engilsnota's nephew the priest Erchanbert: see *TF* 144 (ca. 791), *TF* 159 (792–808), and *TF* 532 (826). Jahn, *Ducatus*, 484, has suggested that Engilsnota's nephew Erchanbert was identical with the future Bishop Erchanbert of Freising (836–54). If that is correct, these records give a hint of what happened to the family property in the long run: it was absorbed into the direct control of the see of Freising through a kindred member's becoming bishop.

This phenomenon shows up clearly in a dispute that erupted sometime between 806 and 811 over properties near Isen. A priest named Arperht had given the properties to Freising in 792 and had arranged have his nephews, the priests Jacob and Simon, receive them as a benefice after his death.[73] When Arperht died, however, a "most contentious Salomon" claimed that Arperht had given the property to him before he had given it to Freising. Salomon took his case before the *missus* Audulf and Archbishop Arn of Salzburg (who is not labeled as a *missus*). Audulf ordered Count Job and the judge Ellanperht to carry out an inquiry. Job and Ellanperht accordingly collected "a multitude of noble men" who swore an oath on relics in Salomon's presence. Count Job himself testified at the head of the group. The witnesses swore that the disputed properties should belong to Freising and that Salomon had no legitimate rights to them.

Both the challenger, Salomon, and the men who headed the inquiry, Job and Ellanperht, belonged to Arperht's wider kin group. This kin group was centered in the area around Isen and had a visible taste for Old Testament names.[74] The evidence for Salomon's connection to the group goes beyond the simple fact of his name and his challenge; his name appears in other charters at about this time in connection with Jacob, Count Job, the judge Ellanperht, and the location of Arperht's property.[75] Count Job, the first of

73. *TF* 247. The properties were in Frauenvils and Elsenbach. Arperht's original gift charters apparently survive as *TF* 151 and *TF* 152, produced on February 6 and 7, 792, respectively. In *TF* 151, Arperht gave his allodial property and a chapel "at Isen" (*ad Isna*) to Freising. It is possible that this coincides with the property in Elsenbach mentioned in *TF* 247; Elsenbach lies ca. eighteen kilometers northeast of the monastery of Saint Zeno at Isen itself, but it lies only two kilometers north of the river Isen. In *TF* 152, Arperht gave a church together with all his inherited property at Frauenvils to Freising. We learn that Jacob and Simon were Arperht's nephews from *TF* 235 (815), in which Bishop Hitto of Freising forced the two men formally to renew the terms of their benefice after hearing charges that they planned to alienate it; see Chapter 5.

74. Most of the members of this group with biblical names were clerics, placing them within a broader tradition of giving such names to those destined for an ecclesiastical career. As Count Job's name indicates, however, this tradition does not account for all the names. Störmer has suggested that some may represent an attempt to connect to the traditions of sacral kingship in the Old Testament. On the Arperht kindred and the broader Isen kin group, see Störmer, *Früher Adel*, 1:42–43, and *Adelsgruppen*, 82, 121–36; Josef Sturm, *Die Anfänge des Hauses Preysing* (Munich, 1931), 89–91.

75. A deacon named Salomon, for example, appears at about this time with a deacon named Jacob as a witness to a dispute carried out at Frauenvils; the dispute was

the pair delegated by the *missus* Audulf to carry out the inquisition, also testified as its leading witness with good reason: he was the leading witness to one of Arperht's original property gifts in 792.[76] Likewise, the judge Ellanperht appears in the Freising charters frequently with Job; a dispute record from the year 849 explicitly identifies him as a relative of a deacon named Arperht.[77]

In short, the kin group involved in the dispute, the see of Freising, and the official forum for dispute resolution all interacted symbiotically. Arperht and his nephews Jacob and Simon used Freising's rights over donated property to define and protect their property holdings with Bishop Atto's cooperation. Their kinsman Salomon challenged the arrangement but lost in the face of Freising's formal rights to the properties. In order to resolve the dispute, the *missus* Audulf ordered an inquisition to be carried out by two officeholders, Job and Ellanperht, who were themselves connected to the kin group involved in the dispute. Job allied himself with Jacob and Simon by witnessing the terms of Arperht's original gifts.[78]

A complex array of factors was at work in the sudden blossoming of disputes in the Freising charters after the Carolingian takeover of Bavaria. On the one hand, we have the disputes over rights to donated properties between Bishop Atto and the heirs of property donors. In these disputes, Atto asserted Freising's canonical rights to the properties against expectations of continued control by the heirs. In other words, two ways of understanding church property ownership clashed, one based on customary practice and the other on a strict interpretation of property gifts. This conflict stands out most clearly in the disputes surrounding the Scharnitz-Schlehdorf monastery.

overseen by Count Job and the judge Ellanperht: *TF* 245 (806–11). A priest named Jacob and a Salomon *clericus* also appear together on the witness list for a dispute that occurred in 811; see *TF* 299.

76. *TF* 151.

77. *TF* 704. The dispute record lists the entire family group involved: father Hartwic, son and priest Rihhart, and then (in an unknown kin relationship) the deacons Heimperht and Arperht, the judge Ellanperht, and Hemmi.

78. This phenomenon is also apparent in the Lantfrid dispute, *TF* 184; the count Reginhard who appears alongside the imperial *missi* belonged to the Scharnitz-Schlehdorf kindred. Not only does he share the name *Regin-* with the founder Reginperht; two years after the Lantfrid case, he himself gave property to Schlehdorf; see *TF* 199 (804).

Before the Carolingian conquest, the founding kindred exercised effective and peaceful joint control of their foundation with the see of Freising. Afterward, Bishop Atto's change of course produced conflict. The dispute between Freising and the Mohingara shows that one kindred was satisfied in the end with ensuring continued de facto control of donated property by one of its own. Freising's violation of this expectation, not Freising's de jure ownership of the property itself, touched off the dispute.

On the other hand, we have the disputes between members of donor kindreds and members of the same kindreds holding the donated property as a Freising benefice. These disputes represent inheritance struggles between lines of the donor groups sheltering property holdings under the umbrella of Freising's property rights and co-heirs shut out by such arrangements. The appearance of such disputes in the decades after the Carolingian conquest was no accident. It is precisely at this point that the political weight shifted in Bavaria to a normative and institutional framework that supported using church rights to defend property holdings. It is not that Bavarian landholders had never hit on the idea before of making gift/benefice arrangements with a church. Both the charters we looked at in Chapter 1 and the story of the Saint Maximilian monastery in the Salzburg property catalogs show well enough that this was a common Agilolfing-era practice. What changed was the use to which the practice could be put. No conflict over arrangements of this sort appears in the charters before the arrival of Carolingian authority in Bavaria; benefice holders under the Agilolfings were not using church rights to protect their holdings from relatives. The one Agilolfing-era example we have of conflict surrounding an arrangement of this kind, the dispute over the Saint Maximilian monastery, does not involve one branch of a founding kindred versus another. It instead involves a descendant of a donor kindred fighting off a claim to control raised by the church holding de jure rights to the property—a claim that turned out to be a dead letter as long as the Agilolfings reigned.[79] Only after the fall of the ducal family did de jure church rights to donated property become a re-

79. There is some evidence that the Albina kindred did indeed fracture in the course of Virgil's dispute with Odilo and Ursus over the Oberalmer property. The list of witnesses who provided Virgil with his information on the Saint Maximilian foundation, which the *Libellus Virgilii* preserves (*BN* 8.14, 114), includes several people who were very likely members of the kindred. Wolfram, *Salzburg, Bayern, Österreich*, 134, speculates that the dispute may have represented a conflict between the ducal and episcopal unfree branches of the kindred or within the ducal unfree branch itself. If that is true, we have an example of one branch of a kindred playing the game in reverse, that is, using the customary norms upheld by the Agilolfings to

source that one branch of a kindred could successfully use against another; it is from this point on that gift/benefice arrangements with a church become flash points for dispute.

In disputes pitting landholders directly against the bishop, the evidence for divisions within the kindreds is not as obvious but is nonetheless unmistakable. In the Lantfrid dispute, some members of the Scharnitz-Schlehdorf kindred lined up with Freising against the expectations of their relative. Embedded in the dispute between Freising and the Scharnitz-Schlehdorfer Reginperht we find a dispute between Reginperht and his own cousin Keio. It becomes very difficult, therefore, to distinguish between conflicts pitting a kindred against Freising and those pitting one branch of a kindred against another.[80]

The church and its rights and offices were thus serving as strategic resources in the competition for property. The church's usefulness changed across the period of the Carolingian takeover. After 787, Bishop Atto's assertion of the letter of episcopal rights outraged older expectations of cooperative control held by some but appeared as a new resource for others. Consequently, the character of conflict also changed. Before 787, some disputes within kindreds were handled through violent feuds. Others, particularly those that explicitly concerned property, were resolved either by a gift of property to a family church or monastery or by resort to family councils. The bishop served as a mediator; he could also help end conflict by receiving disputed property as a gift. After 787, however, with the ducal authority missing and the Carolingian authority very much present, the church and its formal rights themselves became part of the tactical repertoire of conflict. Consequently, members of the kindreds realigned themselves with or against the bishop.

Bishop Atto of Freising, himself inseparable from the aristocratic society from which he came, dealt opportunistically with the new situation. In some cases, he set himself and his church against the claims of some members of the donor kindreds, in cooperation with other members of the same kindreds. In other cases, he helped one branch of a kindred against another

---

defend their rights against the view of church property ownership asserted by Virgil and his allies from the other branch.

80. Fouracre, "Placita," in *Settlement of Disputes*, ed. Davies and Fouracre, 32, suggests that whereas disputes within a kindred might be settled within the group, a dispute with the church was more likely to mean a formal contest and thus a formal record. In view of the evidence described earlier, this statement needs to be extended somewhat: since members of kindreds used the church to carry out disputes with one another, a dispute with the church could still be a dispute within a kindred.

branch by wielding his legal rights to donated property to the advantage of the people holding that property as a benefice. In all cases, he asserted the letter of his rights in his own interests. The office of bishop thus appears itself as a prize in the aristocratic game, with its own inherent set of interests and resources for advancing them.

Bishop Atto and the landholders allied with him were able to use church rights in this fashion because of the position taken by the Carolingian judicial assemblies. The *missi* and other officeholders did not simply act in a black and white fashion against the supporters of the Agilolfings or against property arrangements made under Agilolfing authority. They did, however, act to change fundamentally the relationship between the landholding aristocracy and the church by upholding the strict terms of property gifts. Accordingly, they acted to Atto's advantage in a great number of cases and helped change the nature of the church as a resource in the competition for property. By doing so, the judicial assemblies themselves became resources that Bishop Atto and his allies could exploit in their own interests. Here we find our explanation for the puzzle posed in the Interlude by Bishop Atto's sending of the Huosi inheritance dispute on to the *missi*. By encouraging the legitimacy of the Carolingian judicial assemblies as a forum for resolving disputes, Atto hoped to turn them to his advantage.

The competition for property within the landholding kindreds penetrated into both the church and the judicial assemblies. Neither the church nor the courts can be seen as institutions separate from the disputes themselves. Bishop Atto, for example, himself connected to the Scharnitz-Schlehdorf founding group, disputed with other members of the same group in a way determined by the interests of his position. On a smaller scale, so did the archpriest Ellanod and many other clerics holding property from the church that had come from their kindreds. The same can be said for the officeholders in judicial assemblies: the inquisitor Count Job and the judge Ellanperht were connected to the kindred that was divided over the issue of the property given to Freising by the priest Arperht.

Put together, these findings help explain the sharp increase in the number of conflict charters after the Carolingian conquest. The increase is to a large degree an artifact of the source. Before 787, when disputes were handled by violence or by family councils, or both, there would have been little reason for conflicts within kindreds to show up in a church charter collection. Only when the responses to such conflicts touched on church rights would traces appear in church records. After 787, however, when church rights themselves became part of the repertoire of conflict and the bishop began to act as a player rather than as a mediator, there would have been every reason for conflicts to appear in the charters—suddenly a great many more disputes directly affected church property rights. In other words, although the Carolingian conquest undeniably produced tensions that provoked disputes as well as opportunities that encouraged them, at the same time it changed the parameters for competition in ways that moved a preexisting world of conflict into the light of the church charters.

This evidence also has consequences for our understanding of how the Carolingian takeover of Bavaria worked. As Jahn has demonstrated from other evidence, it becomes very difficult to argue for a uniformly pro-Carolingian aristocracy in western Bavaria that dropped Duke Tassilo in 787 and welcomed Charlemagne with open arms.[81] The evidence of the dispute charters shows a messier situation. Kin groups marked by competition before 787 continued their competition afterward. In the division within kin groups visible after 787, some aristocrats took advantage of the new regime, but others fought it.

81. Jahn, *Ducatus*, 494, 585–86.

CHAPTER THREE
THE NATURE OF AUTHORITY IN CAROLINGIAN BAVARIA
THE EXAMPLE OF ARN OF SALZBURG

T he next step toward understanding what happened to disputing in postconquest Bavaria involves the issue of authority. As we have seen, the Carolingian regime brought with it a new resource for handling disputes, the judicial assemblies headed by officeholding authority figures. Disputants apparently accepted these assemblies without hesitation, beginning in 791 with the Huosi, who at the urging of Bishop Atto of Freising brought their inheritance dispute to the royal *missi* gathered with Charlemagne at Lorch.[1] We have learned that self-interest played a large part in this move. Bishops supported the legitimacy of the judicial assemblies because the authority figures running them upheld the formal terms of property gifts over customary patterns of property holding. Landholders allied with the bishop went to the assemblies because they could turn both the church and the assemblies to their own advantage. These findings still leave open the question, however, where the men heading the assemblies derived their authority. Who exactly were these authority figures, and why did anyone pay attention to their decisions beyond the point of self-interest?

In this chapter, I try to answer these questions by looking at one such figure: Arn, archbishop of Salzburg. Arn appears as an authority figure in the charters between 791 and 811 with a frequency that positively invites scrutiny.[2] Moreover, he personified the connection between Charlemagne's

1. *TF* 142; see the Interlude.
2. Arn's appearances in the Bavarian charters have been most recently examined by Eric J. Goldberg and Herwig Wolfram; see Goldberg, "'Dilectissimus Pater Aquila Transalpinus': Archbishop Arn of Salzburg and Charlemagne's 802 Administrative Reforms" (master's thesis, University of Virginia, 1994); Wolfram, "Arn von Salzburg und Karl der Grosse," in *1200 Jahre Erzbistum Salzburg: Die älteste Metro-*

regime and the Bavarian landholding aristocracy. Arn came from a Bavarian aristocratic family. He was born probably in 740 or 741 in the area south-west of Freising, possibly in Bittlbach near Erding. As we saw in Chapter 1, his father, Haholt, dedicated him to the ecclesiastical life at the Freising cathedral church in 758. Haholt himself moved at the highest levels of Agilolfing society; he enjoyed kinship connections to the aristocratic kindreds in the immediate circle of the Agilolfing dukes, especially the Huosi.[3]

In this regard, Arn was typical of Charlemagne's representatives in post-conquest Bavaria. A great many, if not all, of the authority figures involved in disputes in Bavaria in this period, whether *missi*, counts, or judges, belonged to kin groups present in Bavaria before the Carolingian takeover.[4] The most famous example is the Bavarian prefect Gerold, who appears as a *missus* with Arn twice between 791 and 793.[5] Gerold, who served as count, *missus*, and prefect until his death in 799, came from a branch of the Agilolfing family itself—a gesture on Charlemagne's part to Agilolfing legitimacy.[6] Another example is the Count Reginhard who served alongside Arn at the assembly hearing the dispute between Freising and the Scharnitz-Schlehdorf heir Lantfrid; as discussed previously, he himself came from the Scharnitz-Schlehdorf founding group.[7] Likewise the *iudex* Ellanperht: through his kinship with the priest Arperht, Ellanperht belonged to the aristocratic community attached to the monastery at Isen, which is visible from the earliest entries in Cozroh's collection.[8]

---

pole im deutschen Sprachraum: Beiträge des Internationalen Kongresses in Salzburg vom 11. bis 13. Juni 1998, MGSL Ergänzungsband 18 (Salzburg, 1999), 21–32, and Salzburg, Bayern, Österreich, 185–88.

3. For the prosopography on Arn and his father, see Jahn, *Ducatus*, 330–33; Störmer, *Adelsgruppen*, 66–67 and 133; Sturm, *Preysing*, 95–97, 223–25; Mitterauer, *Karolingische Markgrafen*, 42–44.

4. The qualified statement that "a great many, if not all," officeholders came from Bavarian kindreds stems from the fact that the identities of some Bavarian office-holders are difficult if not impossible to grasp. The judge Orendil (*TF* 184) is a good example. The count and *iudex* Orendil appears in the charters only from 802 on; no record provides explicit evidence for his kindred affiliation. An Orendil, however, shows up as a witness to a Freising charter of 779 (*TF* 97a); this kind of circumstantial evidence suggests that our Orendil's kindred had been in the area before the Carolingian takeover and that Orendil rode the Carolingian tide to office. On Orendil, see Sturm, *Preysing*, 196; Störmer, *Adelsgruppen*, 19.

5. *TF* 142 and 143b.

6. See the Introduction, n. 36.

7. *TF* 184ab; see Chapter 2, n. 78.

8. See the discussion of Ellanperht and the Arperht group in Chapter 2.

What raised Arn above most of these men was a conspicuous role as one of the most influential figures in the Carolingian Empire and a confidant of Charlemagne himself.[9] Arn entered this role via an ecclesiastical career that took him from Bavaria to the Frankish monastery of Saint Amand, where he became abbot in 782.[10] During his stay at Saint Amand, Arn developed a deep friendship with the Anglo-Saxon intellectual Alcuin, who probably brought him into contact with Charlemagne. In 784, as political events in Bavaria headed toward their final crisis, Arn became bishop of Salzburg, without, however, giving up his position as abbot of Saint Amand. Although the elevation of Arn to the see of Salzburg most likely came at Charlemagne's instigation, he seems to have remained in Duke Tassilo's good graces. In 787, Arn and Abbot Hunrich of Mondsee traveled to Rome as ambassadors of the Agilolfing duke to appeal for the mediation of Pope Hadrian I in Tassilo's worsening relations with the Frankish king.

After the Carolingian takeover of Bavaria, Arn moved smoothly and intensively into the Frankish royal service. To give a few examples: in 797, Charlemagne sent Arn along with twelve other *missi* to deal with a dispute between Pope Leo III and the Roman nobility. While in Rome, on April 20, 798, Arn received the *pallium* from Leo as archbishop of Salzburg and metropolitan of Bavaria at Charlemagne's request. Arn also helped return Pope Leo to power in early 800 and participated as Leo crowned Charlemagne emperor on Christmas Day of that year. In 811, Arn served as the third signatory, behind the archbishops of Cologne and Mainz, to Charlemagne's will.

Arn also played an important role in administrative and judicial planning not only in Bavaria but at the imperial level as well. Several scholars have remarked on the evidence contained in Arn's correspondence with Alcuin that in 802 Arn helped create and systematize the formal *missatica*, that is, defined territories in the western part of the empire that were policed by pairs of *missi*.[11] Although there is no direct evidence that any territorial *missatica* were set up in the East, Arn's intense activity as a *missus* in Bavaria has led

9. Arn shared this characteristic with Gerold, who was Charlemagne's brother-in-law.

10. On Arn's career, see Wolfram, "Arn von Salzburg und Karl der Grosse" and *Geburt Mitteleuropas*, 206–10; Heinz Dopsch, "Die Zeit der Karolinger und Ottonen," in *Geschichte Salzburgs: Stadt und Land*, ed. Heinz Dopsch, vol. 1, part 1 (Salzburg, 1981), 157–228 and esp. 157–73.

11. Wolfram, "Arn von Salzburg und Karl der Grosse," 26–27; Dopsch, "Zeit der Karolinger und Ottonen," in *Geschichte Salzburgs*, ed. Dopsch, 165 and n. 67, 68. On the *missi* and *missatica*, see the literature cited in the Introduction, n. 19.

some to speculate that he established the former duchy as a *missaticum* in its own right.[12] Arn's efforts on behalf of Carolingian centralization were not, of course, restricted to the secular sphere. As we see from references in the Freising charters and in the surviving synodal acts, Arn presided over a battery of church synods in Bavaria between 794 and 810. The main goal of this activity seems to have been the reorganization of the Bavarian church along Frankish and Roman lines. Arn's efforts had the support of a grateful Pope Leo, who did his best to stifle resistance with a letter to the Bavarian bishops warning them to obey their metropolitan.[13]

Archbishop Arn thus served as a point of intersection for Charlemagne's imperial authority, the Bavarian regional aristocracy, and the Bavarian church. Nevertheless, questions still remain. What kind of impact did Arn have in Bavaria and how did he make his authority felt? Here the evidence of the Bavarian charters proves crucial. A look not only at Arn's dominant presence in the dispute charters but also at the quality of his participation in disputes shows that authority in Carolingian Bavaria had a great deal to do with the person wielding it. To be specific, Arn's impact on disputes depended less on his titles and more on his personal and political connections to both the Bavarian aristocracy and the sources of imperial power.

THE RANGE OF ARN'S ACTIVITIES

The term *authority figure* for our purposes simply means someone whom a charter singles out as one of the heads of an assembly gathered to deal with a dispute, with statements such as "the venerable *missi* of the lord emperor Charles the Great, namely Archbishop Arn and Adalwin his co-bishop and the judge Orendil, were in residence for the purpose of examining diverse cases and ending them with law and justice," or "there were Bishop Arn, Gerold, Meginfrid, Wolfolt, and the judge Rimicoz, and into their presence came the priest Eio with his co-heirs."[14] In the two decades following the Carolingian takeover of Bavaria, Arn of Salzburg served as such a person

12. Goldberg, "Dilectissimus Pater Aquila Transalpinus"; Wolfram, "Arn von Salzburg und Karl der Grosse," 28, and *Salzburg, Bayern, Österreich*, 185–88.

13. See esp. the *Concilium Rispacense* and the *Concilia Rispacense, Frisingense, Salisburgense*, with links given in the apparatus of the latter to Charlemagne's *Admonitio Generalis* (789), ed. Alfred Boretius, *MGH Capit* I (Hannover, 1883), 52–62. See also the various references to synods in the Freising charters mentioned throughout this book. On Arn's synods in general, see Dopsch, "Zeit der Karolinger und Ottonen," in *Geschichte Salzburgs*, ed. Dopsch, 167–68.

14. *TF* 186 and 142.

with unusual frequency. Between 791, when Arn appears for the first time in the Freising charters in a judicial capacity, and 811, when he heads a judicial assembly for the last time, the Salzburger bishop and metropolitan appears in roughly half—fifteen—of the thirty-five surviving Freising dispute records.[15] When we take into account only those Freising charters that record the actions of formal judicial assemblies—that is, subtract descriptions of informal settlements or simple notes of a dispute's outcome with a witness list—Arn's presence becomes even more overwhelming. In the period 791 to 811, he appears in fifteen of nineteen such records.[16] Arn was particularly active between 802 and 807; twelve of his appearances come in this five-year period alone.[17]

Arn does not appear in any of the conflict records in the Mondsee charter collection; that is not surprising since only one Mondsee conflict notice exists for the period before 811.[18] Arn also fails to appear in the badly loss-damaged collection from Regensburg, which likewise contains only one conflict record from the years in question.[19] According to the Freising records, however, Arn acted at assemblies held in Regensburg at least twice.[20] He also figures in all three of the surviving dispute records for this period from Passau.[21]

The Salzburger archbishop in fact has a more consistent presence in the Bavarian charters for these years than anyone except Bishop Atto of Freising, who appears frequently simply because he was a party to almost all the disputes in question.[22] Arn also operated over a wider geographical area

15. *TF* 142, 181, 183, 184ab, 186, 193ab, 197, 227, 231, 242, 247, 248, 251ab, 258, 299; note that duplicate or two-version records are counted as one.

16. There is some play in the ratio of Arn's appearances to the total number of formal judicial assemblies recorded in the charters. Some records that give only an outcome and a witness list may also have stemmed from formal assemblies because they state that *missi*, counts, etc., were present; see *TF* 223, 235, 239.

17. The list in n. 15 less *TF* 142, 181, and 299. This still represents just over half the twenty-two Freising dispute records from the period 802–7. See Wolfram, *Salzburg, Bayern, Österreich*, 186.

18. *TM* 10.

19. *TR* 11.

20. *TF* 181 and 231.

21. *TP* 13, 50, 54.

22. Bishop Adalwin of Regensburg and the judge Ellanperht follow Arn in judicial appearances. Adalwin shows up nine times, each time with Arn (*TF* 181, 183, 184ab, 186, 227, 231, 242, 248, 299), and is after Arn the ecclesiastic most frequently found at nonsynodal judicial assemblies and most often called a *missus*. The only other churchman so labeled is Bishop Waltrich of Passau, who shows up once as a

than anyone else. Even leaving out his easternmost appearance, in Lorch on the Enns in 791, because it came in connection with Charlemagne's Avar campaign,[23] his judicial activities cover the length and breadth of Bavaria.[24]

Arn acted in a variety of forums and dealt with many different kinds of disputes. Most of his appearances come in records of regular assemblies convened expressly for the purpose of handling disputes.[25] Other records listing Arn as present infer that such an assembly took place but note simply that the disputants brought the case "into the presence" of the authority figures or the like.[26] One dispute handled by Arn took place at a gathering convened for an entirely different purpose, namely, to celebrate the translation of the relics of Saint Quirinus to the monastery at Tegernsee.[27] In addition, Arn served as an authority figure for three disputes settled at ecclesiastical synods.[28] One of his judicial appearances defies categorization; the record

---

missus in the Passau records (*TP* 50). Ellanperht appears with Arn five times (*TF* 231, 242, 247, 251, 299) and without Arn in other records of judicial assemblies, or in short notices that imply that such an assembly took place, four more times (*TF* 223, 232, 235, 245). Next come Audulf, Gerold's successor as Bavarian prefect (five times, always with Arn, labeled either *missus* or count: *TF* 183, 227, 231, 242, 247), the judge Kysalhart (four times, also only with Arn: *TP* 50, 54; *TF* 231, 251), and Count Job (four times, twice with Arn: *TF* 242, 247; twice without Arn: *TF* 232, 245). Arn also acts at judicial assemblies with a variety of colleagues who appear only two to three times each: Judge/Count Orendil (three times); Count Werinharius (twice); Count Reginhard (twice). Other officeholders appear in dispute charters only once, except for the bishops and abbots who were present at the synods.

23. *TF* 142.

24. For example, he shows up in Regensburg in the north (*TF* 183, 231), in Salzburg (*TF* 248) and Inzing near modern-day Innsbruck (*TP* 50) to the south, and in Mattighofen, southeast of modern Braunau, to the east (*TP* 54); see Map 2. The judge Kysalhart has nearly the same range—he too shows up in Regensburg, Inzing, and Mattighofen—but he appears far fewer times than Arn. Adalwin, Ellanperht, and Audulf appear only in the area between Freising and Regensburg, that is, in a triangle formed by Regensburg, Altötting, and "ad fluvio Rotae," probably on the Roth northwest of Dachau. The differences may stem in part from the accidents of source survival; more material from Passau, Regensburg, and Mondsee would certainly expand our picture of these men's activities. Nevertheless, Arn was the only judicial figure who operated over the entire area covered by the Freising charters.

25. *TP* 50 and 54; *TF* 183, 184ab, 186, 193, 227, 251, 258.

26. *TF* 142, 242, 247.

27. *TF* 197.

28. *TF* 181: Reisbach; *TF* 231: Regensburg; *TF* 248: Salzburg.

describes it as taking place "in a public gathering of bishops, and abbots and counts."[29]

At these different forums, Arn headed assemblies dealing with purely internal church conflicts, disputes involving ecclesiastical institutions and laymen, and disputes among laymen alone. This pattern holds true even for assemblies explicitly identified as synods.[30] Similarly, Arn himself appears with a variety of titles. He is frequently identified as the leader of a group of *missi*.[31] In other cases, he is listed as bishop or archbishop, or *pontifex*.[32] This title naturally obtains for the synods. Interestingly, after 806, Arn appears in two records as archbishop or bishop in explicit contrast to a *missus*, namely Audulf, who succeeded Gerold as prefect of Bavaria.[33] One of these records, produced sometime between 806 and 811, places Arn second behind Audulf. The vague dating of this record vis-à-vis the others in which Arn appears makes it impossible to tell whether this lower standing represents a slip over time in his importance or prestige.[34]

THE FORM OF ARN'S DISPUTE CHARTERS

Arn of Salzburg was thus the dominant figure in the resolution of property disputes throughout Bavaria in the period 791–811. Now we need to look at how he was involved in these disputes. Right away, however, we face the issue of formula. Since dispute charters use formulaic language, is it possible to learn anything from them about an authority figure's real activity? In this case, we can learn a great deal first by simply observing the formulas rather than trying to penetrate them. It seems that Arn in fact had the power to

29. *TF* 299. Wolfram, *Geburt Mitteleuropas*, 170n. 13, views this gathering as a synod.

30. *TF* 181, from the synod held at Reisbach in 800, concerns a dispute between Abbot Cundharius of Isen and Bishop Atto of Freising over "four parochial churches"; *TF* 248, from a synod held at Salzburg in 807, records the settlement of a dispute among the Bavarian bishops and abbots over the division of tithes. In contrast, *TF* 231, from a synod held at Regensburg in 806, concerns a conflict between the see of Freising and a layman.

31. *TP* 50, 54; *TF* 142, 183, 184, 186, 227.

32. *TP* 13; *TF* 181, 193, 231, 242, 247, 248, 251, 258, 299.

33. *TF* 242, 247.

34. *TF* 247. Wolfram, *Salzburg, Bayern, Österreich*, 187, suggests that the change in Arn's title was due to Audulf's succeeding Arn as head of a Bavarian *missaticum*.

influence the kinds of charter formulas scribes used to record the actions of assemblies at which he was present.[35]

Arn's dispute charters come in a variety of shapes and sizes. Some simply state the issue, the verdict, the authorities present, and the witnesses.[36] Others give more or less lengthy narrative descriptions of a dispute. Several describe compromise settlements, which by their very nature defy categorization. A number of Arn's records, however, stand out from the others because they use similar formulaic language and follow a similar narrative pattern. With minor variations, the language and pattern look something like this: the record first introduces Arn and the other heads of the assembly as in residence in a given location for the purpose of hearing disputes.[37] The plaintiff then steps forward and charges the defendant with holding some of his property unjustly. Either the defendant makes some kind of reply[38] or the record simply notes that "he stood up and tried to retain the properties as his own"[39] or that "he stood up in their presence and stoutly defended that property,"[40] depending on whether he was a villain or a hero. The authority figures next carry out an inquisition. Sometimes they gather witnesses and make them swear they will tell the truth.[41] In other cases, they view documentary proof of the witnesses' existence brought forward by one of the parties, as, for example: "They brought forward his gift charters into their presence and displayed the true witnesses written in them."[42] The testimony produces either a simple statement—"that [the property] ought more legitimately to remain in the gift of the above-named man to that church than to be returned to them as their own"[43]—or an extensive collective quote from the witnesses.[44] Arn's final appearance in the charters in 811 provides the only quirk in this part of the structure: Arn and Abbot Cundharius of Isen themselves act as witnesses by stating that they saw a disputed church given to Bishop Arbeo of Freising with their own eyes.[45] After the

35. Goldberg, "Dilectissimus Pater Aquila Transalpinus," 59–80; Wolfram, "Arn von Salzburg und Karl der Grosse," 28, and Salzburg, Bayern, Österreich, 186–87.

36. TF 231, 242.

37. See, for example, TF 186.

38. TF 183.

39. TF 186.

40. TF 227.

41. See, for examples of the latter, TF 183, 247.

42. TF 227.

43. TF 183.

44. TF 186.

45. TF 299.

inquisition, the heads of the assembly announce a judgment. The defeated party, "convicted with law and justice,"[46] returns the disputed property to the victor and promises never to raise any further trouble about it. Then the record declares the dispute to have ended in the presence of the entire assembly and lists the witnesses, who were in general "pulled by the ears according to the use of the Bavarians."[47] A dating clause follows, sometimes with an affirmation by the scribe.[48]

Two of these records add a narrative description of the people, places, and issues involved to the beginning of the pattern.[49] For example, one begins, "Notice concerning the church in the place called Auerbach," and tells the story of the acquisition of this church by Freising and the beginnings of Freising's dispute with the sons of the grantor. Then it slides into the characteristic narrative structure just described, reporting the inquisition, testimony, verdict, and witnesses. Several other notices, discussed later, begin with the characteristic formulaic opening but then depart from the formula in order to accommodate compromises.

The particular formulaic language and narrative pattern of these records stem from a form of judicial document common in the Frankish West, the so-called *placitum* report.[50] Such records stand in marked contrast in the

46. *TF* 186.

47. Ibid.

48. Some of these records have spaces left blank. The spaces reinforce the conclusion that the scribes derived the records from a preexisting formula or intended the records themselves to serve as formulas. For example, in *TF* 183 (802), Freising's advocate Kaganhart rebuts the charge by the nun Engilfrit and her brother Kundperht that the bishop of Freising unjustly held their paternal inheritance by saying, "The properties you seek were given to us so-and-so many years ago by the illustrious man named [blank]." *TF* 251a (807) states that "the advocate of Bishop Atto named Ainhart sued a certain man named Oadallant for a church and house pertaining to it at [blank]." Cozroh copied the blanks into his manuscript, which testifies to his accuracy; there is no sign of any scraping on the parchment.

49. *TF* 247 and 299.

50. Fichtenau, *Urkundenwesen*, 75 and n. 11. Several articles in the Davies and Fouracre dispute collection also deal with *placita* of this kind, showing how widespread and long-lived the form's use in the Frankish West was. Fouracre, "Placita," in *Settlement of Disputes*, ed. Davies and Fouracre, 24–25, points out that *placita* are unlike any form of late Roman document and suggests they developed in the early seventh century to meet the needs of new centers of royal justice in northern Francia. For an opposing view, see Peter Classen, "Fortleben und Wandel spätrömischen Urkundenwesens im frühen Mittelalter," in *Recht und Schrift im Mittelalter*, ed. Peter Classen (Sigmaringen, 1977), 13–54. See also Nelson, "Dispute Settlement," 48–49,

Bavarian charter collections to the more common and more flexibly constructed notices that begin with phrases such as "Notice of how," "Notice concerning," "So that it not be unknown," "Concerning the contention that was . . . ," and so on.[51] The formulaic nature of the Frankish-style *placitum* makes it difficult to get at real people and behavior in disputes. In the final analysis, *placitum* reports reveal only the issue and the identity of those present at an assembly and report a verdict that the parties concerned may or may not have followed.[52]

These records nonetheless provide us with three very interesting bits of information. First, the Frankish-style *placitum* report first appears in Bavaria after the Carolingian takeover, specifically, beginning in 802. Second and much more important, in the period up to 811, this kind of dispute record appears only in connection with Arn of Salzburg.[53] Third, seven *placita* bill themselves as having been written by the scribes Bertharius and Egipald,

---

52–53, and Wickham, "Land Disputes," 106–7, both in *Settlement of Disputes*, ed. Davies and Fouracre.

51. *Notitia qualiter . . .*, TF 145; *Notitia de . . .*, TF 181; *Dum non est incognitum . . .*, TF 235; *De contentione qui fuit . . .*, TF 245. See Fichtenau, *Urkundenwesen*, chap. 4, on *notitiae* and the variations in their construction.

52. This point remains debated. On the one hand, Fouracre, "Placita," in *Settlement of Disputes*, ed. Davies and Fouracre, 29–30, and 41–42, points out the ways in which late-seventh-century *placitum* formulas had to be adapted to individual cases. He argues that the evident trouble scribes often had in selecting appropriate formulas and the care they took to adapt the formulas to specifics make their case reporting trustworthy. Wickham, "Land Disputes," in *Settlement of Disputes*, ed. Davies and Fouracre, 107, on the other hand, feels that the formulaic phrases of the *placitum* homogenized what happened. Real information, he suggests, comes when records, even those produced by the same court, differ from one another, as they generally do in his Lombard evidence before ca. 880. After ca. 880, that is no longer true; Wickham's records become more rather than less formulaic, making them in his view much less useful as social-historical documents (112). As becomes clear in the following chapters, the Bavarian evidence leads me to believe that the *placitum* reports reflected real procedure (see esp. the discussions of TF 514 in Chapter 5 and TF 898c in the Conclusion). Nonetheless, the world beyond the charters is undeniably most accessible when two versions of the same case differ or when a compromise forced the scribe outside the formulas.

53. Goldberg and Wolfram, as n. 35. Wolfram suggests that the "transmission vector" for the form was the *Formulae Salicae Lindenbrogianae*, a formula collection that Arn himself brought to Bavaria. See *Formulae Salicae Lindenbrogianae*, in *Formulae Merowingici et Karolini aevi*, ed. Karl Zeumer, *MGH Legum* Sectio 5 (Hannover, 1886), no. 21, 282 (which deals specifically with a case of contested freedom); Bernhard Bischoff, "Salzburger Formelbücher und Briefe aus Tassilonischer und

who appear only with Arn.[54] Another was written by a cleric named Adalperht; circumstantial evidence suggests he came from Freising.[55] Still another *placitum* report was produced at Passau by a cleric named Waldpert at the orders of Bishop Waldric.[56]

In short, Arn of Salzburg had the power to influence how his judicial notices were written, both by his own scribes and by scribes from individual cathedral churches. He had in particular the weight to introduce Frankish practice into Bavarian judicial records.[57] The other men who appear as authority figures in this period, in disputes in which Arn was not involved, were not able to do this; Freising scribes wrote notices describing their actions in the looser Freising notice style.[58]

Karolingischer Zeit," in *Sitzungsberichte der bayerischen Akademie der Wissenschaften: Philosophisch-Historische Klasse*, 1973, no. 4 (Munich, 1973), 9–12 and 31n. 13.

54. The *notarius* Bertharius appears five times in Arn's records between 802 and 804, four times in the Freising collection, and once in a notice from Passau. Two of Bertharius's records are straightforward *placita* recording clear verdicts (*TF* 183; *TP* 54); the other three contain elements of the *placitum* form but diverge from it to record compromises (*TF* 184b, *TF* 193a, *TF* 197). See Wolfram, *Salzburg, Bayern, Österreich*, 187. Bertharius's transdiocesan connection with Arn has led scholars to label him an "archiepiscopal notary"; see Wolfram, *Mitteleuropa*, 209; Fichtenau, *Urkundenwesen*, 76n. 13, 79 and n. 30. The only evidence indicating another kind of connection for Bertharius, namely, to Freising, is a sentence in the report discussed later of a dispute between Freising and the monastery at Tegernsee (*TF* 197). While describing an earlier attempt by Freising to lay claim to the disputed properties, Bertharius makes the remark, "But nothing became of all these things that they had pledged, nor could we make good any of our rights to them" (*Sed nihil profuit de his omnis, unde wadium dederunt nec quicquam de iustitia nostra ad illos invenire potuimus*). This statement suggests that Bertharius identified with Freising's interests. Nonetheless, the fact that Bertharius appears only with Arn and the marked differences between his notices and those written by scribes easily identifiable as Freising clerics (discussed later) support the idea of his archiepiscopal service. Egipald wrote two records in the Freising collection, one a complete *placitum* and the other a compromise couched in *placitum* language (*TF* 227 and *TF* 258).

55. Adalperht appears in two Freising records, each time in connection with Arn: as the scribe for *TF* 186 (802) and as the authority behind *TF* 184a (802), written at his orders by the Freising scribe Horskeo. See Chapter 2, n. 12.

56. *TP* 50.

57. Albeit with some modification to reflect Bavarian custom, as the references to validating witnesses by pulling on their ears indicate.

58. All the notices from this period recording the actions of judicial assemblies in which Arn was not involved come from the Freising collection; see, for example, *TF* 143b and 232ab, headed by the *missi* Gerold, Meginfrid, Wolfolt, and Rimigerus.

Things get really interesting, however, when we turn from the formulaic records of simple judgments to the records of compromise arrangements in which Arn participated. Compromises forced Arn's scribes to bend and rearrange the *placitum* formulas in order to include nonstandard information or even to abandon them altogether when events simply would not fit. This process resulted in the survival of some fascinating information. In several of these cases, the archbishop himself acted directly to mediate or arrange settlements. In one case, he even brought about a compromise by means of a threat.

The first of these compromise records deals with a dispute between the see of Freising and the monastery at Chiemsee over a parish and the six churches belonging to it. Written by one of Arn's notaries in 804, the record begins in the formulaic manner outlined above: it notes that Arn, a count, and two judges were in residence at Aibling for the purpose of hearing disputes.[59] In their presence, Bishop Atto's representative sued Abbot Liutfrid of Chiemsee, claiming that the abbot held the churches unjustly. The abbot resisted the charge. Then the archbishop and the other members of the court launched an investigation. They found that Chiemsee's first abbot had in fact wrongfully appropriated the churches.[60] So far, the narrative has followed the familiar pattern. At this point, however, it jumps the tracks. The two disputing parties, at their request, "made an agreement in the presence of the pontiff Arn in the following fashion": Chiemsee would keep four of the disputed churches as well as their tithes,[61] and Freising received from Chiemsee the remaining two churches plus a say in what Chiemsee did with its tithes.[62] The notice ends with the injunction, "Let there be peace and unshakable concord between them in the future without any conflict or contention."[63]

---

59. *TF* 193a (Bertharius). Aibling lies ca. twenty-five kilometers west of the Chiemsee.

60. Dobdagrecus, the Irish companion of Virgil of Salzburg; see Jahn, *Ducatus*, 147.

61. At Willing, Berbling, Mietraching, and Tattenhausen.

62. At Högling and at "Perch" (identity not clear).

63. Since Bertharius appears only with Arn of Salzburg, it is possible that his account of this compromise was biased by Salzburg's historical ties to Chiemsee. These ties appear already under Duke Odilo; an early priest of a church on the island "Auua" in the Chiemsee appears to have been sent out from Salzburg, and the abbot Dobdagrecus came to Bavaria with Virgil of Salzburg and served himself as bishop of

This account of the dispute explicitly singles out Arn as the mediating authority who helped the two parties work out a settlement. It seems that Arn did more than just oversee negotiations, however; he apparently had to put some pressure on Bishop Atto of Freising to bring the compromise about. As in the Lantfrid dispute discussed in the previous chapter, Freising produced its own description of this dispute. Written by an unknown scribe, this version not only changes the results of the hearing in Freising's favor but also politicizes the dispute by depicting the abbot of Chiemsee as an enemy of the Carolingian regime.[64] To start, it lists only four churches as under dispute, not six.[65] The two that are missing are those that Chiemsee received as its share of the compromise in the version written by Arn's notary.[66] The disputed churches had originally belonged to the see of Freising. They had been unjustly taken away not by Chiemsee's first abbot but by Duke Tassilo and his wife, Liutpirg. The duke and his wife had also robbed Freising of many other things because of the hatred they bore for Atto's predecessor as bishop of Freising, Arbeo. The ducal couple hated Arbeo because he was "more faithful to the lord king Charles and to the Franks than to them."

After having thus charged Chiemsee with benefiting from Tassilo's malice toward a pro-Carolingian bishop of Freising, Freising's account next changes the outcome of the hearing. There was no compromise. Instead, certain "old and truthful men who knew this case well" were ordered to swear on sacred relics that they would reveal the truth of the matter. These witnesses unanimously testified that Freising had the more just claim. The

---

Salzburg until 749. Real influence over Chiemsee in the Agilolfing period was wielded not by the bishops of Salzburg but rather by the Agilolfing dukes, however. Chiemsee's importance to the Agilolfings was recognized by Charlemagne in 788; stressing that Chiemsee had been an integral part of the Bavarian *ducatus*, Charlemagne gave the monastery not to Arn of Salzburg but to Bishop Angilram of Metz (*MGH D Karol* I, nr. 162, 219–20). Chiemsee did not come under Salzburg's control until 891, when it was taken from Metz and given to Salzburg by King Arnulf. Moreover, Bertharius's account of this case is similar to his accounts of other Arn-brokered compromises that did not involve Chiemsee: see the discussions later of *TF* 197 (Freising v. Tegernsee) and the Scharnitz-Schlehdorf case, *TF* 184. See Störmer, *Früher Adel*, 2:435; Jahn, *Ducatus*, 144–49.

64. *TF* 193b. This second version survives only in the twelfth-century copy made by the Freising sacristan Conrad: Bayr. Hauptstaatsarchiv, Hochstift Freising Lit. 3c, fol. 38'.

65. At Willing, Mietraching, Högling, and "Perch."

66. At Berbling and at Tattenhausen.

court then declared that the churches ought to be returned to Bishop Atto. Abbot Liutfrid is represented as accepting this result. The abbot returned three of the churches, including one that the first version had given him as part of the compromise.[67] The fourth, which Chiemsee had likewise received in the first version, it also kept in the second.[68] Not because of any compromise, however—Abbot Liutfrid is described as holding on to it because he wanted another inquiry. There is no mention of concord or peace.

Freising's rearrangement of events has an obvious purpose.[69] It represents Chiemsee not only as having infringed on Freising's rights but as having benefited from the actions of an enemy of the Carolingian regime. Two of the churches Freising had to give up in the first version were simply not mentioned in the second, which left the door open for another attempt to get hold of them later. Of the remaining four churches, two that Chiemsee received in the first version are also presented in the second in such a way as to make a future attack possible; the court had supposedly awarded one of them to Freising, and Abbot Liutfrid himself had allegedly requested another hearing on the second. It appears, therefore, that Arn had exacted a compromise settlement of the dispute that did not go down well with Freising. Freising accordingly drafted its own version of events so that it might rearrange things later more to its liking.

Thus, it is likely that a Freising scribe wrote the second version not at the time of the hearing in 804 but rather later, after Arn had left the Bavarian judicial scene, in order to undo the settlement Arn had imposed.[70] A later

67. At Willing, Högling, and "Perch."

68. At Mietraching.

69. *TF* 193b is one of the principal texts used to argue for a fundamental opposition between Arbeo of Freising and Duke Tassilo: see Glaser, "Bischof Arbeo," in *Vita Corbiniani*, ed. Glaser, Brunhölzl, and Benker, 71 (in the context of a longer discussion on pp. 67–76 of the evidence for Arbeo's political leanings), with a reference to Friedrich Prinz, "Arbeo von Freising und die Agilulfinger," *Zeitschrift für bayerische Landesgeschichte* 29 (1966): 581. Jahn, "Virgil," 231–33, takes the view presented here of *TF* 193b as a "Freisinger Interpretation pro domo"; he points out that the passage quoted earlier matches in content, and in some places literally, the accusations leveled against Tassilo in the *ARF* a. 787, 54.

70. Jahn, in his extensive discussion of this case ("Virgil," 231–33), suggests as he does for the Lantfrid case, *TF* 184ab, that Freising's version represented an attempt to influence the *missi* beforehand (see Chapter 2, n. 21). The attempt to look more pro-Carolingian certainly supports this idea; here as in *TF* 184, however, the fact that Freising's rewrite presents a finished case rather than a set of charges indicates an effort to influence events after the fact, possibly by appealing to other Carolingian officeholders after Arn's withdrawal from judicial activity.

Freising notice places this idea on firmer footing and provides an approximate date for the Freising rewrite.[71] This notice comes from the year 816, that is, after Arn disappears from the Freising records and five years before his death in 821. It reveals that Freising finally gained possession of one of the properties which the original compromise had given Chiemsee and which Freising had let quietly disappear, namely, a church at Berbling. The record concerns the transfer of property in Berbling as a benefice to a Count Oadalschalk in exchange for the count's gift of all his property in the same place. It begins:

> Let it be known to the many residing in the bishopric of Saint Mary, how the venerable lord Bishop Hitto recovered, with great labor, the property of the house of Saint Mary in the place called Berbling which . . . had unjustly been handed over to his monastery in the place called [Chiemsee] in the time of the duchess Liutpirg. But now that has been recovered by the testimony of truthful and good men which had been taken away by the enemies of the house of Saint Mary.

Although the record does not explicitly mention the church that Freising and Chiemsee had fought over, it nonetheless concerns property at Berbling formerly held by Chiemsee. It represents Bishop Hitto's successful effort to claim the property for Freising in the way left open by Freising's version of the original dispute, namely, by an assertion of Chiemsee's unjust possession with the implicit participation of the Agilolfings tacked on via the reference to the Duchess Liutpirg.[72]

The Freising-Chiemsee dispute, therefore, shows Arn acting as an authority figure with the power to bring about a compromise against the will of at least one of the disputing parties. Arn wielded enough authority, ap-

71. *TF* 368.

72. Just how Bishop Hitto got hold of the property at Berbling is unclear. It appears he may have exploited tensions between Chiemsee and the family or families propertied in Berbling. There was certainly a quid pro quo in his arrangement with Count Oadalschalk. Freising had its title to the disputed property at Berbling secured in the form of the written benefice grant to Oadalschalk; it also gained ultimate title to Oadalschalk's own property there. Oadalschalk in turn had Chiemsee's former holdings in Berbling united to his own for his lifetime use. Supporting the idea that Freising was exploiting stresses in the relationship between Chiemsee and the aristocrats propertied in the area is the fact that this arrangement required at least one person to turn coat. One of the witnesses to *TF* 368, Paldachar, appears as the last witness to *TF* 193a, which had explicitly awarded the church at Berbling to Chiemsee.

parently, that Freising had to wait until he had withdrawn from active judicial activity before trying to undo his work.[73]

A second and more spectacular dispute record from the year 804 deepens our picture of Arn's authority. It shows the archbishop deliberately intervening in a judicial process to prod the disputing parties into negotiating a settlement.[74] This record begins by relating the history of a lengthy dispute between Freising and the monastery at Tegernsee. At some unspecified time in the past, Bishop Atto of Freising had sued the abbot of Tegernsee over some churches that he claimed Tegernsee had taken unjustly. The abbot pledged to return the property, but nothing came of his pledge. After some time had passed, a man named Maginhard became abbot of Tegernsee. Maginhard and Bishop Atto agreed that the dispute over the churches needed to be resolved. Accordingly, they asked for a public hearing (*publicum placitum*) on the matter at a great assembly to be held at Tegernsee for the translation of the monastery's patron saint, Saint Quirinus.

The record then slips into the narrative structure of the *placitum* report. It lists the ecclesiastical and lay dignitaries who were present—Arn heads the list—and describes Bishop Atto's claim and Abbot Maginhard's counterclaim. Next, however, instead of an inquisition, we get a rare first-person statement from Arn directed at Maginhard:

73. Another Freising notice, *TF* 206 (804–6), suggests that Freising may have been bold enough to try something similar with another church while Arn was still very much on the scene. This notice concerns the church at Willing, which the compromise recorded in Bertharius's *TF* 193a assigned to Chiemsee but which the pro-Freising *TF* 193b awarded to Freising. One Toto gave what he represented as his "own inheritance and acquisition" in Willing, namely, a church and a house, to Freising. After listing the witnesses to the gift, the notice gives a second list of men who "testified to their and to Toto's inheritance and declared that this gift was valid": Hiltiperht, Adaluuart, Uoio, Herimot, Coteschalch, Waldpehrt, Ratolf, Paldachar, Otlant, Hroadmunt, Eparachar, and Alprih. Of these, four are conspicuous for their presence on the witness list to Bertharius's *TF* 193a: Coteschalch, Otlant, Hroadmunt, and Alprih. Coteschalch appears in both *TF* 193a and *TF* 193b. If the church here is identical with that under dispute in *TF* 193 (and it may very well not be), it would follow that Freising, with the cooperation of the church's founding family, used Toto's gift as a way to get around the terms of *TF* 193a and have its claim to the church at Willing secured only a few years after the original hearing. *TF* 206 certainly bends over backward to stress that Toto had the right to make the gift, which suggests a need to protect the transaction from charges that it was invalid.

74. *TF* 197.

So speaking, the pontiff Arn said, "If you wish to have those churches and all those things that the lord bishop Atto has claimed from you, let your advocate come into our presence and let him act according to the law, and let him acquire from that house of God whatever he is legitimately able to acquire according to the law. If not, let that be returned which you should not legitimately seek to possess."

It appears that Arn was threatening Maginhard with the rest of the *placitum* process, that is, with the interrogation of witnesses and a formal judgment.[75] Faced with this prospect, Maginhard chose compromise; the two parties "came together again among themselves and agreed on how they could recall themselves to the concord of peace." The resulting settlement was ritually enacted. Abbot Maginhard formally returned the disputed properties to Bishop Atto, who was represented by Arn and the Freising archpriest Ellanod.[76] Maginhard did so under the condition that if he wanted, he could open another formal investigation into the matter at a later date. Then Arn asked (*supplicavit*) Bishop Atto to return the churches as a benefice to Abbot Maginhard, excepting the tithes, which Atto would take "just as the bishop ought to take them up for the priests of his parish." Atto agreed, under the conditions that Freising keep one of the churches and that if Abbot Maginhard caused any trouble in the future, Freising would be able to resume control of all of them.

Arn thus openly intervened to bring about a negotiated settlement. Once the two parties had reached an agreement, the archbishop took part in a set of public gestures that underlined his role as the mediator. He participated

75. The passage reads in the original, *et faciat inde legem et conquiratur ad ipsa casa dei quicquid legitime secundem ordinem conquiri potest; sin autem, reddatur qua legitime possidere non queas.* Taken literally, the reference to law (*lex*) could refer to the procedure outlined in the Bavarian Law for asserting rights to disputed property, namely, swearing an oath with a specified number of oath-helpers (see *Lex B* C. XVII/1–2, which refers specifically to disputed fields or meadows). I have chosen not to interpret the passage this way, however, because the oath-helping procedure appears in practice in the charters only once, in marked contrast to the relatively common *placitum* process. In its single appearance, in *TF* 277 (808), the oath-helping procedure is invoked using similar language (*ut ipsi secundum legem exinde fecissent*) but not at a *placitum*. Instead, Bishop Atto of Freising appeals to it directly while working out a bilateral arrangement with his opponent. In a Passau charter, *TP* 13 (785–97), Arn presides over the settlement of a dispute by oath, but without oath-helpers. See Warren Brown, "The Use of Norms in Disputes in Early Medieval Bavaria," *Viator* 30 (1999): 25–26, and the discussion of *TF* 277 in Chapter 4.

76. Maginhard returned the churches *per manus Arnonem pontificem ed* [sic] *Ellanodeum arcipresbiterum* [sic].

in Abbot Maginhard's formal return of the churches to Freising. Then he publicly asked Bishop Atto to carry out his end of the bargain by returning the churches to Maginhard as a benefice. This public request from the archbishop of Bavaria, in the presence of a large group of distinguished witnesses (and on the occasion of the translation of Tegernsee's patron saint), put Atto in the position of bowing to his superior's wishes. Thus, Atto was allowed to make the compromise without losing face. Arn's request added force to the agreement by placing Atto in a position in which he could hardly refuse to accept it. In other words, Arn deftly staged a compromise settlement that gave everyone something: Tegernsee kept de facto possession of all but one of its churches, and Freising preserved its formal rights and saved face.

The two disputes we have examined so far pitted one ecclesiastical institution against another, suggesting that Arn's ability to settle disputes depended on his position as head of the Bavarian church. Arn's authority reached farther, however. First, the two disputes took place not at synods but at judicial assemblies headed by both ecclesiastics and laymen. Second, many of Arn's judicial records involve disputes not between two churches but between a church and laymen. Some of these ended in compromise settlements that also reveal Arn's fine hand at work.

A good example is provided by the Lantfrid dispute discussed in Chapter 2. This dispute, which engaged Freising against the Scharnitz-Schlehdorf heir Lantfrid, also comes to us in two versions, one written by a notary attached to Arn and the other by a Freising scribe.[77] The account written by Arn's notary describes a compromise settlement arranged under the auspices of two *missi*, Arn and Bishop Adalwin of Regensburg. The "*missi* and those making the agreement decided among themselves" that Lantfrid could return the property that belonged to the church at Scharnitz without penalty while keeping the properties to which he was legitimately entitled.[78] That the *missi* exercised a bit of muscle in the process comes out in the fact that Freising did not like the outcome and wrote its own version of events to change it. Freising's account paints Lantfrid as a willfully contentious person and an enemy of the Carolingian house. The disputing parties did not work out a compromise under the aegis of the *missi*; instead, Bishop Atto graciously assented to a settlement that the *missi* asked him to approve. Moreover, Freising's version changed the compromise so that it included only the remission of fines. Lantfrid is represented as giving up his claim to

77. *TF* 184b: Bertharius; *TF* 184a: Horskeo; see Chapter 2.
78. *TF* 184b.

all the properties under dispute, an outcome that, as in Freising's version of the Chiemsee dispute, left the door open for Freising to take up the case again later. In other words, in this dispute between Freising and a layman, the *missi* apparently had enough authority to force Freising to accept a compromise it did not like. The similarity between this dispute and the ones discussed earlier suggests that the authority lay with Arn of Salzburg.

Arn of Salzburg acted as a powerful magnet for property disputes in the years between 791 and 811, and in particular between 802 and 807. Arn not only attracted disputes but had the ability to settle them, often in the face of resistance, in a way matched by no other authority figure in the charters. None of the other officeholders from this period steps out of the dispute charters with the same immediacy and authority; they remain instead hidden behind the mask of the records. Even in cases handled by other *missi*, the records simply list the *missi* as present.[79]

We need to explain Arn's unique influence over judicial processes in these years. One possible explanation attributes his power to his position as a *missus*. In other words, people brought their disputes to Arn and obeyed his judgments because he had the authority of his office as an imperial legate behind him. That must have been true to some degree, but it does not entirely explain the evidence. First, the records do not always label the Salzburger archbishop a *missus*, even in the period 802–6 when his appearances as *missus* cluster.[80] For example, in the two compromise cases discussed earlier, Arn appears not as *missus* but as *pontifex* or *archiepiscopus*.[81] Plainly, he did not have to be a *missus* to wield authority over disputes. Moreover, when Arn withdrew from judicial activity after 811, Freising felt free to alter the results of at least one of his settlements despite the continuing presence of imperial *missi* in Bavaria.[82]

79. See, for example, *TF* 143b (791–93); *TF* 232ab (806–7). An exception is Audulf, who in *TF* 247 (806–11), acting as a *missus* alongside Arn *episcopus*, is described as personally giving the order to Count Job and the *iudex* Ellanperht to carry out the inquisition that settles the case.

80. Wolfram, *Salzburg, Bayern, Österreich*, 185–88.

81. *TF* 193a: Arn *pontifice*; *TF* 193b and 197: Arn *archiepiscopus*.

82. In all fairness to the post-Arn *missi*, they appeared much less often in Bavaria after 811, which may have provided Freising with some room for maneuver. *TF* 368, which records Freising's final success in obtaining Chiemsee's property at Berbling, comes from the year 816; *missi* show up again in Bavaria in 822; see Chapter 5.

A second possibility derives Arn's authority from his position as the metropolitan of Bavaria. The dispute records all concern church rights to a greater or lesser degree, and Arn represented the highest ecclesiastical authority in the region. This argument also has merit but likewise fails to extend farther than Arn. Arn's successor as archbishop of Salzburg, Adalram, shows up in the charters only once, in a Freising dispute record from the year 822.[83] Adalram takes no active role in the proceedings; he appears only in the list of authority figures present. He certainly shows no signs of having inherited a judicial authority inherent in his office as archbishop.[84]

The explanation for Arn's unique presence in the charters, therefore, must lie in the person of Arn himself. Here the evidence makes sense. Arn was connected both downward into the Bavarian aristocratic network and upward to the sources of imperial power. The combination of his regional ties with the prestige stemming from his imperial activities gave him the muscle to make his will felt.[85] Like a modern judge, Arn threatened disputing parties with a formal hearing in order to force a compromise, a practice that sounds perfectly familiar to the modern ear. A modern judge, however, has the weight of the state with all its coercive power behind him. Arn of Salzburg apparently had similar weight behind him, embodied not only in his offices but also in his position as the most visible and powerful member of the regional aristocracy, with the ability to advance careers or hinder them, to give or withhold favors, and, perhaps most important, with the ear of Charles the Great.[86] Even if Arn had a great deal to do with the creation

83. *TF* 463; see Chapter 5.

84. In his letter to the Bavarian bishops warning them to obey their new metropolitan (see Dopsch, "Zeit der Karolinger und Ottonen," in *Geschichte Salzburgs*, ed. Dopsch, 167–68), Pope Leo III asked the bishops to take canonical disputes to Arn rather than to the secular courts. This they plainly did, at least in the synodal cases that dealt with purely church affairs. A legalist turn of mind might prompt one to see this statement as the source for Arn's authority over disputes in the Bavarian charters, since all the disputes in one way or another concerned church property. The wide variety of cases that Arn dealt with, however, as well as the variety of different hats he wore and venues he worked in, would make his canonical authority over church disputes an unlikely single basis for his overwhelming presence in the dispute charters.

85. Wolfram ("Arn von Salzburg und Karl der Grosse," 22) implies as much when he points out that Arn, through his ties to the Huosi (see n. 3), almost certainly had personal and kinship interests in settling the dispute the Huosi brought him and the other *missi* at Lorch on the Enns in 791 (*TF* 142; see the Interlude).

86. Davies and Fouracre ("Conclusion: Dispute Processes and Social Structures," in *Settlement of Disputes*, 232) reach a similar conclusion that relations between state

of the territorial *missatica* in 802, he did not act in Bavaria within the framework of an institution that by itself gave him the authority he displayed. In Bavaria, Arn was not simply a *missus*, he was The *Missus*; not simply an archbishop but The Archbishop. His involvement in imperial efforts to centralize the administration of the empire would simply have made this more, not less, true.[87]

The Arn charters thus provide a fascinating glimpse of how Carolingian centralization in Bavaria worked. For this period of twenty years, Arn produced a burst of very centralized-looking activity. Arn's charters resemble the products of a centralized system, the procedures seem more formal than before, and Arn himself acts with a measure of coercive authority.[88] Nevertheless, things begin to change after Arn's withdrawal from active political life and after his death in 821. Some of the formal elements he introduced—that is, the *placitum* formulas and judicial assemblies headed by *missi*—remain visible in the charters. But they start to change subtly, and then more

---

and community were often simply represented by relationships among local aristocrats acting in various capacities. Nelson, "Dispute Settlement," in *Settlement of Disputes*, ed. Davies and Fouracre, 48, after noting that a West Frankish *missus* was also usually a local magnate, comments that "the jurisdiction of the count or *missus*, in principle delegated from the king, in practice became the acceptable face of local power."

87. Arn of Salzburg's clear interest in promoting settlements in the context of judicial assemblies becomes more interesting when compared with the evidence that Carolingian policymakers viewed anything but strict judgment according to the law with suspicion. See Charlemagne's *capitulare missorum generale* (802), ed. Alfred Boretius, *MGH Capit* I (Hannover, 1883), c. 26, 96: "That judges should judge justly according to the written law, not according to their own will"; Geary, "Extra-Judicial Means of Conflict Resolution," 600–601. Evidently, Arn, despite his own role in the making of Carolingian policy, acted in Bavaria according to the realities of the situation before him rather than according to the strict dictates of imperial prescription.

88. Arn is even remarkable when compared with the evidence assembled in the Davies and Fouracre dispute collection. Davies and Fouracre ("Conclusion: Procedure and Practice in the Settlement of Disputes," in *Settlement of Disputes*, 216) discuss the role of the court "president" in bringing authority to bear on judicial process and in providing facilities for dispute settlement. They suggest it did not matter whence the "president's" authority derived; it mattered only in the immediate situation that his power was sufficient to deter defiance of the court's rules and rulings. It follows from this, they argue, that presidents tended to appear as passive figureheads. Arn, in contrast, had enough power and authority that scribes frequently did not treat him as a passive figurehead.

rapidly, over time, in ways that reflect an evolving perception of imperial or royal authority on the ground. No one after 811 appears in the charters with Arn's power to attract so many cases and particularly to act as a settler of disputes. Arn's unique status suggests that Carolingian power in Bavaria after the conquest did not reflect the successful construction of a centralized institutional apparatus but rather depended on a combination of certain persons with the prestige that flowed from Charlemagne.

CHAPTER FOUR
A SUBCULTURE OF COMPROMISE

U p to this point, we have looked mainly at disputes resolved in the context of formal judicial assemblies. These assemblies served as a place where Carolingian authority, embodied in officeholders such as the royal *missi*, came to bear on local conflicts. Although the assemblies and their leaders profoundly affected Bavarian disputing, Bavarians did not always resort to them. Disputants in postconquest Bavaria frequently chose instead to resolve matters themselves, that is, without resorting to a formal venue and without any meaningful intervention by officeholding authority figures.

This layer of extrajudicial dispute resolution is dominated by compromise settlements.[1] There appear to have been as many different kinds of settlements as there were issues to fight over. Bishops bought off property claims with money or other kinds of compensation. Neighbors resolved boundary disputes with a gift to a church that redrew the disputed boundary. People accused of theft by a church compensated the church to avoid judicial proceedings. In one remarkable case, a bishop and a landowner exchanged property gifts to end low-level warfare.

---

1. See *TR* 11; *TM* 10; and *TF* 176, 181, 232ab, 240, 259, 275, 277, 284, 286ab. On such bilateral dispute settlements, or *convenientiae*, in western Europe from late antiquity through the early Carolingian period, see Geary, "Extra-Judicial Means of Conflict Resolution," 575–85. Wendy Davies, "People and Places in Dispute in Ninth-Century Brittany," in *Settlement of Disputes*, ed. Davies and Fouracre, 82, notes that in Brittany the means of ending disputes varied according to the status of the parties involved; informal arrangements were more typical for those of lower status. Such a link is impossible to prove in the Bavarian records; in most cases, one cannot tell whether the status of the parties prompted the resort to an informal vs. a formal venue. As the following examples attest, it appears in some cases that the relative strength of one side or the other had something to do with it. In general, however, we must be content with simply noting, as Wickham has for Lombardy ("Land Disputes," in *Settlement of Disputes*, ed. Davies and Fouracre, 122), that in disputes not brought before royal officials, the proportion of compromise increases.

Despite the variety, however, there are some common threads. All these settlements involved some degree of negotiation. Moreover, they generally depended on symbolic expression. Rather than simply tell us the results of negotiations, the charters narrate the ritual steps by which those results were made public. That point is a crucial one because how a compromise was made to appear was as important as the substance of the compromise itself. Disputing parties carefully crafted their compromise settlements to balance image against substantive concessions. One side had its rights honored or appeared to be the victor while the other received at least part of what it was after. Concessions by one or sometimes both sides were represented as voluntary gestures rather than as actions compelled by a weak position.

Since representation was so important to peacemaking, church scribes spent a great deal of effort to control it in their written accounts of extrajudicial settlements. In addition to reporting how a settlement was publicly staged, they blasted or extolled opponents with demeaning or flattering language and strategically withheld or disclosed information about their motives in order to undermine or give credit to their positions. Whether the scribes did one or the other depended on whether a settlement left the disputing parties hostile and divided or in a positive and ongoing relationship with each other.

In a few cases, scribes from Freising wrote their compromise narratives according to a familiar pattern, the "act of mercy" script from Bishop Arbeo of Freising's *Life of Saint Corbinian*. As we saw in Chapter 1, this script couched a peacemaking gesture or concession by Freising's patron saint as a strictly voluntary act of Christian charity. Although this way of describing dispute settlement first appears in an Agilolfing-era saint's life, it provided Freising's scribes in the postconquest period with an important tool. Faced with Freising's new role as a direct party to property disputes, the scribes used the script to record compromises in a way that both saved face for their church and avoided giving up any of its general rights.

The "act of mercy" pattern did not benefit just Freising, however. One Freising charter reverses it to favor Freising's opponent rather than Freising itself. A second uses it to describe a dispute not between Freising and a Bavarian aristocrat but rather between an aristocrat and Charlemagne. These examples suggest that the script reflected a culture of extrajudicial dispute settlement, in which rights and face were negotiated along with the substantive issues under dispute, that was held over from the Agilolfing period and was common to Bavarian aristocrats in general. The Carolingian conquest transposed this culture into the new arena of property disputes involving the Bavarian churches.

In the year 810, a Count Ekkibert wanted to give property to the monastery of the Holy Savior at Spalt, to the west of Regensburg.[2] The monastery stood under the authority of the bishop of Regensburg, Adalwin. Ekkibert first gave the property to his vassal Deotpert so that Deotpert could give it to the monastery.[3] Deotpert then went to Spalt and carried out the gift on his lord's behalf. Afterward, Bishop Adalwin himself visited the property with Deotpert and a group of witnesses in order to be formally invested with it and to survey its boundaries. The party found that on the east the property bordered that of an Abbot Deotkarius,[4] and to the south it bordered the lands of a man named Gundbert. At the latter boundary, the group left a mark.

It is at this point that trouble arose in the form of a boundary dispute with Gundbert. Gundbert and two other men claimed to own part of the property Count Ekkibert wanted given to the monastery. Faced with this problem, the two sides came up with a simple and elegant solution. After discussing the matter among themselves, Gundbert and his co-claimants decided to give the part of the property that they claimed to the monastery at Spalt for the salvation of their souls.

This settlement left each side with what it wanted. Gundbert and his co-claimants (probably his kinsmen)[5] in no way recognized Count Ekkibert's property rights. They thus saved face and had their own rights to the disputed property tacitly acknowledged. Moreover, by voluntarily giving the property to the monastery, they gained a position as its benefactors. Bishop Adalwin and Ekkibert's vassal Deotpert for their part achieved what they had originally wanted, namely, that all the property go to the monastery. In other words, the settlement respected the claims of one side while allowing the other side to realize its substantive goals.

---

2. *TR* 11. Spalt lies ca. thirty kilometers southeast of modern-day Ansbach. The charter locates Ekkibert's property in the area northwest of Ansbach called the Rangau, where two streams named "Piparodi" met—now Unterbibert; see Widemann's notes to *TR* 11.

3. Deotpert is referred to as Ekkibert's *vassus et missus*. See Störmer, *Früher Adel*, 1:61–62, for the prosopography on Ekkibert, esp. his possible links to the Huosi and his possible kinship with Deotpert.

4. Of Herrieden; Störmer, *Früher Adel*, 1:61.

5. The two co-claimants, named Hunrih and Gomar, not only shared an interest in Gundbert's property; they also appear with Gundbert at the beginning of the witness list.

A number of compromise settlements in the Freising charters similarly balance rights and face against material concessions. In these cases, the balance depended not only on the steps taken by the disputing parties but also on how those steps were characterized in writing. Freising's scribes went to great lengths to control information and image in their accounts of negotiated settlements. We find them in particular couching opponents' actions in hostile or friendly rhetoric and selectively hiding or revealing details about opponents' identity and motives. How Freising's adversaries were made to appear—that is, whether they were cast in a negative or positive light—depended on whether or not a settlement left them in a positive and ongoing relationship with the Freising cathedral church.

In 798, for example, Bishop Atto of Freising had to give money to a man named Selprih in order to get him to relinquish disputed property.[6] The notice describing the settlement begins by putting Selprih in the wrong: it claims he had "illegally disputed land and forest in the place called Hettenshausen." The record says nothing whatsoever about the reasons for Selprih's behavior. If we read between the lines, we find that Selprih probably had a kinship claim of some sort on the property.[7] We have seen previously that Bishop Atto could bring even very powerful opponents before the royal *missi* and force through his claims to property that their relatives had given to Freising. The fact that here Atto had to buy off Selprih indicates that this opponent had a strong case. That would also explain why Selprih was able to have the dispute resolved in a way that respected his rights. The record states that "after money had been accepted, [Selprih] gave [the property] completely to the church of the blessed virgin Mary in Freising." In other words, despite the hostile scribal rhetoric, Selprih did not have to admit he had raised his claim unjustly. His transfer of the disputed property to Freising is described instead as a voluntary gift.

In a second example, Bishop Atto likewise settles a property claim by buying off the claimant. In this case, the claimant was someone who had strong and ongoing ties to Atto's church. Sometime between 806 and 810, the bishop resolved a dispute with his own advocate Einhart over property

6. *TF* 176.

7. This conclusion stems from the evidence that both Selprih himself and the property were connected to the Huosi. Selprih appears frequently in the Freising charters in witness lists with men bearing Huosi names; see *TF* 208, 211, 255, 277, 290, 315, 334, 336, 371, 721a, and 855a, as well as Störmer, *Adelsgruppen*, 92, 100, and Jahn, *Ducatus*, 324. The property at Hettenshausen = "Hittinhusir" takes its name from the Huosi name Hitto and lies near property that later belonged to Bishop Hitto of Freising.

in Schwindkirchen that had been given to the church there in the time of Bishop Arbeo.[8] In sharp contrast to the notice recording the dispute with Selprih, this record makes no effort at all to hide the reasons for Einhart's claim. Quite the contrary: it states openly that according to Bishop Atto's other advocates, the property had originally been given to the church by Einhart's father. The advocates could produce neither a charter nor witnesses to support their statement, however. Bishop Atto then stepped in and arranged to give Einhart "agreeable" property in another place as a benefice "so that that dispute might be ended." Einhart duly received other property "appropriate and well pleasing to him" on the condition that he and his wife would enjoy the use of it for their lifetimes. Both Atto and Einhart then pledged never to raise the issue again.

On a substantive level, this settlement looks very much like the previous one; Bishop Atto ended his dispute with Einhart by compensating him. The compensation consisted not of money but rather of a benefice somewhere else. Einhart thus remained in a lasting relationship with Freising on two levels: as an advocate and as a holder of a Freising benefice. The document recording the settlement correspondingly differs from the previous one. It openly justifies Einhart's position and is remarkably free of hostile rhetoric. Moreover, it twice stresses how acceptable Einhart found the compensation. The whole affair leaves the impression less of a confrontation than of a perceived injustice amicably resolved by common consensus.

Atto's settlement with Einhart also differs from the previous one in that it involved a mediating group, namely, Bishop Atto's other advocates. In the notice, the advocates unanimously support Einhart's claim. Their failure to produce either a charter or witnesses implicitly awarded the de jure right to Freising. Nevertheless, Bishop Atto, faced with a uniformly held and expressed set of expectations, agreed to a settlement that left honor satisfied all around. Einhart received equivalent property as a benefice and thus an implicit recognition that his claim was valid. Bishop Atto lost nothing and retained control of the church at Schwindkirchen.

Just how much Freising's written representation of a settlement depended on the relationship between Freising and its opponent comes out clearly in a third such "buyout" case. Here we are allowed to watch the relationship between Freising and a single set of opponents change over time. When the relationship changed from a negative to a friendly and ongoing one, the story told by the records also changed, from one that concealed information and cast Freising's adversaries in an unfavorable light to one that let information and justification flow in abundance.

8. *TF* 240.

This story unfolds over two charters, one produced sometime between 807 and 808 and the second much later, in 819.[9] The first tells us that Bishop Atto reached a compromise agreement with two brothers named Patto and Tetti over part of an estate. Atto persuaded the brothers to drop their claim to the property in exchange for property elsewhere, a horse with a lance and shield, and a partial money payment.[10] There is no mention of the basis for the brothers' claim or of their relationship to the property. Like Selprih, however, they must have had a strong case to force the bishop to buy them off.

The second record tells us that the matter resurfaced in 819. Here the whole story of Freising's dispute with Patto and Tetti suddenly leaps into view. We now learn that Patto and Tetti had originally sued Freising over property given to Freising by their ancestors. The brothers had claimed that among the properties in the original gift had been mixed property belonging to them that the unnamed grantor had not been legally entitled to give. Bishop Atto had stepped in and compensated the brothers with other property. Now, in 819, the brothers came to Atto's successor, Bishop Hitto, and took counsel with him for the protection of their souls. They then gave the property Bishop Atto had given them back to Freising "lest the house of Saint Mary be in any way defrauded or damaged because of them." The record remarks gratuitously that this decision to follow good counsel and protect their souls was pleasing to everyone. The brothers formally carried out their gift at the altar of the Freising cathedral church under the condition that after their death Freising's possession of the property should remained unchallenged by their offspring or by any other relative.

In this second stage of the dispute, Patto and Tetti entered an enduring relationship with Freising on two levels: in this world through their property, which they would continue to use for their lifetimes, and in the next world through Freising's prayers. In the written record that memorializes this new relationship, each party made concessions to the other. The brothers admitted they had originally injured Freising. Freising in turn recorded the causes and relationships lying behind the brothers' original challenge, thus justifying their actions.

9. *TF* 268ab and 423.

10. According to *TF* 268a, Bishop Atto persuaded the brothers to drop their claim to part of an estate in Sünzhausen in exchange for some property in Haselbach, namely, forty *iurnales* of land, meadows rated at a production of six cartloads of hay (*pratas VI carradas*), and a horse with lance and shield. *TF* 268b records a similar arrangement in which the brothers dropped their claim to a piece of woodland in Sünzhausen in exchange for seven silver solidi.

Several Freising accounts of extrajudicial settlements follow a specific narrative pattern. According to this pattern, one party made a material concession to the other but couched it as an act of mercy or compassion. The concession appears as a one-time, strictly voluntary act of generosity, compelled not by the merits of the opponent's case but rather by the pleas of friends of one or both parties or by the dictates of Christian duty. Thus, the side making the concession could do so without giving away any of its rights or losing face.

One such account from the year 807 concerns not disputed property rights but theft. A landowner named Hermperht gave Freising part of his inherited property near a place called "Cella," most likely a small dependant monastery.[11] After describing the property, which consisted of two tracts of woodland, the scribe who wrote the record made a remarkable statement. "We do not dare omit," he wrote, "the reason [Hermperht] made this gift":

> It happened that, persuaded by the ancient enemy, [Hermperht] unjustly and in a furtive manner stole one horse and two cows from the above-mentioned Cella; then, after many friends (*amici*) from both sides interceded and entreated, we forgave him that crime, and then the above-named Hermpehrt spontaneously made this gift to the house of Saint Mary at Freising into the hands of the lord bishop Atto in the presence of these named witnesses.

This story placed Freising entirely in the right. Nevertheless, the scribe had his unspecified "we" respond to the pleas of the *amici* with a Christian act of forgiveness that placed mercy ahead of justice. The narrative also served to make the arrangement palatable to Hermperht. Hermperht does not look coerced; he rather appears to have compensated Freising "spontaneously." The comment to the effect that "the devil made him do it" also tends to let Hermperht personally off the hook. Hermperht had little actual choice, however. The alternative was a judicial hearing with potentially stiff consequences provided by the Bavarian Law.[12] In other words, everyone involved,

11. Cella lay on the Inn, in the so-called *pagus inter valles*, or Sundergau, at the extreme southeast edge of the Freising sphere of influence; according to Bitterauf, it is now Bayrischzell. See Störmer, *Adelsgruppen*, 134.

12. *Lex B* C. I/3 and 6, as well as C. IX/2 and 3, give procedures and penalties for the theft of church property, including animals. They prescribe judicial duels or the swearing of oaths by accused thieves and a variable number of supporting oathhelpers to determine guilt or innocence. C. I/6 specifies that if a thief was caught, he was to provide a guarantor and pay a pledge (*wadium*) of forty solidi for the "peace

including the scribe who wrote the record, played his part to satisfy Freising's injured honor and rights, at the same time avoiding a judicial proceeding and leaving no seeds for a future dispute behind.

We have seen this narrative pattern before. It is essentially the "act of mercy" script that Bishop Arbeo of Freising used in his *Life of Saint Corbinian* to describe how Freising's patron saint handled conflict.[13] According to Arbeo, Corbinian resolved his disputes bilaterally, without resort to any third-party authority. The saint first compelled his opponents to admit their guilt and surrender completely. Once he had thus restored what he saw as right order, he responded with mercy: he made peace and in some cases offered compensation that met some or all of his opponent's needs. In one case, Arbeo added the plot device of the "begging" group. At the end of Corbinian's dispute with the citizen of Pavia who had stolen his Spanish horse, the Lombard court and the Lombard king joined the citizen's wife in pleading with the saint to accept compensation and forgive the dead man. Their combined entreaties provided Corbinian with both the opportunity and the excuse to let mercy take precedence over justice.

The "act of mercy" script allowed Arbeo to have his saint follow the dictates of Christian charity while upholding both his own rights and those of God. In the Hermperht charter, the same script, complete with a "begging" group, shows up in a Freising dispute record. There is a good reason for this: here too the script served a useful purpose. Both Freising and Hermperht plainly felt it was in their interest to come to a mutually palatable arrangement without getting involved in judicial proceedings. By couching the concession necessary to achieve such an arrangement as a voluntary act of generosity, the "act of mercy" pattern allowed Freising's scribes to record the compromise in a way that upheld Freising's version of events and protected its rights.

At this point, it becomes important once again to recall the dispute between Freising and the Scharnitz-Schlehdorf heir Lantfrid.[14] In that case, which was handled at a formal judicial assembly, we were faced with two written descriptions of the same dispute. The first was produced by a notary attached to the *missus* Archbishop Arn of Salzburg, and the second was written by a Freising scribe. In the first version, the heads of the judicial assembly brokered a compromise in which the defendant Lantfrid kept some of

money" due the fisc and on top of that pay such a fine as the judge might order—the clause ends by encouraging a high penalty. On the ways Bavarian landholders could choose how to respond to the Bavarian Law, see Brown, "Use of Norms."

13. See Chapter 1.

14. See the discussions of *TF* 184ab in Chapters 2 and 3.

the disputed property and escaped paying the applicable fines. Freising plainly did not like this compromise and wrote its own version, which undermined the first one. The Freising version essentially followed the "act of mercy" pattern. The court suggested a compromise not because Lantfrid had any justice on his side but because it wished, "considering his foolishness," to restore him to the mercy of the church and the emperor. The compromise included only the remission of the fines; it did not encompass the disputed property. The *missi* submitted the settlement to Bishop Atto of Freising not as a fait accompli but as a request to which Atto graciously agreed. In short, the Freising version of this dispute restored Freising's lost face and upheld what Freising saw as its rights. It did so not only by altering the settlement itself but also by making it look like an act of generosity on the part of Bishop Atto.

It turns out, however, that the "act of mercy" narrative was more than just a hagiographic device employed by church scribes to protect their interests. The pattern appears once in the Freising charters in a situation in which someone else's interests, not Freising's, were being protected. In the year 808, a Freising scribe wrote an account of the only dispute in the Freising collection that Freising lost.[15] A man named Isangrim claimed property from the see of Freising in a place called "Egino's church." Bishop Atto and his advocates chose to respond to this claim by leaving "the dispute in the hands of Isangrim and his relatives so that they might then act according to the law." Following a procedure that is in fact contained in the written Bavarian Law, Isangrim and his kindred came to Freising and swore with oath-helpers that the disputed property belonged to Isangrim, "and the matter was thus resolved among them."[16] The story did not end there, however. Isangrim, "compelled by the divine mercy, gave the same property, which he had acquired with contention, to the house of Saint Mary and of Saint Corbinian the confessor of Christ for the salvation of his soul and of those of his relatives." He stated further that no dispute should ever arise over the property again.

This case is a mirror image of the ones just discussed. Isangrim and his relatives successfully asserted their rights to the disputed property by taking an oath. After winning, Isangrim made a gracious gesture; prompted by the

15. *TF* 277.

16. Isangrim and his kin swore *cum legitimis sacramentalibus*. Cf. *Lex B* C. XVII/1–2, which specifies an oath by the plaintiff and six oath-helpers (*iuret cum VI sacramentalibus*) in the case of disputed possession of land; see Brown, "Use of Norms," 25.

divine mercy, he voluntarily gave the disputed property back to Freising (it is in all likelihood this gift that we have to thank for the fact that the record remained in the Freising archives at all). By enabling Isangrim to cede the property gracefully without giving up his formal victory, the divine mercy played a role similar to that of the "begging" group in the Hermperht dispute. As for Freising's image, Bishop Atto had to remain satisfied with the description of Isangrim's gift as a voluntary atonement for his earlier "contention." The settlement nonetheless left the status quo the way Freising wanted it—Freising still had its property.[17]

The "act of mercy" script also appears once in a situation that had little to do with Freising. A Freising record produced in 793 describes a settlement between a layman and Charlemagne.[18] The record concerns a gift to Freising by one Count Helmoin, a member of a prominent aristocratic kindred whose members had been among the closest followers of the Agilolfings.[19] At some point in the past, the count had wanted to give something for the salvation of his soul. He could not, however, because he was involved in a dispute with the royal fisc over certain properties. It is evident that Helmoin had been trying to secure the disputed properties by giving them to Freising and getting them back as a benefice.[20] The dispute came before the royal *missi*. Helmoin was duly defeated, and the properties were removed from his possession, "to which I was forced to consent, whether I wanted to or not."

At this point, the familiar pattern emerges. "Hearing this, the most clement and Christian king Charles the Great, the divine grace inspiring

17. It is entirely possible, but unfortunately unprovable, that Isangrim and his kindred retained the de facto possession of the property.

18. *TF* 166a, produced when Charlemagne was actually in Bavaria (*ARF* a. 791, 58–61; a. 792, 60; a. 793; 60–63).

19. On the roles and connections of the various bearers of the names Helmo, Helmoin, and Helmuni, see Jahn, *Ducatus*, 262–76, esp. 272–73, 320–21, 388; Störmer, *Adelsgruppen*, 49–59.

20. The properties were located in the Sualafeldgau, that is, the area north and west of the Danube where Alemannia, Franconia, and Bavaria met; see Map 1 as well as Gertrud Diepolder, ed., *Bayerischer Geschichtsatlas* (Munich, 1969), 14a. Their location suggests they belonged to the Frankish royal fisc: see Störmer, *Adelsgruppen*, 55. Störmer concludes that Helmoin must have been holding a Frankish office and that he was therefore brought into a crisis of interest by the Carolingian conquest of Bavaria. From the timing of the case, it would be tempting to conclude that Helmoin was trying to cement his control over former Agilolfing fiscal property. The properties' location far from any known Agilolfing holdings, however, makes this improbable; see Jahn, *Ducatus*, 378–79.

him to his eternal salvation, granted me in his mercy that which I sought, and which had been returned into his possession by a most just examination, as [my] perpetual property." The king took this action, according to Helmoin, under the terms that it "be in my power, just as it was with my other properties, to transfer and to give [the property] wherever I might wish for eternal favor and for the salvation of my soul." Helmoin got the implicit message: "The power therefore having been granted me by the most clement king, I resolved to give property to the see of Freising for the work of Saint Mary ever virgin." Helmoin made the gift as alms for King Charles and his sons and for the redemption of his own soul.

This compromise was carried out and expressed in a manner precisely in line with the previous examples. After his rights were publicly vindicated, Charlemagne bowed to the duties of the Christian ruler and made a concession.[21] The king further gained a place in Freising's prayers for himself and his sons. Helmoin appears as the humbled recipient of royal mercy. He nonetheless was able to make the gift he originally wanted to with all its memorial and prayer benefits.[22] When placed alongside the Isangrim case, this charter reveals that the "act of mercy" pattern was not just a hagiographic script designed to protect the rights and honor of the Freising cathedral church. Rather, it was a way of narrating compromise that Bavarian aristocrats in general and the Frankish king understood as a means to balance image and material concessions.

The Helmoin dispute also shows how an apparently open and shut judgment by royal *missi* could have an afterlife, in this case an afterlife that substantially modified what the *missi* had done. It moreover gives us another example of Charlemagne's modus operandi in Bavaria after the conquest; the king forced the recognition of his de jure rights but in return recognized the de facto expectations and desires of the regional aristocracy. The outcome of the dispute thus helps explain the smooth transition in Bavaria from Agilolfing to Carolingian rule.

A brief look at Charlemagne's only other personal appearance in the Freising collection provides a contrasting glimpse of how the king could and did behave when he stood above two disputing parties.[23] In a charter produced in 806 or 807, a priest named Otker claimed that a Count

21. See Althoff, "*Ira Regis*," on clemency as a virtue in royal dealings with the nobility, a virtue first visible under the Carolingians.

22. Although perhaps not under the precise terms he would have chosen; there is no mention of a *post obitum* arrangement, and his heirs were explicitly blocked from making claims on the property.

23. *TF* 232ab.

Cotehram had illegally seized property he had given Freising during the reign of Duke Tassilo. Otker, who must have been a person of some importance himself (and who must have been holding the property from Freising as a benefice),[24] went to Charlemagne and told him the story. The emperor "in his mercy" responded by appointing two special *missi* to deal with the matter: Bishop Atto of Freising and a deacon named Hwasmotus.[25] Atto and Hwasmotus had the job of delivering a flat order: they demanded the property from Cotehram. The count in response "unwillingly returned to me all my property according to the order of the king."[26]

THE TALE OF KYPPO'S PIG

In the period from 791 to 811, the "act of mercy" pattern is not the only way to represent compromise in the charters. As we saw at the beginning of this chapter, descriptions of informal settlements could sometimes take highly individual paths. A good example can be found in perhaps the most entertaining charter in the Freising collection, one that moreover highlights the importance of ritual to compromise and peacemaking. Produced in May 808, the record tells how a certain Kyppo gave property to Freising.[27] At some earlier point, there had been a dispute (*contentio*) between Kyppo and Bishop Atto over an exchange agreement; "Kyppo sadly nullified this exchange, for which reason they disputed." Bishop Atto apparently lost his nerve first: "Then the pious pontiff Atto returned the exchanged property to [Kyppo] and further gave him one horse and a woolen garment and an-

24. The fact that the conflict is represented as between Otker and Cotehram rather than between Freising and Cotehram indicates that Otker was holding the property as a benefice. The property was in Wörth; see also *TF* 389 (817), where Otker renews a benefice arrangement over property in the Wörth area on behalf of himself and his brother.

25. By noting that "at that time, Wolfolt and Rimigerus were the *missi* of the lord king in Bavaria," the charter reveals that Atto and Hwasmotus were special *missi* appointed to deal with this case. Jahn, "Virgil," 249, interprets Charlemagne's actions as simply referring the matter to a *missi* court rather than imposing a settlement. As indicated earlier, I do not agree.

26. A second version of this case, *TF* 232b, differs substantively from *TF* 232a only in containing a renewal by Otker of his original gift to Freising. Otker and Cotehram may have been related to each other; if so, Otker would have brought in the king to help him in an inheritance dispute with a powerful relation: see Störmer, *Früher Adel*, 1:226, and *Adelsgruppen*, 49–59; Mitterauer, *Karolingische Markgrafen*, 61–63.

27. *TF* 275.

other of linen for the buildings that had been destroyed in the course of the dispute, and they made peace among themselves in the presence of many people."

Next comes an astonishing line from Kyppo: "Kyppo said, 'If you do not give me one pig, nothing is affirmed between us, neither concerning the peace nor concerning the gift I have made.'" Bishop Atto promptly ordered a pig to be produced. Both men placed their hands on the animal, "and they were pacified in this manner." Kyppo then carried out his property gift.

This jewel of a conflict notice provides the first flicker of evidence for what could lie behind the frequently used word *contentio*. Most appearances of this term in the records leave an impression of orderliness; at the most, extended *contentiones* suggest perhaps repeated court hearings. Here, however, violence—at least toward buildings—appears as part of the disputing process for the first time since the Agilolfing period. Moreover, Bishop Atto's men carried out at least some of the destruction since the bishop had to offer compensation. The violence led to negotiations. Whether it was targeted to bring about negotiations is impossible to say, although it seems likely.[28] If it was, Bishop Atto seems to have come off the worse, because he made the first move toward peace. The resulting compromise settlement consisted of an exchange: Atto's horse and clothing for Kyppo's property.

This record shows as well as any the public, ritual nature of peacemaking. First, the parties publicly reached an agreement; then the agreement was sealed, at Kyppo's behest, by the ritual laying of hands on a pig.[29] The pig itself is something of a mystery. Its appearance as a ritual peacemaking object is unique, not only in the Freising charters but also in general. The ritual likewise sends a unique message. In contrast to most other Freising conflict notices, in this record little effort is made to save face for Bishop Atto, except for the brief statement that Kyppo was "sadly" responsible for starting the dispute. On the contrary, the bishop comes off very poorly: he had to initiate the peace, and he had to compensate Kyppo for the de-

28. See Geary, "Living with Conflicts," in *Living with the Dead*, 144, and White, "Feuding and Peace-Making," 260, for violence in feuds in eleventh- and twelfth-century France as intended to reestablish a balance of honor or to influence bargaining positions by inflicting economic damage. See also Gerd Althoff, "Königsherrschaft und Konfliktbewältigung im 10. und 11. Jahrhundert," in *Spielregeln*, 21–56, for tenth- and eleventh-century East Francia.

29. Jahn, "Virgil," 249, defines as *pacho* as a "Mastschwein," that is, a "fattened pig."

stroyed buildings. The pig ritual added to Atto's loss of face. Kyppo made a threatening statement whose substance was, "If you don't give me a pig, the whole deal is off." Atto complied with the demand humbly and without protest.

There are two possible ways to explain this mystery. The proceedings may have been a joke. That is, the parties reinforced the peace by means of a lighthearted burlesque of more common affirmation rituals such as laying hands on relics or on a charter. Alternatively, Atto's position with respect to Kyppo was really so bad that Kyppo could demand and receive all honor both in the proceedings themselves and in the written record. Because of a lack of information, we cannot tell one way or the other by establishing Kyppo's identity and social position; there is no evidence that Kyppo was any particularly powerful person.[30] The fact that in other cases Freising scribes dealt much more roughly and condescendingly with much more powerful people, however, supports the idea that Kyppo was dealing from a strong hand.

The key to the puzzle would seem to lie in the meaning of the pig to the participants. Unfortunately, here too a lack of information on pigs, other than as economic assets, cripples the investigation before it gets started. The only helpful hint comes in a passage from Jacob Grimm's nineteenth-century *Deutsche Rechtsaltertümer*. In the context of a discussion of oaths taken on various animals, Grimm notes that pagan Scandinavians used the boar as a sacrificial animal; oaths carried out on it were considered inviolable. He then quotes this Freising charter as evidence for the practice in the Carolingian period.[31] If Grimm is correct (and this has to remain speculation), his theory turns Kyppo's demand into something very serious. Kyppo did not trust Bishop Atto. To seal the agreement to his satisfaction, he reached back to a pagan ritual. The bishop agreed to take part in the ritual despite its conflict with Christian practice. If true, this interpretation opens up fascinating avenues for speculating about Atto's participation in a mythological inheritance shared by the members of the aristocratic network to

---

30. The prosopographical record on Kyppo is very thin. The name appears in only one other charter; a "Chippo" is last on the witness list to the dispute record *TF* 268a, which pits the brothers Patto and Tetti against Bishop Atto of Freising. Common names in the witness lists of *TF* 268a and *TF* 275 make it likely that the two bearers of the name were the same man, but beyond that Kyppo's identity and social position remain hidden.

31. Jacob Grimm, *Deutsche Rechtsaltertümer*, 4th ed., ed. A. Heusler and R. Hübner, 2 vols. (Leipzig, 1899), 2:551.

which he belonged and about his evident respect for, or at least tolerance of, pre-Christian belief.

◉

The disputes discussed in this chapter reveal a varied and colorful culture of extrajudicial compromise in operation alongside the more formal world of the judicial assemblies and Frankish-style *placitum* reports. This culture came into play in two related situations: first, when the disputants decided not to seek out a third party with the power to adjudicate or to force a settlement, and second, when the two disputing parties were closely enough matched or good relations between them important enough that one side did not simply overwhelm the other (as Freising did, for example, when it sued a layman and won a decision based on its formal rights).

The compromise settlements reported by the charters did not look the same in all cases. Instead, they were crafted to meet the specific needs of the parties involved in a specific set of circumstances. Nevertheless, they display some common elements. For one, they all depended on publicity. The disputing parties did not negotiate settlements and fix the result by written contract but rather carried them out ritually in front of witnesses. The public expression of settlements blended in with the written records that recorded them; the records do not tell us the specific terms of agreements but instead reveal them through descriptions of their public enactment.

How agreements were characterized also played a crucial role. Here the written record itself served as part of the settlement process. A settlement's success depended on whether a concession looked forced or spontaneous, whether property claims were implicitly acknowledged or remained unrecognized, or whether actions were represented as justified or prompted by greed or diabolical interference. Awarding the proper amount of justification to one side could counterbalance an actual property concession made to the other.

In a few cases, Freising scribes resorted to a narrative pattern that harks back to the "act of mercy" script from Arbeo of Freising's *Life of Saint Corbinian*. According to this pattern, one side in a dispute successfully asserted its rights and then made a concession to the other side couched as a voluntary act of mercy. Describing settlements in this fashion enabled the more powerful of the two parties to meet its opponent halfway without losing face or creating a precedent that would undermine its future rights. In the case pitting Freising against the cattle thief Hermperht, the scribe added the plot device, likewise familiar from the *Life of Corbinian*, of a supplicating group. The pleas from this group on behalf of mercy enabled Freising to come to an agreement with Hermperht, at the same time protecting its honor. The "begging" group would thus seem to have acted not to broker or mediate a compromise but rather to give Freising the opportunity or excuse necessary to make its concession gracefully.

The "act of mercy" script appears in the charters after the Carolingian conquest because it served a useful purpose for Freising's scribes. In the new political climate of postconquest Bavaria, the see of Freising found itself frequently and directly involved in conflict with its landholding neighbors. When Freising and its opponents chose to settle their quarrels extrajudicially rather than take them before a judicial assembly, the "act of mercy" script enabled the scribes to record settlements without giving up any of Freising's general rights or claims. As a result, a narrative pattern that had previously served Arbeo as a way to uphold the rights of God and Saint Corbinian was now employed by charter scribes to protect the rights and image of Saint Corbinian's church.

The script was not simply an Agilolfing-era hagiographic device that Freising scribes wielded only in their church's interests. A single record documenting a compromise in which Freising had to surrender, and which was thus constructed to favor Freising's opponent, follows the same pattern. Moreover, the pattern appears in a charter describing a dispute between a Bavarian count and Charlemagne himself. These two charters indicate that both Arbeo and the scribes were drawing on an older tradition governing negotiated dispute settlements, a tradition that Bavarian aristocrats in general understood and that they continued to follow after the Carolingian conquest.

This way of representing compromise becomes more pronounced, and then finally dominant, in the Bavarian charters in the years after 811. Most interesting, it begins to appear not only in records of extrajudicial settlements but increasingly often in records of formal judicial assemblies. The following chapters illustrate this phenomenon and work out its consequences.

CHAPTER FIVE
DISPUTING UNDER THE
CAROLINGIANS, 812-835

I n 811, Bishop Atto of Freising died. Cozroh marked the accession of Atto's successor and his own employer, Bishop Hitto, with a page dominated by beautifully decorated capital letters.[1] Like Atto, Hitto appears to have enjoyed kinship connections to the Huosi. He remained in office for twenty-four years and was succeeded after his death in 835 by his kinsman, and possibly his nephew, Erchanbert.[2]

Hitto's reign as bishop of Freising coincided with changes at the Carolingian court that profoundly affected Bavaria. In 814, Charlemagne died. He was immediately succeeded by his only surviving son, the forty-one-year-old Louis the Pious. Louis remains a controversial figure. It is clear that he intended to be a reformer. He understood himself to be the Christian emperor of a Christian people whose job it was to promote the health and salvation of the society he ruled. On taking office, he launched a series of efforts to reform and further unify the Frankish Church and the Frankish Empire, efforts that built on and extended similar reform programs already visible under his father. What has provided fodder for controversy is the question of Louis's effectiveness. A long-lived historiographical tradition sees him as the "the great emperor's little son"—as a pious and well-meaning but weak and politically inept ruler whose mistakes fatally undermined what Charlemagne had built.[3] More recent scholarship has tended to rehabilitate Louis. Many now view the second Carolingian emperor as a competent commander and an effective administrator who was quite able to use the

---

1. Hochstift Freising Lit. 3a fol. 187.

2. Störmer, *Adelsgruppen*, 91n. 12 and 106–7; Jahn, *Ducatus*, 333; Strzewitzek, *Sippenbeziehungen*, 189–92. On Atto, see Chapter 1, n. 31.

3. N. Staubach, "Des großen Kaisers kleiner Sohn," in *Charlemagne's Heir*, ed. Godman and Collins, 701–22.

military and administrative resources left him by his father to achieve his own ends.[4]

Louis the Pious certainly began his reign on a strong note. On assuming the throne, he cleaned house at the imperial court, surrounding himself with advisers and court officials drawn primarily from his former life as sub-king of Aquitaine. Most members of Charlemagne's former court circle withdrew from public life, including the now elderly archbishop Arn of Salzburg. Arn met Louis the Pious only twice, at assemblies held in Paderborn in 815 and at Aachen in 816. Arn died on January 24, 821, at the advanced age of eighty.[5]

The relationship of Bavaria itself to the imperial court also changed.[6] Where Charlemagne had replaced the Agilolfing dukes with prefects, first Gerold and then Audulf, Louis the Pious reconstituted the former duchy as a sub-kingdom. In 814, he gave it to his eldest son, Lothar. In 817, as part of his first effort to regulate the imperial succession, he reassigned it to his youngest son, the eleven-year-old Louis the German. Accordingly, when the Bavarian prefect Audulf died in 819, no new prefect was named to replace him. Bavaria remained essentially under Louis's direct control until 825, when Louis the German took up the reins of his kingdom. The younger Louis proceeded to forge close ties to Bavaria that would serve him well for the rest of his career. He was able to rely on Bavarian support during the rebellions that temporarily unseated his father in 829/830 and again in 833. Bavaria remained the basis for his power even during the brief period from 833 to 838 when he was first able to claim dominion over all the Frankish territories east of the Rhine.

These developments at the imperial level are reflected by several important changes in the Bavarian dispute evidence. To begin with, the character of the authority figures heading formal judicial assemblies in Bavaria has changed. Although in other parts of the empire Louis the Pious used *missi* frequently and to good effect, in Bavaria the *missi* no longer dominate the judicial stage.[7] Their place has been taken by local bishops and counts,

---

4. Godman and Collins, *Charlemagne's Heir*; McKitterick, *Frankish Kingdoms*, 109–27; Janet L. Nelson, "The Frankish Kingdoms, 814–898," in *NCMH*, 110–19, and *Charles the Bald*, 75–104; Timothy Reuter, *Germany in the Early Middle Ages, 800–1056* (London, 1991), 45–51. As suggested earlier, not everyone has agreed to rehabilitate Louis the Pious; see, for example, Roger Collins, *Early Medieval Europe, 300–1000* (New York, 1991), 290–301.

5. Dopsch, "Zeit der Karolinger und Ottonen," in *Geschichte Salzburgs*, ed. Dopsch, 167–73.

6. See the outline of Bavarian history in the Introduction.

7. See McKitterick, *Frankish Kingdoms*, 126–27, and Josef Semmler, "*Renovatio Regni Francorum*: Die Herrschaft Ludwigs des Frommen im Frankenreich,

including bishops who are themselves party to the disputes at issue. When imperial *missi* reappear in Bavaria in the year 822, they show no sign of acting under a general mandate to dispense justice as Arn of Salzburg did. Instead, they serve in an ad hoc fashion in connection with a specific set of disputes.

These disputes concerned the emperor's property rights. The appearances of the *missi* in Bavaria during this period can be directly linked to an effort by Louis the Pious to find out whether the imperial fisc had unjustly usurped any property. Bishop Hitto of Freising saw this effort as an opportunity to challenge the fisc's property rights in an area where Freising also had property interests. As a result, *missi* suddenly appear in Bavaria to deal with a new kind of dispute, that is, between Freising and people claiming not kindred rights but rather fiscal rights in their defense.

There are also visible changes in the way dispute records are written and in the stories they tell. The Frankish-style *placitum* report, which had previously appeared only in connection with Arn of Salzburg, is now more widespread; documents written this way record the actions of judicial assemblies headed by a variety of people. This development reveals that Arn's efforts to standardize the way disputes were carried out and recorded had a strong and lasting impact. Just as important, however, are the signs that this world of formal dispute resolution was being influenced by the informal world we looked at in the last chapter. The scribes go to greater lengths than before to record how *placita* fit into much longer and more complicated relationships between the churches and their opponents. In the course of these relationships, other kinds of settlements, settlements that continue the same bartering of appearance for substance we saw before, could substantially modify or even overturn what the formal assemblies had done.

CONTINUITY AND CHANGE

Roughly the same number of dispute charters have survived from Hitto's reign as from the preceding two decades.[8] The disputes these charters

---

814–829/830," in *Charlemagne's Heir*, ed. Godman and Collins, 130, on Louis's use of *missi* for special missions and to police defined *missatica*.

8. The number of Freising dispute records drops somewhat; twenty-four from the period 812–35 directly or indirectly concern conflict, as compared with thirty-seven for the period 791–811: *TF* 304, 318ab, 327, 345, 351, 345, 401abc, 402, 403, 430, 437, 438, 463, 466, 473, 475, 507, 514, 562, 563, 579, 585ab, 592ab, 604. The evidence from the other Bavarian charter collections improves, however: three Passau records (*TP* 73, 74, 78), five Regensburg (*TR* 15, 16, 19, 20, 25), and one Mondsee record (*TM* 102) preserve information about conflict, bringing the total for the

record resemble in many respects those we have looked at so far. Most continued to be driven by the tension between hereditary claims to property and church rights to property gifts. As before, this tension played itself out in conflicts between disgruntled heirs and the church or between heirs and co-heirs holding property as a benefice from the church. A good example of the former is provided by a dispute settled in Linz in 821 and recorded in a Passau charter.[9] A priest named Odalschalch gave all his possessions in a certain location to the church of Saint Stephen at Passau.[10] After Odalschalch's death, his brother Ruodolt "unjustly" took the property for himself, claiming that the property by right belonged to him and that his brother had had no right to give it to Saint Stephen in the first place.[11] Passau's scribe, who was just as capable as a Freising scribe of using the written record to destroy an opponent's image, informs us that at a public hearing Ruodolt "contended in an evil dispute in the presence of many." After several days, he literally "returned to his senses,"[12] admitted that he had acted unjustly toward God, and returned the disputed property to Passau's bishop, Reginharius.

A Freising case from the year 828 shows that the tactic of using a church benefice to protect property from a relative was alive and well.[13] A nun named Engilpurc and her mother had given property to Freising from their inheritance and had received it back as a benefice. Engilpurc's cousin, however, a priest named Wicharius,[14] wanted to take the property for himself.

---

period to thirty-three. Interestingly, in the Freising collection, the proportion of dispute charters to the total number of surviving charters drops significantly: twenty-four in 308 charters, as compared with thirty-seven in ca. 180 for the period 791–811. To explain this drop, one would need to know why the total number of Freising charters increased so sharply during Hitto's reign, a subject for a different study.

9. *TP* 78.

10. Odalschalch's original gift charter survives as *TP* 36 (791–803).

11. The fact that Ruodolt waited until his brother had died to raise his claim indicates that Odalschalch had made his initial gift *post obitum*, with the property to revert to Passau after his death. Ruodolt had possibly been sharing the use of the property during his brother's lifetime. He either felt his rights were violated when Passau asserted its rights after his brother's death or saw his brother's death as an opportunity to gain control of the property.

12. *Postea vero post multis diebus in se reversus.*

13. *TF* 562.

14. *Nepus eorum.* It is unclear just exactly what this means. I am assuming that it means Wicharius was the nephew of Engilpurc's mother and thus Engilpurc's cousin.

Engilpurc came before a synod headed by Bishop Hitto to ask for help. Hitto responded by renewing the benefice for as long as Engilpurc and her mother might live and forbidding Wicharius to preach in the church there without their license.

This evidence for continuity notwithstanding, the disputes from this period differ from those that came before in some important ways. The first and most obvious difference has to do with the authority figures heading formal judicial assemblies. By far the most common head of a formal assembly in the records after 812 is the bishop who was himself involved in the dispute.[15] This says nothing about who were really the most common heads of judicial assemblies in the world beyond the charters. We are, after all, dealing with episcopal charter collections that record conflicts over episcopal rights and that, at least in Freising's case, were designed to memorialize episcopal deeds. When we compare them with the charters from the preceding two decades, however, we find a striking difference. In the period 791–811, the authority figures that appeared most often at judicial assemblies were the royal *missi*, usually but not exclusively Archbishop Arn of Salzburg. Bishop Atto of Freising occasionally showed up on a list of authority figures with *missi*. In general, however, he actively handled his own disputes only in extrajudicial settlements.[16] The other Bavarian bishops likewise appeared at assemblies only in the company of *missi*. In contrast, in the period after 812, Bishop Hitto appears himself as the head of a formal assembly seven times, whereas Bishops Baturic of Regensburg and Reginharius of Passau each headed such assemblies once.[17]

The reverse side of this coin is more significant. What we are really looking at, rather than a serious increase in bishops as authority figures, is an overwhelming absence of *missi*. In sharp contrast to the period 791 to 811,

15. On the roles and sources of authority of bishops in early medieval dispute resolution, see Geary, "Extra-Judicial Means of Conflict Resolution," 596; Wilfried Hartmann, "Der Bischof als Richter nach den Kirchenrechtlichen Quellen des 4. bis 7. Jahrhunderts," in *La giustizia nell'alto medioevo (secoli V–VIII)*, vol. 2 (Spoleto, 1995), 805–37.

16. In the single exception of *TF* 288 (809), Atto headed a *placitum* in company with Count Heriperht, Abbot Cundharius, and Abbot Maginhart. Note in view of the following discussion of the *missi* in the period 812–35 that *TF* 288 took place in the gap between Arn of Salzburg's main period of judicial activity (802–7) and his last appearance in the Freising charters (811).

17. Bishop Hitto heads four *placita*, along with one or more counts, and three synods: *TF* 327, 351, 401ab, 437, 507, 514, 562; Baturic and Reginharius each head one *placitum*: *TR* 16, *TP* 78.

missi appear in the charters for the period 812 to 835 only four times. These four appearances cluster at widely separated points: three come in the spring and summer of the year 822, and one in the year 829.[18] It turns out that in the three cases from 822, the *missi* acted not in response to a general mandate to settle disputes but rather to deal with a specific issue. This issue, the rights of the imperial fisc versus those of the see of Freising, was played out in a series of individual disputes between Freising and people claiming to hold fiscal benefices. When considered as a group, these disputes show how an element of the emperor Louis's reform program—in this case, a new policy toward the fisc—provided a major player on the Bavarian stage, Bishop Hitto, with the chance to exploit that policy to his own advantage.

The *missi* in this period differ from their predecessors in another important respect: they make a much weaker impression than Arn of Salzburg made. Although they could still render clear verdicts, they were unable or unwilling to uphold the rights of the fisc against Freising's claims. Moreover, one of their verdicts was later modified by a compromise. The compromise came about not through the intervention of the *missi* themselves but rather through a classic "act of mercy" settlement arranged directly between Bishop Hitto and his opponent outside the context of the judicial assembly.

THE *MISSI* AND THE IMPERIAL FISC

The story of the imperial legates' appearance in Bavaria in 822 actually begins seven years earlier, in 815. A dispute record from that year shows Freising preparing for a possible conflict with the imperial fisc in the area around Föhring, about twenty-six kilometers south of Freising on the right bank of the Isar River.[19] The record tells a curious tale. A deacon named Hwezzi, "acting faithfully with respect to the house of Saint Mary," came before Bishop Hitto and his clergy, who were gathered in a synod at Freising. There the deacon learned that a church he had accepted as a benefice from the emperor, the church of Saint John at Föhring, had earlier belonged to Freising. Freising's scribe carefully dodged the issue of how the emperor had acquired the church; he wrote only that it had been taken away from Freising by "some people" (*aliquis*). After seeking advice "from many,"[20] Hwezzi promised that if in fact it should be found that the church belonged to Freising, he would not act contrary to Freising's rights. Before a mixed

18. 822: *TF* 463, 466, 475. 829: *TF* 579.
19. *TF* 351.
20. Hwezzi acted *cum consilio multorum*.

group of lay and ecclesiastical witnesses, Hwezzi then pledged the church to Bishop Hitto, repeating that he would respect Freising's rights only if Freising acquired the church legally. In return, Bishop Hitto gave Hwezzi the church back as a benefice from Freising under the condition that Hwezzi keep faith with Freising and pay a specified yearly rent.

Freising's opponent in this affair was not Hwezzi himself but the fisc, from which Hwezzi thought he was holding the church as a benefice. The record of the dispute does not, however, describe a direct conflict between Freising and the fisc. What it does describe is Freising's attempt to strengthen its own hand with respect to the fisc, in advance of a conflict that it must have seen coming, by creating a document and witness trail in its favor. Bishop Hitto persuaded Hwezzi to profess his loyalty to Freising publicly and to ritually receive his church as a Freising benefice. The charter also stresses the deacon's faithfulness to Freising every step of the way. Hwezzi was no pushover, however; he recognized Freising's rights over the church only on the condition that the bishopric was actually shown to have any. In return, Bishop Hitto left him in de facto possession of the church.

Fast forward seven years, to April 3, 822. On that date, according to a formal *placitum* report written by an unknown Freising scribe, Freising's uneasy relationship with the fisc in the Föhring area erupted into outright conflict.[21] At a formal judicial assembly headed by four laymen and five bishops (including Bishop Hitto himself), two imperial *missi* named Nidhart and Freholf sued Bishop Hitto for another church at Föhring.[22] The *missi* stated that a cleric named Gregorius had appealed to the emperor Louis, saying Hitto had unjustly seized the church.[23] Gregorius must have claimed to hold the church as a fiscal benefice because the emperor had ordered the two *missi* to find out whether it belonged to Freising or belonged in the im-

21. *TF* 463.

22. This conflict unfortunately does not deal with the same church in Föhring as the one held by the deacon Hwezzi in 815. Later documents show that two neighboring churches stood in the Föhring settlement complex. The one dedicated to Saint John in the Hwezzi notice, *TF* 351, later formed the center of Johanneskirchen; the other, dedicated to Saint Laurentius, was situated in what is now Oberföhring. See Jahn, *Ducatus*, 305; Sturm, *Preysing*, 119; Alexander Freiherr von Reitzenstein, *Frühe Geschichte rund um München* (Munich, 1956), 42–43; Helmut Stahleder, "Bischöfliche und adelige Eigenkirchen des Bistums Freising im frühen Mittelalter und die Kirchenorganisation im Jahre 1315," *Oberbayerisches Archiv* 104 (1979): 175.

23. Although the record does not explicitly call Gregorius a cleric, he must have been one of some kind because the record tells us he had an advocate.

perial service. The assembled bishops, abbots, counts, and other "good and truthful men" testified against Gregorius. They declared that the church had belonged to Freising since the time of Charlemagne's father, Pippin. On hearing this, the *missi* acknowledged that they could not take the church away from Freising. Gregorius likewise admitted defeat and agreed to raise the issue no further.

The *missi* involved in this case, Nidhart and Freholf, did not act to uphold imperial rights with the force and authority that Charlemagne's *missi* did. In the single instance in which we saw Charlemagne assigning special *missi* to a specific case, the dispute between Otker and Count Cotehram, the emperor sent the *missi* not to investigate but rather to order Count Cotehram to deliver up the disputed property. In the only previous dispute over the rights of the fisc, that involving Count Helmoin, the *missi* forced the count to return the disputed property to the fisc before receiving it back as an act of mercy from Charlemagne himself.[24] Here in 822, however, the *missi* sent by Louis the Pious were compelled by common testimony to admit that the fisc had no claim.

Eleven days later, on April 14, 822, Freising clashed with another person claiming to hold a fiscal benefice near Föhring.[25] The dispute was brought before a judicial assembly at Föhring headed by Bishop Hitto himself, his colleague Bishop Baturic of Regensburg, and the *missi* Hatto and Kisalhard. These last two men also appear in the list of authority figures who oversaw the Gregorius case, Hatto with no title and Kisalhard as a judge; we now learn that they held *missi* commissions. Bishop Hitto and his advocate sued a man named Adaluni for a church at nearby Hinterholzhausen.[26] They claimed that the bishops of Freising had possessed the church "from olden times" and had granted it out to a sequence of junior clerics as a benefice until Adaluni "unjustly contested that church and took possession of it." Adaluni responded that he held half the church by right of inheritance and the other half as an imperial benefice. "Truthful and honorable men" immediately declared this statement to be false. Thereupon the *missi* Hatto and Kisalhard gathered a group of witnesses and ordered them to swear on relics that they would reveal the truth about the matter. At this point it emerges that Adaluni's family was divided against itself. The first to swear was Adaluni's own brother Regindeo; "with one voice" he and the other wit-

24. See the discussions of *TF* 232ab and *TF* 166a in Chapter 4.
25. *TF* 466.
26. Bitterauf in his notes to *TF* 466 identifies "Holzhusun" with Hinterholzhausen near Erding, which lies ca. eighteen kilometers northeast of Oberföhring.

nesses supported Freising's claim.[27] In the face of this testimony, Adaluni's appeal to fiscal rights failed. "Convicted and confounded by right justice," Adaluni was forced to return the church to Bishop Hitto. He also pledged to pay a fine of forty solidi "for the altar" (*pro altare*).[28] The record then grandly states that "at the end the entire people cried out with one voice that this was law."

After this stirring declaration of legal consensus, however, Freising's scribe added a twist to what is otherwise a perfectly formulaic *placitum* report. In its final sentences, the report states that "urged by many, the abovementioned bishop [Hitto] remitted the fine of forty solidi" on the condition that Adaluni make no further trouble and formally invest Freising with the church. This small tag represents a classic "act of mercy" compromise. After Hitto had upheld Freising's formal rights, an interceding group asked him to be merciful, giving him the opportunity to make a conciliatory gesture. This is the first time in the Freising charters that this compromise script appears in a formal *placitum* report.

27. Other circumstantial evidence deepens our picture of this interkindred conflict. The witnesses against Adaluni testified that Bishop Atto had first granted the disputed church as a benefice to one Adalfrid, who shares a name part with Adaluni, before it came to a cleric named Deotperht. This testimony, together with Adaluni's claim to have inherited half the church, strongly suggests that a branch of the kindred, led first by Adalfrid and then by Deotperht and supported by Adaluni's brother Regindeo, had secured the church via a benefice arrangement with the bishops of Freising. Another branch of the same kindred, represented by Adaluni, had tried to win it back by appealing to the imperial fisc. Especially interesting is a puzzling reference in this charter to the cleric Deotperht as Bishop Hitto's "brother." If Deotperht really was Hitto's biological brother rather than a "spiritual brother," the whole affair would be a dispute between Adaluni and Hitto as kinsmen. Strzewitzek, *Sippenbeziehungen*, 252–53, in his tabular representation of Hitto's kinship connections, does not identify Deotperht as a biological brother. He does, however, place a Deotrat and a Deodolt as Hitto's ancestors two and three generations before him, respectively.

28. It is not clear exactly what this fine is or where it comes from. It appears nowhere in the surviving normative texts. The fine most closely resembles the forty-solidi peace money due the fisc that appears with some frequency in the Bavarian Law (see, for example, *Lex B* C. I/6, I/7, and I/9) and the forty-solidi compensation due a church for seizing someone by force who had sought sanctuary there (*Lex B* C. I/7). Taking a cue from this last, we can infer that the forty solidi *pro altare* represents compensation for the church, perhaps the compensation mentioned only to be waived in the Lantfrid case, *TF* 184ab (see Chap. 2). See Wilhelm Störmer, "Ein Gerichtstag an der Pfettrach im Jahre 818," *Amperland* 4, no. 3 (1968): 65–69.

These three charters do not tell us exactly why Freising was competing with the fisc for property around Föhring. The competition probably had its origins in the Agilolfing past. The area on the right bank of the Isar centered on Föhring originally contained a great deal of Agilolfing fiscal property. In 755, Duke Tassilo gave some of this property to Bishop Joseph of Freising.[29] The tension between Freising and the fisc, therefore, very likely resulted from the ambiguity inherent in Agilolfing ducal property gifts. In other words, the dukes may well have given property in and around Föhring to Freising without relinquishing their rights to grant it as benefices to loyal followers (as Duke Odilo did with his chaplain Ursus in the case of the Saint Maximilian foundation in the Pongau). Since these followers had received their benefices from the duke, their descendants still understood them to be fiscal benefices after the Föhring fiscal complex fell to the Carolingians.[30]

Whatever the original cause, the trigger for these disputes and the reason for their timing lay with a change in policy at the imperial level. To be specific, among the emperor Louis's early reforming initiatives was an effort to make sure the fisc was not holding any property unjustly. Immediately after coming to power in 814, Louis sent *missi* throughout his realm "to inquire and investigate whether any injustice had been done to anyone."[31] The next year, 815, Bishop Hitto of Freising leaned on the deacon Hwezzi to declare his church at Föhring a Freising benefice. In 818 or 819, the emperor issued a capitulary requiring that church property be neither divided nor diminished under him or his successors.[32] In his instructions to the *missi* of 819, he declared that if any count, official, or other palatine legate had done any injustice that had benefited the fisc, the *missi* were to investigate and refer the

29. *TF* 5: Tassilo met with the leaders of both the Fagana *genealogia* and the "Feringas" or "people from Föhring" to give property in Erching (ca. fifteen kilometers north of Föhring and about the same distance northwest of Hinterholzhausen) to Bishop Joseph of Freising. Jahn, *Ducatus*, 304, points out that Cozroh placed *TF* 5 at the front of his charter collection, right after the Prologue; this suggests that the tension over rights in the Föhring area was important enough for Cozroh to advertise Freising's claims.

30. Jahn, *Ducatus*, 304–6. The Föhring fiscal complex did not come to Freising in its entirety until 903, via a gift from the last of Charlemagne's descendants to rule in the east, Louis the Child.

31. *Thegani Vita Hludowici Imperatoris*, ed. Reinhold Rau, *Quellen zur karolingischen Reichsgeschichte* 1, AQ V (Darmstadt, 1987), c. 13, 224; *Anonymi Vita Hludovici Imperatoris*, ed. Reinhold Rau, AQ V, c. 23, 292.

32. *Capitulare ecclesiasticum* (818–19), MGH Capit I, c. 1, 275–76.

matter to him for judgment.[33] In a capitulary of 821, Louis again required the *missi* to investigate complaints about property occupied by the fisc, with the reservation of final judgment for himself.[34] In 823, the emperor issued a diploma in Frankfurt restoring property that had been unjustly drawn into the fisc to the nearby monastery at Hornbach.[35] In the spring of 822, in the middle of this evident imperial concern for the fisc's relationship with regional landowners, *missi* appeared in Bavaria to deal with this relationship in the area around Föhring.

In other words, what Louis the Pious said and did mattered in Bavaria, at least insofar as his policies benefited someone. When Louis declared his intent to investigate possible unjust holdings by the fisc, Bishop Hitto seized the opportunity to assert Freising's property claims in the old Agilolfing fiscal area around Föhring. As a result, a battery of disputes erupted in which we see for the first time Freising's opponents claiming fiscal rights in their defense. These disputes thus reveal in miniature the same kind of ground-level reaction to political change as took place immediately after the Carolingian conquest.[36] After Charlemagne imposed his authority on Bavaria, the Bavarian churches exploited the new political climate to redefine property relationships to their own advantage. As a consequence, conflicts pitting the churches directly against landowners showed up in the charters for the first time. In the early years of Louis the Pious's reign, Bishop Hitto did the same thing on a smaller scale. Disputes between Freising and the fisc appear in the Freising charters in 815/822 because the new emperor's policy toward the fisc made it possible for Hitto to challenge fiscal rights successfully.

Just as important are the changes in the way the *missi* appear in these records. Louis the Pious seems to have continued Charlemagne's practice of using Bavarian aristocrats as his *missi* in the region; the *missi* Hatto and Kisalhard, for example, share names with members of the established Bavarian aristocracy.[37] Nonetheless, the *missi* no longer display a general mandate

33. *Capitulare missorum* (819), *MGH Capit* I, c. 1, 289.

34. *Capitula missorum* (821), *MGH Capit* I, c. 2, 300.

35. Rudolf Hübner, *Gerichtsurkunden der Fränkischen Zeit* no. 242 (1891–93; reprint, Aalen, 1971), 42.

36. See Chapter 2.

37. The name Hatto appears in connection with the Huosi often enough in the Freising collection as far back as the 750s to make it likely that our Hatto was a member of the established Bavarian aristocracy; see the name index to Bitterauf's edition. A Count Hatto appears in both the Regensburg and the Freising charter collections at about this time heading judicial investigations, so it is as good as certain that he is identical with the *missus* Hatto; see *TR* 16 (819); *TF* 507 (824). Other

to handle disputes. The link between the *missi* and Freising's conflict with the fisc is unmistakable; one cannot escape the conclusion that the emperor had commissioned them specifically to deal with this issue. Moreover, Freising's scribes have the *missi* acting in a qualitatively different way than they did before. In the case of Gregorius, the *missi* sent to investigate fiscal rights in response to Gregorius's appeal had to concede the right to Freising. This outcome most likely reflects the emperor's almost apologetic attitude toward fiscal abuses. Nonetheless, it is the first time we see a judicial assembly deliver a verdict against the imperial authority. In the Adaluni case, the scribe tacked a small "act of mercy" compromise onto the formal proceedings of a judicial assembly headed by *missi*. This settlement stands in marked contrast to the settlements reached at Arn of Salzburg's assemblies, which were mediated or imposed by the *missi* themselves, not arranged afterward by the disputing parties. Thus, it seems that extrajudicial methods of dispute settlement were beginning to compete directly for scribal attention with the actions of formal courts. In some of the cases that went before the *missi*, Freising's scribes evidently felt that what happened outside the assemblies was as important as what took place at them.

Once they had been given their commissions, the *missi* could still attract cases unrelated to their original purpose. Hatto shows up once more as a *missus* at an assembly held a few months after the fiscal disputes, on August 31, 822. The assembly dealt with a conflict between Bishop Hitto of Freising and Bishop Nidker of Augsburg over possession of a church. Hatto was joined by Bishop Hitto himself, two other Bavarian bishops, and Kisalhard (who is once more called a judge rather than a *missus*). The dispute had

---

Hattos among the Bavarian elite are Bishop Hatto of Passau and Abbot Hatto of Mondsee. See Jahn, *Ducatus*, 324, on connections between the name Hatto and the Huosi/Scharnitz-Schlehdorf kin group; Störmer, *Adelsgruppen*, 70–77, on connections of the name to the (Huosi) founders of the monastery at Schäftlarn and to the grouping around the monastery at Isen. Likewise Kisalhard: the *iudex* and *comis* Kisalhard appears in *placitum* reports going back to 802. Prosopography links the name, which appears as early as 759, to the interconnected Scharnitz-Schlehdorf and Benediktbeuern founding groups; see Jahn, *Ducatus*, 458–60. The two special *missi* in the Gregorius case, *TF* 463, are a bit harder to pin down. Freholf bears a name that appears in Freising witness lists as far back as 765/766 (see inter alia *TF* 26). A Nidhard *comis* appears in 802 among a large group of counts witnessing *TF* 183, a formal *placitum* headed by Arn of Salzburg, and the name Nidhart appears in Freising witness lists from 804/809 (see inter alia *TF* 216). Thus, it is likely that the special *missi* in *TF* 463 were also drawn from among the regional aristocracy.

nothing to do with fiscal rights.[38] It indicates, therefore, that once a *missus* was around, he attracted other disputes.

After 822, the *missi* disappear from the charters until 829.[39] In that year, a Count Anzo headed a judicial assembly in company with Bishop Hitto and a Count Liutpald. The record of the assembly explicitly labels Anzo a *missus* of the emperor Louis's son, the Bavarian sub-king Louis the German.[40] The assembly dealt with a dispute between Bishop Hitto and a certain Alprih, who had given property to Freising that was not in his power to give. After Alprih returned the property to its rightful owner, Anzo ordered him to compensate Freising, which Alprih did by giving equivalent property in another location. The next *missus* does not appear until 837.

FORMAL *PLACITA* AFTER ARN OF SALZBURG

Although the imperial *missi* acted in a more ad hoc fashion in this period than they did immediately after the Carolingian conquest, other reflections of Carolingian judicial authority continued to lead a vigorous, even expanded life. One of them was the Frankish-style *placitum* report. In the first two decades after the Carolingian conquest, this formulaic way of describing disputes depended entirely on the *missus* Archbishop Arn of Salzburg. In some cases, the *placitum* reports were written by Arn's own scribes. In others, they were written by scribes attached to other churches but only in cases where Arn was present.[41] In the period 812 to 835, however, this is no longer true; local scribes wrote entirely typical *placitum* reports to record the

38. Bishop Nidker of Augsburg and his advocate claimed that the previous bishop of Augsburg had successfully sued a certain Adalhard for rights to the church before imperial *missi* at Paderborn. Bishop Hitto's advocate replied that Adalhard had accepted the church as a benefice from Freising before the hearing in Paderborn. Hatto and Kisalhard summoned witnesses who supported Freising's version of events.

39. In 825, Louis established a new set of *missatica* that between them covered all the old three Frankish kingdoms of Neustria, Austrasia, and Burgundy. Bavaria was left out, along with Italy and Aquitaine, possibly to respect the subregnal authority of Louis's sons; in 825, Louis the German began exercising power in Bavaria in his own right. See the literature cited in n. 7.

40. *TF* 579. Count Anzo appears three times in the Freising charters between 828 and 864, in *TF* 561, 579, and 890, in the area to the south and west of Freising. There is not enough information to determine whether he was a member of the established Bavarian aristocracy.

41. See Chapter 3.

actions of judicial assemblies at which no *missi* were present. It seems, therefore, that the standardized procedures introduced and promoted by Arn of Salzburg had found their way into wider Bavarian practice and had survived his retirement from the Bavarian judicial scene.

A Freising record from the year 814 provides a good example.[42] It begins with the typical opening line: "Bishop Hitto and Count Engilhard and Count Liutpald were in residence at the church named Bergkirchen, and many others came to this *placitum*." Then comes the charge: "Hunperht and Hroadleoz and Ermanrih came into their presence and sought the church in Odelzhausen which the priest Freido had given to Freising for the salvation of his soul." Defense: "Then Kaganhart and many others with him stood up and testified that they had seen Freido give the above-mentioned church into the possession of Bishop Atto and to Freising when Bishop Atto consecrated that church." Testimony: After Hunperht and Hroadleoz and Ermanrih denied this accusation, Count Engilhard demanded that a group of noblemen swear to the truth of the matter. The nobles responded that Freido at the end of his life had called them to him, given the church to Freising, and charged them with going to Freising and carrying out the gift. Finally, the surrender: "The men who sought that church saw that they were unable to obtain what they sought and that they had been overcome by right justice, and they admitted they had acted unjustly." Both the losers and the witnesses then went to Freising and carried out Freido's original gift in the presence of the entire Freising congregation. The notice ends with a witness list and a dating to the first regnal year of the emperor Louis.

So far, I have treated this narrative structure as a formulaic pattern that makes it hard to say anything about "real" behavior. Scribes took the results of a process whose outcome they knew and fitted those results into a standardized format. Only in the case of compromises did they include enough case-specific information to let us draw conclusions about individual behavior. Another Freising example, however, indicates that the formal *placitum* structure was not just a narrative device but rather reflected a real set of procedures that served an important purpose. Produced in 825, this record begins as usual by noting that Bishop Hitto, Count Heimo, and many other nobles had convened "for the purpose of determining right justice."[43] Bishop Hitto's advocate stood up and sought a priest named Salomon as the serf of the monastery of Saint Zeno at Isen.[44] Salomon made no resistance;

42. *TF* 327.
43. *TF* 514.
44. Hitto's advocate sought Salomon *ad proprio servo et ad servitium*.

he admitted the charge and declared his desire "to hand himself over immediately into the possession of Bishop Hitto."

The scene should have been set for an informal resolution of the whole problem. The good bishop, however, would not allow his opponent to give up. Hitto forced Salomon instead to go through the entire ritual procedure of testimony, judgment, and surrender that is typical of the formal *placitum*. The bishop "refused to accept him [Salomon], before the people had judged and before those who better knew of his birth had confirmed this with an oath." A group of witnesses proceeded to swear on relics that they knew Salomon to be a serf of Saint Zeno from both his mother and his father. The assembly then judged that Salomon must hand himself over to Bishop Hitto and his advocate. Salomon obeyed and publicly admitted he had no choice.

The message here is clear: Hitto wanted his rights over Salomon nailed down in the most secure fashion possible. That meant going through the entire public ritual of a *placitum*. Hitto apparently saw anything less as exposing his rights to a renewed challenge later. In other words, the narrative structure of the *placitum* report reflected real procedure, procedure that Bishop Hitto in this case considered important enough to insist on in order to secure his property rights.

One still has to be cautious, however, about assuming that *placitum* reports tell the whole story. The pat manner in which they describe clear-cut verdicts can mask what really happened and give a false impression both of how effective the judicial assemblies were and perhaps of what their real purpose was. In particular, they can disguise how a *placitum* fit into a longer and more complicated relationship between the two disputing parties.

A *placitum* held in 824 over rights to a basilica in Bachern formed part of just such a relationship.[45] At a judicial assembly headed by Bishop Hitto of Freising, his colleague Baturic of Regensburg, and five counts, Hitto's advocate sued two men named Hroadolt and Engilman. The men had claimed the basilica at Bachern for themselves and had "usurped it as their own."[46] Faced with this charge, the two men directly admitted they had acted unjustly. They pledged to return the basilica, provided guarantors, and promised to pay a fine of forty solidi.

This terse report says nothing about the defendants' relationship to each other, to the disputed basilica, or to Freising. It turns out, however, that Engilman was a deacon, that he and Hroadolt were brothers, and that both had a long association with Freising through the medium of property in Bach-

45. *TF* 507.
46. "Pahhara" = Ober/Unterbachern near Dachau.

ern. Almost a year before the *placitum*, in June 823, the deacon Engilman had made a gift of half his inherited property at Bachern to Freising.[47] Just over eighteen years after the *placitum*, in February 843, Hroadolt pledged to pay Freising an annual rent for a benefice at Bachern. A few years later, sometime between 845 and 851, Hroadolt gave inherited property in Bachern to Freising. He made the gift on the condition that both his and his brother Engilman's shares of the Bachern property be held by himself, by his wife, Svidpurc, and by a deacon named Kernot for their lifetimes.[48] All the people named in this last transaction must have died fairly quickly thereafter. In January 852, a nobleman named Manigolt received a benefice from Bishop Hitto's successor, Erchanbert, consisting of "the ecclesiastical property at Bachern which the deacon Engilman of good memory gave."[49]

In short, Engilman and Hroadolt enjoyed gift/benefice ties with Freising in Bachern both before and well after the *placitum* of 824. Thus, it is very likely that the dispute handled at that assembly ended in a compromise arranged outside the assembly, to the effect that either Engilman or Hroadolt (probably Engilman, since he was a deacon) received the disputed basilica back as a benefice. In any case, what the *placitum* report reveals when placed in its entire context is a dispute regulating an ongoing association. Bishop Hitto had his formal rights to the basilica at Bachern publicly vindicated at the *placitum*. Nevertheless, the two brothers continued to use gift/benefice arrangements with Freising to keep their property together and to pass it on to two other relatives—Hroadolt's wife, Svidpurc, and the deacon Kernot.[50] The *placitum*, therefore, served simply to secure Freising's formal rights to the basilica, before witnesses and in writing, in the context of this longer relationship.

DISPUTES AS PARTS OF ONGOING RELATIONSHIPS

The charters from this period make it much easier to see how conflict fit into ongoing relationships between landholders and the Bavarian churches because the scribes writing the charters have become more interested in documenting such relationships. This new interest is evident in the see of Passau as well as in Freising. Sometime between 818 and 834, a Passau scribe recorded a dispute involving Bishop Reginharius of Passau, a priest

47. *TF* 493.
48. *TF* 656b and 675.
49. *TF* 732.
50. Based on previous cases, one can infer that Kernot was Engilman's nephew.

named Kundalperht, and a man named Plidkis.[51] Kundalperht had held property as a benefice from Passau; he in turn had given the property as a benefice to Plidkis. After Kundalperht died, Bishop Reginharius's advocate sought the property back from Plidkis. Plidkis duly surrendered the property before a group of witnesses. The scribe then resorted to the "act of mercy" script, which we have seen up to now only in the Freising charters. When Plidkis met with Reginharius to invest him formally with the property, the bishop, "moved by mercy," returned it to him as a lifetime benefice. In other words, Bishop Reginharius had Passau's formal rights to the property publicly restated before confirming Plidkis as the benefice holder. As in the Freising examples, the "act of mercy" pattern allowed Reginharius to recognize the status quo—that is, Plidkis's possession of the property—at the same time protecting the rights of his church.

Relationships of this kind were regulated not only by disputes between churches and benefice holders but also by conflict between benefice holders and others with an interest in their property. Several charters from this period report charges by anonymous third parties that a benefice holder intended to alienate his benefice from the church. Such challenges forced benefice holders to reaffirm or redefine their relationship with the church in order to protect their property holdings. Thus, the churches and their rights were continuing to play an important role in the endemic competition for property within the landholding kindreds that we have been tracking from the beginning.

One example derives from a case we looked at earlier, in a discussion of how a benefice arrangement made by one branch of a kindred could protect property from claims made by another branch.[52] In 792, the priest Arperht had given property to Freising and asked that his two nephews, the priests Jacob and Simon, receive it as a benefice. After Arperht's death, a relative named Salomon challenged Jacob and Simon's rights to the property. The

51. *TP* 74.

52. In addition to *TF* 345, discussed here, see *TF* 438 (820): "certain insidious men" charge one Cozpald with trying to alienate his benefice from Freising. Cozpald protests that he "would never say or believe anything" other than that the property belonged to Freising; Bishop Hitto then confirmed his benefice. In *TF* 604 (830), unspecified *aliqui* came to Hitto and complained that a certain Erchanolf was alienating some of his father's property that he held as a Freising benefice. The bishop sent out (his own, not imperial) *missi*, who collected sworn testimony from the local unfree as to Freising's rights. Erchanolf then swore he held the property as a Freising benefice.

pair's successful defense rested on Freising's formal rights to Arperht's gift.[53]

In 815, however, Jacob and Simon themselves ran afoul of Freising.[54] This time, Freising's rights were turned against the two priests. Bishop Hitto of Freising sought Arperht's property back from the two men "because it was intimated to him by many that they wished to cast doubt and to waver about this property with respect to the house of Saint Mary." After witnesses testified to the terms of Arperht's original gift, Jacob and Simon "no longer wished to dispute any further, and they returned to Bishop Hitto and his advocate whatever their uncle [Arperht] had given the house of Saint Mary the mother of God." They went even further and gave themselves personally into Bishop Hitto's service (*servitium*). The two men then asked for the properties back as a benefice with the same rent and dues that had been arranged by their uncle. Hitto granted their request with a stern warning that they not give, alienate, or exchange the property and that it come after their deaths indisputably into Freising's possession.

In the two cases just discussed, a dispute caused a benefice arrangement to be publicly renewed. It is possible, therefore, that we are seeing not real conflicts but rather renewals of benefice arrangements couched as conflicts. In other words, the two parties might have staged a dispute in order to get the public and written restatement of the relationship that both sides wanted.[55] That this was not necessarily true is apparent in a similar case in which a relationship was not renewed but rather broken off. In 820, a layman named Wergant came before a synod headed by Bishop Hitto.[56] There he charged a priest named Altwart with having given away his share (*suam partem*—whether Wergant's or Altwart's is unclear) of ecclesiastical property that actually belonged to Freising. Altwart did not deny the charge. Bishop Hitto then asked for Altwart's side of the story. Altwart responded with the confusing claim that Bishop Joseph of Freising had consecrated a church on the property and had afterward given it to him as "his own for life." This statement smacks of Agilolfing-era assumptions about property holding. Altwart had evidently built the church on family property, invited Bishop Joseph to dedicate it, and then formally given it to Freising while continuing to treat it as his own.[57] Witnesses testified, however, that Altwart

53. See the discussion of *TF* 247 in Chapter 2.
54. *TF* 345.
55. See the literature cited in Chapter 2, n. 29.
56. *TF* 437.
57. There are, unfortunately, no earlier documents that confirm this claim.

had formally returned the church and its property to Bishop Joseph's successor, Atto. Bishop Hitto demanded the church back from Altwart. Defeated, Altwart complied.

In this case, Freising's scribe identified Altwart's accuser, Wergant, by name. It is not possible to connect Wergant directly to Altwart, but the circumstances strongly suggest that the layman, who by implication held a share of the church property Altwart had tried to alienate, was a kinsman.[58] The record does not describe a renewal of Altwart's benefice arrangement. Although there is no way to tell whether such a renewal took place later, the contrast with the cases discussed earlier suggests that Altwart had in fact tried to alienate his benefice and as a result lost it.[59] In short, disputes of this sort were not simply rhetorical devices that couched restatements of benefice arrangements in the language of conflict. Instead, competition for property among claimants was making it necessary for benefice holders to renew their benefices or risk losing their property.[60]

Conflict thus acted as a part of the process of affirming or adjusting long-term relationships between the Bavarian cathedral churches and church benefice holders on several levels. In some cases, the bishop simply called in property and received a public restatement (and archival notice) of his formal rights from the benefice holder. In other cases, the dispute involved not only the bishop and the benefice holder but also third parties who were possibly kinsmen of the benefice holder. Here conflict served to adjust relation-

---

58. The suggestion gets even stronger if *suam partem* means that Altwart had alienated Wergant's share.

59. Property in the location at issue here—Luttenwang—seems to have been firmly in Freising's hands by the third quarter of the ninth century. In *TF* 780 (856–60) and *TF* 878 (860–75), Bishop Anno of Freising swaps property in Luttenwang with lay noblemen.

60. Churches did not need to use conflict as a device for restating or modifying their relationships with landholders; they could do so quite peacefully. *TF* 599 (830) tells the story of two brothers, Kernod and the deacon Kerolt, who shared property inherited from their parents in two locations. With his brother's consent, the deacon Kerolt gave his half of their inherited property in both places to Freising. He must have continued to hold the property as a benefice, for it was not until he died some years later that his brother Kernod came to Bishop Hitto and asked that the bishop share Kerolt's property with him. The bishop agreed; he gave Kernod Kerolt's share of the property in one location, and Kernod gave his share of the property in the other location to Freising. This arrangement, which reshuffled the properties so that both sides had economic units, was carried out in a perfectly amicable fashion; the charter's description of the two brothers positively drips with fraternal affection and religious piety.

ships between the bishoprics and those holding church benefices and also between benefice holders and their competitors. Competition acted as a check on the benefice holders, forcing them to renew or strengthen their relationship with the church. Altwart's case shows what could happen when a benefice holder neglected this task.

PLACITA AND COMPROMISE

In the process of recording these ongoing relationships, the scribes have taken us back into the world of extrajudicial conflict resolution. We have found that they continued to use the "act of mercy" script and learned that the script was not just a Freising device. In the period from 812 to 835, the extrajudicial world is not as distinct from the formal judicial assemblies as it had been earlier. A hint that the two arenas were beginning to mix has already appeared in the disputes over the rights of the imperial fisc; a Freising scribe placed a short but complete "act of mercy" compromise at the end of an otherwise normal *placitum* report. Other charters from this period reveal that church scribes were becoming increasingly preoccupied with disputes that perhaps began at formal assemblies but were resolved outside them by often lengthy processes of settlement.

One of these charters comes from Regensburg.[61] Written in 822, it too shows that the "act of mercy" pattern was not just a Freising script. The record describes a compromise worked out between Bishop Baturic of Regensburg and his adversary in the wake of a judgment at a formal *placitum*. "A long time ago," an abbot named Rihpald and his aunt had given property to Saint Emmeram at Regensburg. The pair expressed a desire to have the property pass as a benefice to Rihpald's nephews Engilmon and Isandeon.[62] Rihpald failed to carry out the arrangement, however, so after his death the two nephews simply took possession of the property themselves. Bishop Baturic responded by suing for the property at a *placitum* headed by a Count Cotafrid. The charter gives no details of the proceedings; it states only that "recognizing the law," Engilmon and Isandeon acknowledged Saint Emmeram's formal rights and returned the property. Next comes a perfect "act of mercy" compromise, complete with the intervention of a faceless third-party group. After the *placitum* had ended, "it was their petition and that of other good men that [the property] be given back to them as a benefice." Compelled by his own "goodness" (*benignitas*), Bishop Baturic granted the request in exchange for their promise to pay a rent.

61. *TR* 19.
62. *Postea ipse Rihpald uoluit conplacitare nepotibus suis Engilmone et Isandeone....*

A much more elaborate example comes from Freising. It too begins in the context of court. Nevertheless, according to the Freising scribe who recorded the case, the most important elements of the dispute took place outside the court in a settlement process that lasted several days. This process likewise followed the "act of mercy" script to the letter. On September 15, 818, Bishop Hitto of Freising and his advocate brought a suit before a judicial assembly headed by the counts Kisalhard and Liutpald.[63] They sought a man named Waldperht as a serf of Freising (*ad servitium*), claiming that Waldperht's father had died a member of Freising's servile community (*in servili famulatu*). The counts sought testimony from witnesses, who swore that Waldperht's father had indeed died as a serf of Freising and that Waldperht therefore ought to be in the same condition. The counts then judged that Bishop Hitto should take Waldperht as Freising's serf.

Waldperht, however, had a free wife: Ermansuind, daughter of Sigiheri.[64] As soon as she heard that her husband was not a free man, Ermansuind raised the issue of her own inherited property: "She said she did not wish to lose her own inheritance because of the fact that her husband had been found out and caught up in servitude." An investigation of Ermansuind's property holdings ensued. Witnesses testified before the assembly that in the time of Bishop Atto, Ermansuind's father, Sigiheri, had divided his property in two parts. One part he had given to the see of Freising and the second part he had left to his daughter as her inheritance.

Looking at the case systematically, one would expect that the two counts present would issue a judgment in line with the valid norm.[65] That did not

63. *TF* 401c.

64. *TF* 402.

65. A norm implicitly expressed by the narrative governed Ermansuind's situation, which we can read out of her resistance to it: if a free woman was found to be married to an unfree man, she stood to lose her property to her husband's owner. In addition, according to Bishop Hitto, her children would become the unfree property of her husband's owner. Whether this norm stemmed from some written source or from commonly understood yet unwritten practice remains hidden. As it appears here, the norm shows up neither in the Bavarian Law nor in the Bavarian capitularies or synodal acts. Other barbarian law codes, however, make it clear that free women ought to have avoided marrying unfree men. The Frankish *Pactus legis Salicae*, for example, declares that a woman in such a position would lose her freedom; if she married one of her own unfree, she would be outlawed and her property would go to the fisc. See *The Laws of the Salian Franks*, trans. Katherine Fisher Drew (Philadelphia, 1991), XXV/4, 87, LXLVIII/1–2, 144. The only Bavarian reference to the situation comes in acts of the Synod of Dingolfing, summoned by Duke Tassilo III in 770. Chapter X states that a free woman found married to an

happen. Instead, the two sides left the assembly and worked out a compromise. Bishop Hitto returned to Freising and went to the chest containing the archives of his church. There he found the charter recording Sigiheri's division of his property.[66] With her property rights clarified, Ermansuind took counsel with her closest relatives. It seems likely that Bishop Hitto also took part in the discussion since the outcome directly affected him. The resulting settlement was ritually staged. On September 17, two days after her husband had been declared unfree, Ermansuind went to the altar of the Freising cathedral and formally gave up her rights to the property left her by her father. In response, "moved by pity" (*misericordia motus*), Bishop Hitto gave her both halves of her father's property back as a benefice. In addition, he agreed to do the same for up to two of her children, who would be serfs of Freising through their father.

Ermansuind, in other words, acted according to the "act of mercy" script. She made a total surrender of her inheritance, thus acknowledging the legitimacy of Freising's claim to it. With his de jure rights acknowledged, Bishop Hitto then responded with a counteraction couched in the language of Christian charity that met Ermansuind's de facto needs for support. This compromise, which awarded Freising the formal victory yet left Ermansuind in possession of all her father's property, followed from the actions of the original judicial assembly but nonetheless took place outside them.

The fact that Ermansuind and her relatives came away with a compromise suggests that she and her kinsmen had some influence.[67] A little prosopographical digging supports this idea. According to Sigiheri's original gift charter,

---

unfree man could regain her free status only by leaving her husband (*Concilium Dingolfingense*, 95).

66. This charter has survived in Cozroh's collection as *TF* 130, dated by Bitterauf to 790–94. It describes Sigiheri's gift of property in Haselbach to Freising for the souls of himself, his wife, and his sons. The property Sigiheri gave represented half his holdings at Haselbach; the other half went to his daughter Ermansuind. Störmer, *Adelsgruppen*, 14, reads the charter sequence as having Sigiheri giving property at Sixthaselbach to Freising in response to Waldperht's descent into unfreedom so his daughter could have it back as a benefice; that is not what *TF* 402 says.

67. How wives came out of situations like this depended on individual circumstance. Cf. *TP* 50 (800–804): at a *placitum* headed by the *missi* Arn of Salzburg and Bishop Waldric of Passau, Waldric sought one Epo as a serf (*ad servitium*) of Passau; Epo surrendered himself with his sons and daughters. Waldric then ordered his scribe to note that Epo's wife, Hrodwar, was free, that no one in the future should infringe on her right to be with her husband as if he was free, and that all subsequent children she might bear would also be free. In contrast, in *TP* 54 (802), a *missi* court again headed by Arn judged that two men named Williperht and Adalperht were

the property concerned was located in Haselbach. A Freising charter of the tenth century describes Haselbach as "Sigiheri's village, which is now called Haselbach."[68] Evidently, Ermansuind's father or a like-named ancestor had founded the settlement. In addition, some circumstantial evidence suggests that Ermansuind enjoyed connections to the Huosi *genealogia*.[69] Bishop Hitto himself has likewise been counted among the Huosi.[70] Putting these pieces together, we find that all parties to the dispute were connected to one another. If we accept this evidence, it seems that underneath the narrative of conflict an interconnected group of people at the highest levels of Bavarian society had resolved an embarrassing situation in the least painful manner possible.

Bavarian property disputes in the period 812 to 835 shared many features with those of the preceding period. As before, the tension between hereditary expectations and church rights to property dominated the disputing landscape. Disgruntled co-heirs continued to challenge church rights to property given by their relatives; others continued to shelter themselves under the umbrella of those rights through benefice arrangements. Nonetheless, some new features have emerged. For one, we have been able to see more clearly what made benefice arrangements work for the church. The endemic competition

---

serfs of Passau; the pair immediately handed themselves over to Passau with their wives and daughters.

68. *Sigiheresdorf, qui nunc Hasalpah nuncupatur*: TF 1203 (957–72). See Störmer, *Adelsgruppen*, 14.

69. We know the names of Ermansuind's three guarantors (*fideiussores*): Esit, Lantperht, and Othoh. Esit and Othoh have not left a paper trail sufficient to provide any useful information. Othoh does not reappear in the Freising charters. Esit appears only one other time, in a witness list to a charter of 821 (*TF* 449). Lantperht, however, bears a name that appears in the highest circles. Arbeo of Freising in his *Life of Saint Emmeram*, for example, identified the son of the Bavarian Duke Theodo as a Lantperht: *Vita Haimhrammi*, 20–50. A Freising charter of 853, *TF* 736, directly links the name with the Huosi; the charter records an exchange of property in *Lantperhttesreode in confinio Hosiorum* that a Count Adalperht had purchased from a Lantperht. Störmer, *Adelsgruppen*, 107, points out *TR* 40 (863/864?), in which an Egilolf with a brother named Lantperht makes a gift to Saint Emmeram; cf. the Egilolf explicitly identified as a Huosi in *TF* 142 (791). A final piece of circumstantial evidence: Störmer, *Adelsgruppen*, 92, has placed the location of the court that condemned Waldperht in *TF* 401c, Allershausen, in an area containing some of the highest concentration of Huosi property—the lower Glonn valley west of Freising.

70. See n. 2.

for property within the Bavarian kindreds lowered the risk involved for the churches in giving out benefices. The competition not only prompted people to shelter property via benefice arrangements; it acted as the best guarantee that people would honor those arrangements. Charges that benefice holders were planning to alienate their benefices forced such holders to reaffirm their relationships with the church or risk losing their property. In short, the churches could give out benefices secure in the knowledge that competition would help enforce their de jure property rights.

In addition, church rights to donated property and kinship rights no longer appear as the only justifications for claiming or defending property holdings. Some people defended their holdings with the rights of the imperial fisc. Bavarians therefore did not see the church and the imperial authority as automatically allied; the two could end up competing with each other. This phenomenon was not necessarily new. People had very likely been holding property they regarded as fiscal benefices all along. What had changed was the political climate surrounding such benefices. As part of his reform program, the emperor Louis the Pious set about investigating possible abuses by the fisc. Louis's policy toward the fisc had an effect in Bavaria; it triggered on a small scale the same reaction that had appeared on a large scale immediately after the Carolingian conquest, that is, an opportunistic response that changed the rules of the disputing game. Bishop Hitto of Freising found himself positively invited to claim property in a fiscal area from people who thought they were holding the property as fiscal benefices.

Connected to the disputes over the rights of the fisc is a visible change in the nature of the authority figures heading formal judicial assemblies. Where before the imperial *missi* and in particular Arn of Salzburg dominated the assemblies, after 812 the *missi* appear only irregularly. The patent connection of three of their appearances in 822 with the disputes over fiscal rights in the area around Föhring strongly suggests that they showed up in Bavaria to deal with the specific concerns of the emperor rather than to administer justice generally. Once given their commissions, however, the *missi* had the authority to issue clear judgments and to attract at least one other high-level case that needed their standing to resolve.

The reverse side of this coin is the more frequent appearance of bishops and/or counts as heads of judicial assemblies in their own right. This observation leads to even more interesting information: the Frankish-style *placitum* form that at first had been exclusively linked with Arn of Salzburg was used after 812 to describe assemblies headed by these bishops and counts. Arn's efforts to standardize how disputes were processed and recorded, therefore, had evidently left a lasting mark on how the bearers of regional authority handled formal disputing and how their scribes recorded it.

At the same time, the records reveal that this world of formal dispute resolution was beginning to connect to the "subculture" of extrajudicial dispute settlement. Previously, the records had made the judicial and extrajudicial layers of dispute resolution look like separate arenas. After 812, however, some scribes began to focus on how the extrajudicial layer connected to the judicial one. This subtle shift in the scribes' attention highlights more clearly how *placitum* reports captured moments in what could be quite lengthy and ongoing settlement processes.

This trend is most apparent in the records of disputes that started at *placita* but ended outside them. The possible connection between *placita* and extrajudicial processes came up for the first time in one of the fiscal cases. At the very end of an otherwise straightforward adjudication overseen by two bishops and two *missi*, Freising's scribe added a little "act of mercy" compromise: a faceless "begging" group asked Bishop Hitto to forgive a mandated fine, and the bishop complied as an act of charity. Other, longer examples from Freising and from Regensburg also describe disputes that began at *placita* but ended in extrajudicial settlements following the "act of mercy" script. In these cases, the scribes regarded the "real" end of the dispute not as what happened in the *placitum* but rather as what happened outside it.

Such blending of the judicial and the extrajudicial had probably been going on long before this time. Arn of Salzburg's *placita* in all likelihood captured moments in ongoing relationships and settlement processes much as these cases did; disputants probably modified court judgments with settlements that followed the rules of the extrajudicial game before 812 as much as they did afterward. What is important is that the scribes are now telling us about it.[71] In the first two decades after the Carolingian conquest,

71. It is possible that several earlier extrajudicial settlements took place in the wake of formal judicial assemblies, because officeholding authority figures took part in them as witnesses. The scribes do not say explicitly one way or the other, however. Figuring out what happened in these cases is made even harder by the fact that the officeholders could have been on the witness lists because they were related to one of the disputing parties, not because they had headed a *placitum*. See, for example, *TF* 176 (Chapter 4) and *TF* 235 (Chapter 2). Jahn has speculated that the investiture notice *TF* 187 following the Reginperht dispute *TF* 186 (see Chapter 2) represents a hidden compromise worked out after the formal judgment because it shows Reginperht returning only part of the properties he had committed to return at the assembly; see *Ducatus*, 443. The only earlier example in which the scribe makes it explicit that an informal settlement modified a formal judgment comes in *TF* 166a (Chapter 4), in which Charlemagne himself stepped in and as an "act of mercy" returned property to Count Helmoin that a *missi* court had taken away.

the scribes represented *placita* as the totality of a dispute; what the judicial assemblies did was the information worth preserving. Although the scribes also recorded informal settlements, those settlements existed in their own separate world. Now, however, we find scribal attention moving in the course of the same dispute from assemblies to settlements. In the career of a single dispute, both what happened at the assembly and what happened outside it were important enough to write down.

The changes in this period, though real, are subtle; they obviously cannot bear the entire weight of an argument for the "informalization" of formal disputing in the period 812 to 835. When compared with the evidence for the period after 835, however, they may be seen as the heralds of much greater changes, changes that show such an informalization taking place on a large scale.

CHAPTER SIX
DISPUTING UNDER THE
CAROLINGIANS, 836-854
THE ART OF THE DEAL

I n 836, Bishop Hitto's kinsman Erchanbert succeeded to Freising's episcopal throne. Like his predecessor, the new bishop was thoroughly connected to the aristocratic kindreds that surrounded his see. This connection is made plain by the names of some of his relatives who appear in the Freising charters. In 843, for example, Erchanbert associated himself in a property transaction with a nephew who bore the Scharnitz-Schlehdorf name Reginperht. In 845, the bishop agreed to help a younger relative named Hitto get started on a clerical career at Freising.[1]

In the course of Bishop Erchanbert's reign, which lasted until his death in 854, Bavaria became part of an independent East Frankish kingdom.[2] On June 20, 840, Louis the Pious died at his palace at Ingelheim. The elderly emperor had just returned from a campaign in which he had stripped his son Louis the German of the East Frankish territories he had claimed after the rebellion of 833 and reduced him again to his sub-kingdom in Bavaria. With Louis the Pious dead, the younger Louis tried again to increase his share of the Carolingian empire, in competition with his elder brother Lothar and in

---

1. *TF* 661 and 674. Erchanbert's loyalty to his kindred was so strong that he advertised his living and dead relatives at the expense of the Freising cathedral clergy in a book recording the members of a sworn prayer association kept at the Alemannian monastery of Reichenau. See Maß, *Bistum Freising*, 83; on the Reichenau confraternity book, see McKitterick, *Frankish Kingdoms*, 210–11; Karl Schmid, "Religiöses und sippengebundenes Gemeinschaftsbewußtsein in frühmittelalterlichen Gedenkbucheinträgungen," in *Gebetsdenken und adeliges Selbstverständnis*, 532–97.

2. Johannes Fried, "The Frankish Kingdoms, 817–911: The East and Middle Kingdoms," in *NCMH*, 142–68; McKitterick, *Frankish Kingdoms*, 169–78; Reuter, *Germany in the Early Middle Ages*, 70–111; *HbG*, 264–77.

cooperation with his younger half-brother Charles the Bald. In the civil war that ensued, Louis was able to rely on the unswerving loyalty of the Bavarian aristocracy. His efforts bore fruit in the treaty signed by the three brothers at Verdun in 843; he regained what his father had taken away and became once and for all *rex in orientali francia*.

In the years following Verdun, Louis the German forged an East Frankish *regnum* anchored in two regions: Bavaria and his share of the Frankish heartlands, which lay in western Franconia around the confluence of the Rhine and Main rivers. The latter represented a rich lode of royal palaces and estates centered on the palace at Frankfurt (where Charlemagne in 794 had forced Duke Tassilo to renounce his family's rights in Bavaria). Because of these economic resources and because its Frankishness helped Louis buttress his claim to rule a greater Frankish kingdom, western Franconia became a major focal point for Louis's rule. It was there, for example, that he held most of his royal assemblies, assemblies that in contrast to those he held in other regions drew magnates from all over his kingdom.[3]

Nevertheless, Louis continued to lavish a great deal of attention on Bavaria. He spent as much time in his former sub-kingdom as he did in Franconia. Regensburg was his favorite residence; it alone of all his residences received the title *civitas regia*—the royal city. In addition, Louis maintained his close ties to the Bavarian aristocracy, including Bishop Erchanbert of Freising. In 843, Erchanbert, his nephew Reginperht, and a large number of other Bavarian aristocrats had taken part in the assembly held at Verdun to divide the empire.[4] A year later, the bishop secured a post for his nephew as a subdeacon in Louis's royal chapel at Regensburg while himself receiving the royal abbey at Kempten. Erchanbert also acted once as an inspector of saints' relics for the king; at Louis's request, he prescribed a regimen of fasting in order to induce God to declare whether or not some alleged relics of the apostle Bartholomew and other saints were genuine.[5]

Erchanbert's reign as bishop of Freising has left us with seven conflict

3. See esp. Eric J. Goldberg, "Creating a Medieval Kingdom: Carolingian Kingship, Court Culture, and East Frankish Nobility under Louis the German (840–876)" (Ph.D. diss., University of Virginia, 1998), esp. 328–49, 354–78, and tables 1–7; Goldberg, "'More Devoted to the Equipment of Battle than the Splendor of Banquets': Frontier Kingship, Military Ritual, and Early Knighthood at the Court of Louis the German," *Viator* 30 (1999): 41–78. After the Treaty of Meersen in 870, Louis added Lotharingia with Charlemagne's palace at Aachen as a third regional anchor for his kingdom.

4. *TF* 661.

5. Maß, *Bistum Freising*, 84.

records in the Freising charter collection.[6] Owing to the accidents of source survival, none has survived in any of the other Bavarian collections. The seven Freising records deal for the most part with the usual varieties of property disputes, that is, disputes between Freising and lay or clerical opponents or disputes within kindreds. In one very important respect, however, they form a distinctly homogeneous group. Although they record disputes handled at venues ranging from formal *placita* to informal gatherings and every shade in between, all seven record compromise settlements. Royal officeholders played little or no role in these settlements, despite Bishop Erchanbert's own close ties to the king. Instead, Erchanbert worked them out directly with his opponents. Moreover, they all followed the "act of mercy" script, which now appears so often that it begins to look formulaic.

FORMAL INFORMALITY

The earliest of these dispute records, from the year 837, makes it clear that we have entered a different world from that of the years immediately following the Carolingian conquest. Nevertheless, it tells a familiar story. Written by Cozroh himself, the record reconnects us to the ongoing history of the Scharnitz-Schlehdorf monastery.[7] It describes the actions of a formal judicial assembly and begins with the formulaic opening typical of a Frankish-style *placitum* report. Bishop Erchanbert of Freising, four counts, and a *missus* of Louis the German named Anternaro were gathered for the purpose of settling disputes. Bishop Erchanbert's advocate stood up before the assembly and sued two nobles (*nobiles viri*) named Isanhard and Ellanhard for property they held in two separate locations, Dürrnhausen and "Pachiltahofa" (not now identifiable). The advocate charged that their grandfather, Isanhart, and their father, Reginhart, had given the property to the monastery at Schlehdorf.[8] The two men resisted the charge, and the

6. Out of a total of 132 charters that Bitterauf dates to Erchanbert's reign: *TF* 626a, 636, 670, 679, 703, 704, 738.

7. *TF* 626a. Cozroh first appears as a Freising scribe in *TF* 440 (820).

8. The records of the original gifts by the grandfather Isanhart and the father Reginhart look with reasonable certainty to have survived as the Freising notices *TF* 75 and 76ab (776). In the former, Isanhart gave his allodial property at Herrsching, Holzhausen, Raisting, and Erling to Schlehdorf *post obitum*. In the latter, the two versions of which are virtually identical, Isanhart's son Reginhart gave property at Raisting and at Dürrnhausen to Schlehdorf *post obitum*. Since Raisting appears alongside Dürrnhausen in this gift, Bitterauf has identified it with the mysterious "Pachiltahofa" of *TF* 626a. If we accept *TF* 75 and 76ab as the original gift charters,

parties "disputed among themselves about this for a long time." Bishop Erchanbert responded by summoning witnesses.

At this point, Cozroh's narrative, like those in Arn of Salzburg's compromise *placita*, breaks free from the familiar formulaic structure. Unlike
Arn's scribes, however, Cozroh does not describe a settlement imposed or
mediated by the authority figures heading the assembly. He gives us instead
an "act of mercy" compromise in its purest form, complete with a supplicating group, arranged directly by Bishop Erchanbert and his opponents.
Faced with the witnesses' testimony, which apparently ran in Freising's
favor, the two defendants "took counsel." Cozroh does not say with whom,
but previous experience suggests they met with their nearest relatives.[9]
They then admitted the justice of Freising's charge.[10] The pair next offered, "for the purpose of peace and reconciliation with the lord bishop," to
return three *colonicas* of property in one of the disputed locations, "Pachiltahofa." In response,

> with the others in that *placitum* begging him, the most benign bishop, moved
> and compelled by mercy, did not wish to deprive them of all their inheritance
> or to disinherit them, but considering their poverty he permitted them to re-
> turn those three full *colonicas* . . . and whatever was seen to pertain to those
> three *colonicas* and over and above this, half of the woods and cultivated forests
> and of all their territories, whatever on that day they were seen to have.

Isanhard and Ellanhard agreed and handed over the property. They then offered to swear on relics that they would give up the rest of their property.
"In his mercy," Bishop Erchanbert declined, on the condition that they
faithfully carry out the main agreement.

This process followed the rules of the bilateral settlement game as we
have seen them before. The defendants admitted the justice of Freising's
claim. Then, with the help of a "begging" group, they made a compromise
offer. Bishop Erchanbert experienced the requisite feelings of mercy; taking

---

it appears that in *TF* 626a the father Reginhart had just died and that his sons Isanhard and Ellanhard wanted to keep using their father's property.

9. Cozroh uses the phrase *inito consilio*; in *TF* 402 (Chapter 5), the same phrase explicitly refers to relatives.

10. *Proinde inito consilio supradicti viri credebant semet ipsis se ad placandum et con-
ciliandum cum domno episcopo profitebantur se reddere domno episcopo. . . .* This statement could also be translated to read that the two men admitted not the full justice
of Freising's claim but only that they wanted to reconcile themselves with the
bishop.

their poverty into consideration and not wishing to disinherit them, he made a higher counterdemand. The defendants accepted. Indeed, it appears that they tried to go the bishop one better by pledging all the disputed property, not just half of it. Erchanbert, again moved by mercy, declined under the condition that his opponents honor the agreement.[11]

The other authority figures present at the *placitum* played no role whatsoever in these proceedings; Cozroh does not even mention them, apart from noting their presence and their service as witnesses. Interestingly enough, the authority figure who comes across as the least important of all is the royal *missus* Anternaro. Cozroh places him dead last in the list of authority figures and, in contrast with the others, does not include him in the witness list.[12] In Cozroh's view of things, apparently, the *missus* was unimportant; the settlement of the dispute was a matter between the bishop and his two opponents. The *placitum* served only as a venue for testimony and as a source of supplicants. In short, Cozroh describes the settlement of a dispute at a formal assembly in terms previously characteristic of extrajudicial arrangements.

This case has been seen as evidence for the self-inflicted decline and fall of both the narrow Scharnitz-Schlehdorf founding kindred and the larger Huosi *genealogia*. According to this interpretation, the protracted infighting within this extended kin group, captured in the long list of Freising dispute charters involving its members, could only end up impoverishing some branches of the group. By 837, this fate had overtaken Isanhard and Ellanhard; the representation here of the brothers as impoverished and needing Bishop Erchanbert's mercy reveals that these downfallen members of a once powerful family had reached the end of their resources.[13]

---

11. *Et aliud quicquid ex parte hereditatis eorum habuerunt cum iuramento super capsam corporis sancti Tertulini confortare et confirmare voluerunt, sed ipsum iuramentum per misericordiam suam supradictus episcopus dimisit eis, si pleniter perfecissent sicut supra prenotatum est.* This line is somewhat confusing. It appears that Isanhard and Ellanhard offered to give up all the rest of their property but that Bishop Erchanbert declined on the condition that the two men honored the primary agreement. The line may thus represent a rhetorical/ritual action on the part of Isanhard and Ellanhard, with an expected ritual refusal by the bishop. Or it may represent an offer to confirm the main agreement itself by means of an oath, with Erchanbert releasing them from the oath in exchange for a simple promise.

12. This appearance of the name Anternaro is unique in the Freising charters; there is no evidence that indicates whether he had links to preexisting Bavarian kindreds.

13. Jahn, *Ducatus*, 445–48; Jahn goes on to draw wide conclusions about the effect such protracted infighting within the kindreds had on Bavarian social development.

We have spent a great deal of time observing how frequently and intensely members of the same kindred could fight over property. The evidence built up over the last few chapters, however, suggests a different way to explain Isanhard and Ellanhard's apparent poverty: this was how a Freising scribe had to represent a negotiated compromise in order to uphold his bishop's rights and prestige. It provides no evidence whatever for the brothers' actual status. The Freising effort to rewrite the Lantfrid case of 802 in a similar fashion (Lantfrid's foolishness instead of his poverty provided the justification there for Bishop Atto's act of Christian charity), in the face of the quite different version of the same case produced by Arn of Salzburg's scribe, serves as a shining example that events represented by Freising in one way could look quite different from another point of view.[14]

Given the substance of this settlement, it looks as if Isanhard and Ellanhard were actually dealing from a fairly strong hand. Had this dispute occurred earlier, say during the reign of Bishop Atto, one would have expected it to be settled according to a strict interpretation of the original gift charters. In other words, the court would have simply awarded the disputed property to Freising, perhaps remitting a few fines along the way. Here, however, Freising's opponents were able to launch negotiations; moreover, they ended up keeping some of the property Freising claimed.

It does not look as though the brothers intended to forge an ongoing relationship with Freising—quite the opposite. There is no way to tell what happened to their branch of the Scharnitz-Schlehdorf kindred. The last we see of the brothers, they have ended up with property in Dürrnhausen and "Pachiltahofa," neither of which locales appears again in the ninth century in the Freising charter collection.[15] The naming tradition of the Scharnitz-Schlehdorf group as a whole survives in the Freising records in the person and immediate kindred of one Piligrim "of Allershausen." Piligrim continued the kindred tradition of giving property (albeit to Freising, not to Schlehdorf) and of serving Freising as an advocate.[16] One wonders whether the disappearance from the records of Scharnitz-Schlehdorfer branches other than Piligrim's reflects their decline into poverty or, alternatively,

14. *TF* 184ab (Chapter 2).

15. Dürrnhausen does not reappear at all; Raisting appears again in the mid-tenth century (*TF* 1192). The names Isanhard and Ellanhard, of course, show up frequently in witness lists in the Freising charters throughout the ninth century, but there is not enough evidence to identify them exactly. It remains entirely possible, therefore, that the two brothers continued in an ongoing relationship with Freising in other arenas.

16. Jahn, *Ducatus*, 448.

their decision not to have anything more to do with Freising.[17] The charters have already provided plenty of evidence that kindreds could fragment into branches that chose to ally themselves or not to ally themselves with the house of Saint Mary.[18]

RENEGOTIATING RELATIONSHIPS

In contrast, in two other Freising dispute records from this period, conflict acts in the way we have seen before, to reinforce or adjust relationships between the see of Saint Mary and people who decided to remained associated with it. These records also rely on the "act of mercy" script. The first, from the year 849, relates a sequence of events surrounding a priest connected to the Huosi.[19] It begins not with the formulaic opening of a *placitum* report but rather with the informal opening characteristic of a *notitia*. The notice states that in the time of Bishop Atto, a noble priest named Erchanfrid had given property to Freising which he had inherited from his father.[20] But then, "urged on by the devil and by other advisers," Erchanfrid tried to renege on his gift. At a *placitum* convened by Bishop Erchanbert, "many of the Huosi and as many other noblemen met together to defeat and to overcome the falseness of this denial, which was then accomplished with truthful witnesses and written documents." Faced with defeat, the priest Erchanfrid met "in a secret place" with Count Fridaratus and Count Rihho and "others with whom he wished to consider his case"—most likely his friends and relations.[21] The group decided that Erchanfrid should reverse himself and

17. It is worth noting in this context that Isanhard and Ellanhard's father, Reginhart, and grandfather, Isanhart, had given their property to Schlehdorf before Freising had completely absorbed the monastery.

18. See Chapter 2.

19. *TF* 703ab.

20. The connections of the *nobilis presbiter* Erchanfrid to the Huosi are implicit in the document. The scribe refers to the presence of "many from the Huosi," Erchanfrid shares part of his name with Bishop Erchanbert, and the Scharnitz-Schlehdorfer Piligrim "of Allershausen" appears as Bishop Erchanbert's advocate.

21. The fact that Erchanfrid met with the two counts indicates some kind of close connection; other, more explicit examples of disputants taking counsel (see, for example, the discussion of *TF* 402 in Chapter 5) suggest kinship. It is impossible to say for certain whether they were related. Count Fridarat appears only in this charter. Count Rihho appears a number of times in the Freising charters beginning ca. 806–10; in 836, he witnessed a property gift by Erchanfrid (*TF* 609; see n. 22). Jahn, *Ducatus*, 529, comments that "one has to see Count Rihho as one of the leading representatives of the Huosi in the ninth century above all because of his connection to

recognize his previous gift. Accordingly, Erchanfrid and his advocate returned to the assembly, surrendered, and handed the property over to Bishop Erchanbert. Two days later, however, Bishop Erchanbert met again with Erchanfrid. The bishop asked the priest "what he had decided concerning his property." Erchanfrid responded by asking to renew his original gift. After he did so, Bishop Erchanbert, "not unmindful of his mercy," granted the property back to him as a lifetime benefice.

This narrative displays many of the same elements as the previous one. A formal *placitum* took place that delivered a clear judgment against the priest Erchanfrid. The scribe's interest, however, lay not only with the *placitum* and its judgment but also with what took place after the *placitum* between Bishop Erchanbert and his opponent: a straightforward "act of mercy" compromise. This compromise represented the heart of the settlement. The *placitum* served as a starting point by providing the defeat that led to the bishop's charitable gesture.

The differences between this case and the previous one lie in the ways Erchanfrid's case continues trends already visible in the charters from Bishop Hitto's reign. First, the settlement started in the context of a formal assembly but reached its conclusion outside it. Second, the dispute regulated an ongoing relationship between the two parties. Not only does the scribe assert that Erchanfrid had originally given the disputed property to Freising in the time of Bishop Atto; another Freising record from the year 836 tells us that he was already holding part of the property as a Freising benefice.[22] This relationship clearly had to overcome some friction. The scribe describes Erchanfrid as having been "instigated by the devil and by other advisers." Nevertheless, he did not plumb the full depths of the hostile representations a Freising scribe had at his disposal; he freely admitted that Erchanfrid had inherited the property from his father. It appears that this dispute enabled the priest Erchanfrid and Bishop Erchanbert, as well as the members of the larger Huosi kindred surrounding them both, to clarify

---

the priest Erchanfrid" (vor allem wegen seiner Verbundenheit mit dem Priester Erchanfrid wird man den Grafen Rihho für einen der führenden Vertreter der Huosi im 9. Jahrhundert halten müssen).

22. The property under dispute here was located (according to the separate investiture notice *TF* 703b) at Singenbach, Ried, and Tannara. Although Erchanfrid's original gift charter from the reign of Bishop Atto does not survive, Erchanfrid appears in 836 giving a benefice in Singenbach and allodial property in Ried to Freising (*TF* 609). This charter also leaves no doubt of Erchanfrid's Huosi connections; the transaction was carried out at "Holzen, which belonged to the priest Eio," one of the parties to the Huosi dispute handled at Lorch in 791 (*TF* 142; see the Interlude).

the terms of their association. The "act of mercy" pattern represented the expected process that everyone went through to do so. It looks as if Erchanfrid surrendered at the *placitum* knowing full well that the next steps in the final settlement of the case would take place not at the *placitum* but rather between himself and the bishop. In other words, in a case involving an interrelated group of people, formal procedures and institutions once more took second stage to the accepted extrajudicial ways of working out and expressing solutions to problems.

Another such dispute from the year 840, again described by Cozroh himself, shows even more clearly how Freising could use the "act of mercy" script to work out tensions in its relationship with a landholding kindred.[23] This tale concerns two brothers named Wichelm and Eigil, sons of a man named Kiso and his wife, Purcswind, who belonged to the extended kin group surrounding the monastery at Isen.[24] The family had already been holding property from Freising for more than a decade; in 827, Kiso had given property in Berghofen to Freising on the condition that he, his wife, and their son Eigil have lifetime use rights.[25] In 840, Bishop Erchanbert and his advocate sued the brothers Wichelm and Eigil for a church and its property at a location south of Berghofen called Strogn.[26] The two men responded that the property belonged to their inheritance. Their defense failed in the face of testimony from witnesses to the effect that their father had previously given the church at Strogn along with the property at Berghofen to Freising. Defeated, the brothers returned the property at Strogn to the bishop.[27]

23. *TF* 636.

24. See Störmer, *Adelsgruppen*, 123–32, esp. 129 and 132.

25. *TF* 541. Berghofen's location is disputed; Jahn, *Ducatus*, 487, places it near Altomünster, that is, in the area northwest of Dachau along the Glonn River. Störmer, *Adelsgruppen*, 132, identifies it with the Berghofen that lies ca. thirty kilometers north of Isen. This location is the more plausible suggestion since, as we see later, it is only ca. eighteen kilometers north of the family's other holdings in Strogn.

26. The record begins with the unusual statement, "How the same Bishop Erchanbert of blessed memory and his advocate Kerhart sought one church at Strogn and whatever pertained to it, namely, whatever the noblemen Wichelm and Eigil had there." This line gives us a rare glimpse into the process by which Cozroh put his charter collection together; although Cozroh wrote the original charter himself, he must have copied it into his collection after Bishop Erchanbert died in 854.

27. The family's original connection to the church at Strogn remains hidden. A church at Strogn appears in four other Freising charters over the period 815–22; the names involved, however, make it almost certain that these charters deal with a different church: *TF* 346, 445, 474a, 474b.

At some unspecified point afterward, however, Wichelm and Eigil appeared before Bishop Erchanbert "with others supplicating him on their behalf." They asked to add property at Berghofen, which their father had left them before making his gift to Freising, to their father's original gift. This they proceeded to do; they then renewed their father's gift. In exchange, Bishop Erchanbert agreed to let Eigil and his mother, Purcswind, have the properties at Strogn as a lifetime benefice.[28]

Cozroh's description of this dispute implies that a formal *placitum* took place, but again the *placitum* is not his primary focus. He does not mention any authority figures; he refers only to the involvement of Bishop Erchanbert and his advocate, the summoning of witnesses, and Wichelm and Eigil's formal surrender of the disputed property. Cozroh concentrates instead on the familiar structure of an "act of mercy" compromise: surrender, supplication with faceless group support, and a counteraction by the bishop (although Cozroh does not explicitly give mercy here as a motivation). This settlement served to update a preexisting relationship between the see of Freising and the family. Bishop Erchanbert agreed to let Eigil and his mother have the church at Strogn and its property as a lifetime benefice. In exchange, they gave him formal title to all Kiso's original property at Berghofen, some of which they had inherited and some of which they held as a Freising benefice. Eigil and his mother thus ended up with lifetime use rights to Kiso's property at Strogn (and very likely all his property at Berghofen—the terms of the arrangement do not specify that, but the terms of Kiso's original gift make it likely). Bishop Erchanbert for his part achieved formal title to all Kiso's property in both places, including the parts he did not already have.

It is important to recall at this point that these disputes, like the similar ones discussed in the previous chapter, do not represent peaceful renegotiations of relationships disguised as conflicts but rather reflect real tensions. Truly amicable arrangements could look quite different.[29] In the year 845, for example, Bishop Erchanbert and his advocate sued a certain nobleman (*quondam virum nobilem*) named Cundpato, son of Albricus, at a formal assembly headed by the bishop himself and a count.[30] Erchanbert's advocate charged that Cundpato was holding property that had previously been given to Freising by someone else. Cundpato responded "that he was neither able

28. The name of Eigil's mother is blanked out here by two cm of empty space in the manuscript; her name survives, however, in Kiso's original gift charter, *TF* 541.
29. See the discussion of *TF* 599 (830) in Chapter 5, n. 60.
30. *TF* 670.

nor did he want to dispute [this]." Thereupon, "filled with longing," he gave the disputed property to Freising along with some other property that had belonged to his father. After accepting the property, Bishop Erchanbert ordered a serf of Freising to hold a vigil for three nights "according to the custom of the Bavarians."[31] He then gave the property back to Cundpato as a benefice under the condition that Cundpato pay an annual rent.

The glowing representation here makes it clear that there was no real conflict involved. Bishop Erchanbert and Cundpato instead used the assembly to confirm Freising's property rights and agreeably restate their relationship.[32] The bishop plainly did not regard the situation as at all threatening. He did not force Cundpato to go through all the steps of a formal *placitum*, as we saw Bishop Hitto do once when he did not trust an opponent's willingness to surrender.[33]

THE BISHOP AS INTERESTED MEDIATOR

Next we turn to something that has not come up since the Carolingian conquest, namely, the mediation by a bishop of Freising of a dispute between two other parties. The record of the dispute states that the case was handled at a formal assembly headed by Bishop Erchanbert; in other words, it represents the bishop as an authority figure to whom the disputants came for a settlement. The dispute's outcome, however, points up once more the two-way flow of interest and negotiation and embeds this case securely in the same world that produced the others discussed in this chapter.

The dispute, recorded in a Freising charter from the year 849, pitted a deacon named Arperht against a priest named Rihhart over a basilica and its

---

31. *Iuxta morem Baiouuariorum*; on the possible meanings of this phrase, see Brown, "Use of Norms," 21–23. According to the *HdR*, this *sessio triduana* or *possessio triduana* represented a legal/ritual act designed to advertise a change in the condition of property, as, for example, when a gift to a church was made and then the same property went back to the original giver as a benefice. It is especially visible in Bavaria and Alemannia (although it does not appear in the Bavarian Law). The ritual visibly broke the original rights of the giver and made clear the change in formal ownership, which would otherwise have been masked by the continuity of possession. This purpose could also be accomplished by reigniting a hearth fire extinguished by the giver or by entertaining guests. In practice, the ritual was carried out not by the new owner in person but by someone designated for the purpose; churches frequently used unfree.

32. See Rosenwein, *To Be the Neighbor*, 65–68, and esp. the conclusion, 202–7.

33. See *TF* 514 (Chapter 5).

property at Geiselbach near Isen.[34] The two men belonged to the broader kin group surrounding the monastery of Saint Zeno at Isen.[35] They, or at least Rihhart, had already enjoyed a long and cordial relationship with Freising. Sometime around 806, Rihhart and a kinsman had given property in the area around Isen to Freising; in 836, Rihhart had received a benefice from Freising in exchange for another gift.[36]

The document recording the dispute between Arperht and Rihhart begins in a way that echoes both the formal *placitum* report and the informal notice and is thus impossible really to classify as either: "So that it is not unknown to all how the venerable man Bishop Erchanbert and many others with him whose names are inserted below gathered in the public place which is called Dorfen."[37] The priest Rihhart and his advocate sued the deacon Arperht and his advocate for the basilica at Geiselbach and the property attached to it. Rihhart claimed that Arperht had unjustly taken the church from him. Arperht's advocate responded that Arperht possessed the property legally according to an agreement that Rihhart himself had entered into. The agreement was as follows: Rihhart himself, his father Hartwic, the

---

34. *TF* 704; "Kysalpahc" = modern Ober/Untergeiselbach, ca. seven kilometers north of Isen.

35. They were connected in particular to two branches of the Isen group that we have encountered before: the Wichelm/Eigil/Kiso branch discussed earlier (*TF* 636) and the branch surrounding our previous acquaintances the priest Arperht and his nephews Jacob and Simon (*TF* 151, 152, 247, and 345). The connection with Wichelm/Eigil/Kiso is apparent in the fact that both groups had property in Strogn (see n. 36). The connection between the Arperht/Jacob/Simon group, which owned property in Frauenvils and Elsenbach, and this one, which concerns a deacon Arperht, his advocate Adalhoh, and property in Ober/Untergeiselbach, is revealed in *TF* 103 (780): one Adalo [*sic*] gave half his property and a church in Ober/Untergeiselbach to the church at Mehnbach; a priest, Arperht (presumably the uncle of Jacob and Simon), acted as the second witness.

36. In *TF* 241, produced sometime between 806 and 810, Rihhart and the deacon Heimperht gave property and a church at Neufahrn to Freising. In *TF* 613 from 836, in a transaction carried out at the monastery at Isen itself, Rihhart gave property at Geiselbach and Strogn to Freising in exchange for a benefice at Strogn. There was another priest Rihhart who in *TF* 211 (804–7) gave property at Gross/Kleinhelfendorf and in *TF* 523c (825) renewed this gift and another he had made of property in Heimatshofen. It is unlikely that the two priests were the same person, since there is no overlap in the witness list with any of the charters mentioned here (save for the priest Eio in *TF* 211 and an Eiio [*sic*] in *TF* 613).

37. According to Bitterauf, "Dorfa" = Oberdorfen, ca. ten kilometers northeast of Isen.

deacon Heimperht, the *iudex* Ellanperht, and a man named Hemmi had originally given the church to Freising. They had done so on the condition that Arpehrt should have it until the day of his death, after him Rihhart, if he should survive him, and after Rihhart the deacon Wolfperht, if he should survive him. After the death of all three, the property would then revert wholly to Freising's control.

At this point, Bishop Erchanbert declared that he wanted to end the dispute, and "it was done so with the consent of both parties." The deacon Arperht and his advocate pledged twenty solidos that they would honor the original arrangement. They immediately handed over forestland and other goods equivalent to the amount of their pledge. Next, everyone connected with the original arrangement swore on a reliquary of Saint Mary to renew it unchanged. Finally, Rihhart gave property of his own to Freising "so that he might merit to receive some solace." The notice ends with a list of the witnesses "who saw and heard that this was legally done according to the custom of the Bavarians."

This is the first time since 791 that we have seen members of a kindred take an internal property dispute to a bishop of Freising for resolution.[38] In this case, the move makes perfect sense because it concerned a preexisting gift/benefice/inheritance arrangement with Freising. On the face of the account, Bishop Erchanbert behaved in much the same way as Archbishop Arn of Salzburg did; he stood above both parties and brokered a settlement.[39] The source of Erchanbert's authority is clear enough. Not only did he act as a bishop overseeing a dispute between two churchmen (the priest Rihhart and the deacon Arperht); as bishop of Freising, he really "owned" the property at issue.

The substance of the settlement, however, places Erchanbert's activity in a different light. The person who was first in line for the property under the original agreement, the deacon Arperht, pledged as part of the settlement to honor the agreement, that is, to allow the property to pass to Rihhart after his own death. Since the issue would presumably arise only after Arperht's death, this pledge rested on a tacit commitment by Bishop Erchanbert to allow what was ultimately Freising's property to pass from Arperht to Rihhart. Moreover, the bishop himself benefited from the settlement, since Rihhart as his part of the peacemaking deal gave some more of his own property to Freising. In short, Bishop Erchanbert did not really stand above the two disputing parties. Instead, all the parties involved, including the bishop,

38. See the discussion of *TF* 142 (791) in the Interlude.
39. See Chapter 3.

came together to bind one another more tightly into the inheritance/benefice agreement concerning the basilica and its property. The bishop himself played an integral role in both the dispute and its resolution and came away with his own reward.

PERSONAL VIOLENCE

I end this chapter by returning to an issue that has cropped up on the margins of our property disputes: violence. Evidence for violence as a way to handle conflict in Bavaria first surfaced under the Agilolfings; people wounded by violent assaults responded with property gifts to a church or monastery.[40] Violence, albeit against property, again intruded into the Freising records in the first decade of the ninth century; in 808, Bishop Atto had to compensate Kyppo for buildings damaged in the course of their *contentio*.[41]

Violence appears in the records in another way, especially in the period under discussion here: in references to wergeld, that is, the blood price paid for personal injury or death. The Bavarian Law contains extensive and detailed provisions for the types and amounts of compensation to be paid for injury or death.[42] The wergeld for killing a free man, for example, was one hundred sixty solidi, in addition to a forty-solidi fine due the fisc.[43] This amount, two hundred solidi, shows up once in the charters between 765 and 767; as discussed in Chapter 1, the brothers Reginolt and Egino had to sell property to Freising in exchange for approximately *CC solidos*. The coincidence of the amount with the terms of the Bavarian Law suggests they were raising wergeld money.[44]

Wergeld surfaces unequivocally in the charters in 814. A Freising charter from that year reads: "These are the witnesses Hleoperht provided concerning the territory he gave Kernand for the wergeld of the priest Hroadolf in Allershausen."[45] This short note implies that Hleoperht had killed Hroadolf, who was related to Kernand. It does not reveal any more than that.[46]

40. See Chapter 1.
41. *TF* 275 (Chapter 4).
42. See esp. *Lex B* C. IV.
43. See Chapter 1, n. 22.
44. *TF* 24b.
45. *TF* 318b.
46. The names of Kernand and the priest Hroadolf appear with some frequency in the Freising charters, but not in any explicit relationship to each other. The prosopographical problem is compounded by the existence of another priest Hroadolf who lived on past 814: see *TF* 356 (816), 412 (819).

Neither does it say with absolute certainty that Hleopert actually killed Hroadolf, since wergeld could also serve as a way to compensate other kinds of injury, such as violating the terms of a charter.[47] If the record does describe murder compensation, the property involved must have been quite valuable, since the Bavarian Law dictates a wergeld for a dead priest of three hundred solidi in gold or equivalent property.[48]

Wergeld does not show up again in the charters until 830; then it appears in 846 and again in 853.[49] It is highly tempting to see these later references to wergeld as evidence that personal violence in Bavaria increased during the reign of Louis the German. This inference would be dangerous. A few scattered references to wergeld merely represent the tip of a greater iceberg of violence that impinged on the charters only when someone decided, or needed, to raise wergeld by selling property to the church. They do not provide enough evidence to say how that iceberg developed over time.

The last two wergeld references, however, lead straight back to the issue we are most concerned with here, the ubiquitous settlement of dispute by compromise during Bishop Erchanbert's reign. These two references to wergeld involve Erchanbert directly. They end not in formal wergeld payments according to the terms of the Bavarian Law but rather in deals that, like the ones just discussed, left the bishop and his opponent in an ongoing relationship with each other.

In 846, a nobleman and local official (*sculdhaisus*) named Isanparto arranged with Bishop Erchanbert and his advocate the wergeld of one of Isanparto's unfree, the barschalk Kaganhart.[50] In other words, someone for whom Bishop Erchanbert was responsible killed Kaganhart, for whom Isanparto was responsible. The two parties settled the incident without fuss, in a manner that apparently satisfied Isanparto's honor and at the same time left him connected to Freising. Bishop Erchanbert compensated Isanparto with

47. For example, *TF* 8 (755) includes a penalty clause in which someone violating the terms of the charter had to pay his own wergeld "as is customary." See also *Lex B* C. VIII/1–2; C. IX/4; C. XVI/5.

48. *Lex B* C. I/9.

49. *TF* 592ab, 679, 738.

50. *TF* 679. A *sculdhaisus* appears to have been a bearer of authority subordinate to a count, responsible for executing comital decisions (and collecting fines—hence the name *sculdhaisus* = Schuldenheischer = "debt collector"); see Ganshof, *Frankish Institutions*, 33, 93, and Hermann Conrad, *Deutsche Rechtsgeschichte*, vol. 1 (Karlsruhe, 1962), 104. On the barschalks, that is, the "noble unfree" possibly descended from the Agilolfing adalschalks, see the Introduction, n. 32.

a benefice consisting of a "suitable" (*aptam*) *colonica*.[51] In exchange, Isanparto agreed to pay Freising a rent of thirty denarii or one gold solidus each year on the feast of Saint Martin.

A similar but much more interesting record comes from the year 853.[52] This record points up again the flexibility of venue that characterized Bavarian dispute settlement; the main requirement was a large gathering of sufficiently prestigious witnesses. A great number of noblemen of the province had gathered at Freising on the feast of Saint Corbinian to pursue "worship with divine prayers as is the custom of Christians." A nobleman named Engilperht came among them and claimed that his daughter had been "murdered by poison through the malevolent exertions and machinations of a maidservant of the *familia* of Saint Mary." After the maidservant in question failed to defend herself, Bishop Erchanbert, "mercifully settling this unjust deed," agreed to compensate Engilperht. The bishop gave Engilperht a *colonica* for his lifetime and for the lifetimes of his sons. In addition, he gave Engilperht a benefice held by another priest under the conditions that he pay the same rent as the priest and agree to serve the see of Freising faithfully. Engilperht was satisfied; "he settled everything that had been done unjustly to him."

As in the previous case, here Bishop Erchanbert compensated a murder carried out by one of his own with property given as a benefice. The benefice arrangement bound Engilperht as well as his sons into an ongoing relationship with Freising.[53] Both these wergeld cases, therefore, fit nicely

51. In a place whose name is unfortunately hidden by a gap in the copy. Since we do not know the location of the property involved, we cannot say whether Isanparto had already been in some sort of relationship with Freising. The names Isanparto and Kaganhart suggest connections to the Huosi. Isanparto is an idiosyncratic spelling that appears three times in Freising witness lists over a period from 810 to 870 (*TF* 200g, *TF* 679, *TF* 899); this fact makes it dangerous to identify it with the much more common (and clearly Huosi/Scharnitz-Schlehdorf) name Isanperht. The name Kaganhart appears twice in charters relating to the Scharnitz-Schlehdorf monastery (*TF* 77, *TF* 184ab), suggesting a possible link between the barschalk Kaganhart and the Scharnitz-Schlehdorf kindred. If there was a connection between Isanparto and the Scharnitz-Schlehdorfer, it is possible that Isanparto's wergeld claim and its settlement did not disturb but rather reinforced an ongoing association with Freising.

52. *TF* 738. This notice has survived only in the twelfth-century copy made by the Freising sacristan Conrad.

53. This particular Engilperht defies exact identification, preventing us from saying for certain whether the settlement adjusted a previously existing relationship in the wake of the murder. See Störmer, *Adelsgruppen*, 70–77, on the name Engilperht.

with the other disputes discussed in this chapter. Bishop Erchanbert and his opponents worked out mutually acceptable settlements, settlements that left honor and material claims satisfied while creating, maintaining, or reinforcing ongoing relationships between the two parties involved.

Between 836 and 854—a period that saw Bavaria become part of Louis the German's newly won East Frankish kingdom—the impact of central authority visible in the Bavarian charters after the Carolingian takeover became extremely diffuse. Not to mislead: the Freising records clearly indicate that formal venues for resolving disputes headed by officeholding authority figures still existed and functioned. The records make it equally clear, however, that the Freising scribes regarded these formal proceedings as more or less irrelevant. According to the records they wrote, the scribes focused their attention instead on settlements worked out directly between Bishop Erchanbert and his opponents. These settlements recognized the formal rights of the bishop while meeting the de facto expectations of his opponents. With only one exception, they left both parties in a strengthened or altered but nonetheless ongoing relationship. In the exception, the dispute between Bishop Erchanbert and the brothers Isanhard and Ellanhard, it seems that the two parties divided up the property at issue and went their separate ways.

Compromises of this sort have shown up before, of course, both in the Freising charters and in the other collections. Before 836, however, they appeared alongside records describing the settlement of dispute by adjudication according to the rules of the formal *placitum* (although the lack of context available for many of these disputes makes it unwise to rule out later compromise).[54] The fact that after 836 the scribes acknowledged the existence of these formal mechanisms only by implication, or as a starting point for the real business of negotiating a settlement, marks a significant change in the evidence. This change suggests that formal adjudication, at least in the eyes of Freising's scribes, was no longer an important part of the repertoire of conflict. The scribes felt instead that the interests of their church were better served by recording the substance of extrajudicial settlements and how those settlements affected relationships between Freising and the people connected to it through property.

54. See, for example, the Hroadolt and Engilman case, *TF* 507, discussed in Chapter 5, where the context suggests a later compromise.

When Freising's scribes wrote their accounts of dispute settlements in this period, they employed the "act of mercy" script almost formulaically to describe settlements reached both in the context of formal assemblies and outside them. As discussed previously, this narrative pattern benefited Freising by upholding its rights while representing (either unavoidable or desired) compromises as voluntary acts of Christian charity. It thus saved face for Freising and preserved its future room for maneuver.[55] The dominant role played in the charters by the "act of mercy" pattern after 836 raises once again the question whether these representations reflect "real" dispute resolution. In other words, do these formulaically constructed compromise narratives simply represent the scribes' efforts to control the memory of a dispute for their church's benefit? Or did the larger society beyond the charters see this ritualistic dance of surrender and merciful countergesture as the accepted way to communicate publicly the balance of rights, face, and concession needed to achieve a lasting settlement? On the one hand, we have already found that charters could serve to control information and image at the expense of competing representations. On the other, Gerd Althoff has argued for precisely such a use of surrender and mercy as a means of ritually communicating dispute settlement among the highest German nobility of the tenth and eleventh centuries. Drawing on a variety of narrative sources, Althoff has put together an impressive array of stories about rebellious nobles undergoing a ritual and abject surrender (*deditio*), only shortly afterward to have the king mercifully restore them to their former lands, rights, and status. Arguing that these stories must have resonated with contemporary audiences, Althoff has made a cogent case for this kind of ritual pattern as a commonly accepted, even necessary, way to represent publicly a dispute settlement.[56]

The Freising charters have given us plenty of evidence that eighth- and ninth-century Bavarians also communicated dispute settlements by means of public ritual (recall, for example, the ritual use of a pig to seal the peace between Kyppo and Bishop Atto). This evidence, when seen in the light of Althoff's findings, makes a strong argument for the "act of mercy" script not just as a way of describing a compromise in writing but also by 836 as

---

55. See Chapter 4.

56. See Althoff, "Das Privileg der *deditio*: Formen gütlicher Konfliktbeendigung in der mittelalterlichen Adelsgesellschaft," 99–125, and "Königsherrschaft und Konfliktbewältigung," 21–56, both in *Spielregeln*, as well as the discussion of the *deditio* in Chapter 7. On the importance of such rituals of supplication to the political order of tenth- and eleventh-century France see Geoffrey Koziol, *Begging Pardon and Favor: Ritual and Political Order in Early Medieval France* (Ithaca, N.Y., 1992).

the accepted way of ritually acting out a compromise in a situation concerning the interest and prestige of someone powerful.

Nevertheless, these Freising records remain Freising productions. It is less easy than for narrative chronicles to argue that they must have resonated with a wide audience. In fact, it is not all that obvious who the audience for these charters was (we have only fleeting references to charters produced at trials), just that there must have been an audience, given the creative effort scribes expended on constructing their records.[57] In short, it is hard to support in a bullet-proof way the claim that the "act of mercy" charters tell stories of settlements in which everyone involved agreed what had happened. Philippe Buc's recent work on the written representation of public ritual has made it quite clear that one aspect of the competition for power in the Carolingian world consisted of the struggle for control over the meaning and representation of events.[58]

Even so, we still learn something very important about the world beyond the records from the changes that took place in how the scribes constructed the records. The fact that after 836 no more *placitum* reports in the classic sense appear in the Freising collection indicates that the mechanisms of extrajudicial dispute settlement between the bishop and his neighbors and kin, not the intervention of a third-party authority, had become for the scribes the most important part of resolving property disputes. This finding in turn points to two more conclusions. First, in the arena of everyday social interaction at the local and regional levels, the Bavarian bishops had by 836 gained a great deal of power at the expense of Carolingian authority. Bishop Erchanbert, despite his own ties to Louis the German, no longer felt it was in his interest to let official judicial assemblies or officeholders tell him how to settle property disputes. Second, the bishop's neighbors and kin had gained a great deal of power with respect to the bishop. The bishop now had to take the interests of his opponents into account in all cases, not just in some.

---

57. For example, in *TF* 227 (806), the cleric Wago displayed charters and the names of the witnesses listed in them before a judicial assembly; see Chapter 2. *TF* 240 (806–10) refers to the advocate Einhard's inability to offer proof of a claim "either in writing or in the form of witnesses"; see Chapter 4. In *TF* 703a (discussed earlier), the priest Erchanfrid is defeated by "truthful witnesses and written documents."

58. See Philippe C. Buc, "Martyre et ritualité dans l'Antiquité tardive: Horizons de l'écriture médiévale des rituels," *Annales ESC* 48, no. 1 (1997): 63–92, and *The Dangers of Ritual: The Politics of Medieval Anthropology* (Princeton, forthcoming), esp. chap. 2.

One need only think of the way Bishop Atto of Freising could make his interpretations of gift charters stick in judicial assemblies immediately after the Carolingian takeover to see the difference.[59] All this tells us that the strong impression made by Carolingian authority and institutions on local Bavarian disputing practices had begun to fade

59. See Chapter 2.

CONCLUSION

THE SOURCES AFTER 854

In the second half of the ninth century, our sources of information about Bavarian disputing change drastically. The rich, detailed ecclesiastical charters characteristic of the late eighth and first half of the ninth centuries disappear. Their place is taken by a vast sea of short exchange notices. These notices, a few lines long at most and highly formulaic, record exchanges of property between a church and another landowner. It is hard to explain why they suddenly dominate the Bavarian charter collections, although several scholars have tried. Heinrich Fichtenau, for example, has suggested that by the 850s landowners had cleared and populated all the land in Bavaria they could. As a result, Bavarian aristocrats simply had no more land left to give; property relationships between them and the churches could continue only in the form of exchanges designed to round out and consolidate holdings.[1] Both Störmer and Jahn, in contrast, have argued that the change represents an aristocratic reaction against the extension of episcopal power. When the Bavarian bishops began after 800 to assert their rights over aristocratic church and monastic foundations, the aristocrats gradually stopped giving property to churches and monasteries. By the second half of the ninth century, such gifts came almost completely to a halt; the exchanges that replaced them served only mutual interests in property consolidation.[2]

---

1. Fichtenau, *Urkundenwesen*, 99–100.

2. Jahn, *"Tradere ad sanctum,"* in *Gesellschaftsgeschichte*, ed. Seibt, 412–13; Störmer, *Früher Adel*, 2:374–81. Störmer also suggests that repeated fighting in the East in this period made it necessary for the Bavarian aristocracy to keep as much of its property as it could. He notes in addition that Louis the German issued a series of privileges granting permission to carry out such exchanges, inter alia to the abbot of Niederaltaich/bishop of Würzburg, the archbishop of Salzburg, and the bishop of Passau; Störmer interprets this royal permission as indicating a sudden need for exchanges. See also Geneviève Bührer-Thierry, "Formes des donations aux églises et stratégies des familles en Bavière du VIIIe siècle aux Xe siècle," *Mélanges de l'École*

The latter explanation in particular leaves some dangling threads. As we have seen, one cannot treat the church and the aristocracy as entirely separate interest groups. The dispute records from the first decades of the ninth century reflect competition among members of aristocratic kindreds as much as the encroachment of the church on aristocratic property. It seems highly unlikely that those aristocrats who had developed profitable cooperative arrangements with the church via property, or the bishops who were themselves regional aristocrats, would suddenly decide in the 850s to end relationships of mutual benefit.

The sources themselves also present a puzzle. Much of the evidence for change comes from the fact that Cozroh's collection of the Freising charters ends and a new Freising collection, a *codex commutationum*, or "book of exchanges," begins.[3] It seems dangerous to argue for a shift from gifts to exchanges based on the testimony of a codex devoted to exchanges. It will take a great deal more work to ascertain how much of the phenomenon rests on a real change in behavior and how much of it reflects an impression created by the surviving sources.[4]

Be that as it may, this change in the nature of the available sources drastically restricts our ability to study disputing. Only three Bavarian documents from the second half of the ninth century have survived that record disputes settled without the direct involvement of a king. Two come from Freising, and one comes from Regensburg. Together these records reveal that despite the dearth of documentary evidence, property disputes similar to those that took place earlier were continuing to occur. The Regensburg record simply states that one Sicca and her advocate had sought part of a

---

Française de Rome 111, no. 2 (1999): 675–99, which places the change in the context of a longer development in Bavaria toward geographically closed territorial lordships; Hammer, "Land Sales," 48n. 3.

3. See Bitterauf's introduction to *TF*: xvii–xxxiii.

4. This is a difficult issue. Störmer in particular, according to his footnotes, seems to base his argument on Bitterauf's arrangement and consolidation of the Freising charter collections. As noted previously, however, Bitterauf's edition homogenizes the material and makes it appear to comprise a unified collection rather than an aggregate of different collections put together at different times for different purposes. Moreover, the Freising notices do not present the entire story for Bavaria; as Fichtenau points out, the Passau records show the continuous presence of gifts alongside exchanges throughout the ninth century (Fichtenau, *Urkundenwesen*, 99–100). One could argue, however, that the Freising *scriptorium* found it necessary to put together and preserve a *codex commutationum* only because exchanges had replaced gifts as the most important transactions for the Freising cathedral church.

church and its property but had dropped their claim.[5] The two Freising records provide a bit more detail. The first, from the year 860, states that a woman named Hiltfrid had held a *colonia* as a benefice from Freising but had tried to claim it as her own.[6] After an investigation by Freising's advocate, Hiltfrid admitted defeat and gave the property to Freising. The second briefly describes the mediation by Bishop Erchanbert's successor, Anno, of a property dispute between two other parties; Bishop Anno was involved because his church ultimately owned the property at issue.[7] Sometime between 860 and 869, one Adalfrid had a property dispute with a local notable (*sculthazus*) named Atto.[8] The two men went to Bishop Anno because "the matter (*causa*) pertained to him." In the bishop's presence, Adalfrid vindicated his rights with an oath to the effect that his wife was to have possession of the property until her death, at which point it would revert entirely to the cathedral church at Freising.

In the only other dispute records available for Bavaria in the second half of the ninth century, Carolingian kings directly participated in the settlement process.[9] It is only in these cases that royal authority has any impact on property disputes. Not surprisingly, it is also only in these cases that we see any remaining traces of the *placitum* form. In 855, for example, King Louis the German dealt with a dispute between Bishop Anno of Freising and Bishop Odalschalc of Trent over some vineyards at Bozen in northern Lombardy.[10] The record, which apparently represents Freising's point of view, charges that Bishop Odalschalc had unjustly seized the vineyards from

---

5. *TR* 67 (863–85).

6. *TF* 862. Cf. the discussion of *TF* 345, 437, 438, and 604 in Chapter 5.

7. *TF* 864. Cf. the discussion of *TF* 704 in Chapter 6. Anno's accession to the episcopal throne at Freising in 854 possibly represented a shift in the balance of power among the kindreds surrounding the see of Freising; according to Störmer, *Früher Adel*, 2:332, Anno stemmed from a different aristocratic kin group than his predecessors, who were connected to the Huosi.

8. On the *sculthazus*, or *sculdhaisus*, see Chapter 6, n. 50.

9. In addition to the two discussed later, see *TP* 88 (887), in which Louis the German's youngest son, Charles III, confirmed Passau in the possession of a disputed piece of forest land; and four diplomas of Louis the German's illegitimate grandson Arnulf that deal with dispute: *Die Urkunden Arnolfs*, ed. P. Kehr, *MGH DrG Karol* III (Berlin, 1940), 75, 112–13 (890); 76, 114–15 (890); 132, 197–99 (895); 175, 264–65 (899).

10. *Die Urkunden Ludwigs des Deutschen, Karlmanns und Ludwigs des Jüngeren*, ed. P. Kehr, *MGH DrG Karol* I (Berlin, 1934), 72, 101–2. The record survives in a copy by Conrad the Sacristan.

Freising during the upheaval surrounding Anno's election as bishop, when "tumultuous events were taking place in the see of Freising." The narrative then begins to follow the *placitum* pattern. While staying at Aibling in Bavaria, King Louis received an embassy that included two *missi* sent by his nephew Louis II, king of the Lombards, as well as two of Bishop Odalschalc's advocates.[11] The embassy disputed Freising's claim to the vineyards. Louis the German asked what the law was concerning the matter; he was told that Freising should produce witnesses to an unbroken thirty-year possession of the disputed property. Bishop Anno promptly produced the witnesses, who swore to Freising's possession of the property before King Louis's right-hand man in Bavaria, Count Ernest.[12] Count Ernest then asked the assembled how justice ought to be done. They responded that the property should remain forever in the possession of Freising, a judgment to which King Louis and the Lombard *missi* (the latter "inevitably") assented.

A Carolingian could also influence a property dispute simply by being present. Sometime around 869, a wealthy nun named Peretkund went to Freising. There she met with Bishop Anno and his leading men (*procerum*) and gave a great deal of property to the Freising cathedral church. Part of the property was in the area to the immediate north and west of Freising itself,[13] and the other part was located at Pitten, in what is now Lower Austria.[14] Shortly afterward, Peretkund found herself embroiled in a dispute

11. Louis II was the eldest son of Louis the German's elder brother Lothar; he became king of Italy in 840. This charter identifies Louis II not by name but simply as *rex Longobardorum*.

12. Count Ernest, who most likely came from a Frankish family, first appears in Louis the German's entourage in a Regensburg charter of 829 (*TR* 24). By 849, he is described in the Annals of Fulda as "duke and first among the friends of the king." In the dispute record under discussion here, Ernest is referred as the leader (*ductor*) of a Bavarian army sent into Bohemia; in the Annals of Fulda for 861, he appears again as "first of all the nobles." Ernest's prominence has led some to suggest that Louis the German installed him as a subregnal governor of Bavaria; see *HbG*, 265.

13. *TF* 898a: the property was in Rohrbach and in Rudlfing.

14. *TF* 898b. On the property locations in *TF* 898ab, see Bitterauf, notes to *TF* 898; Störmer, *Adelsgruppen*, 114n. 10. Peretkund's behavior supports the conclusion that Bavarian landholders in the second half of the ninth century were striving to consolidate their property holdings. The following year, Peretkund gave more property in Lower Austria to Freising in exchange for benefices in Kienberg, Allershausen, Langenpettenbach, and Weil—all locations to the immediate west and south of Freising (*TF* 899). She was evidently trying to divest herself of her property in Lower Austria in favor of concentrated benefices to the west of Freising.

over the property at Pitten with a count named Kundharius, to whom she may have been related.[15] In the fall of 869, she went to Baden, also in Lower Austria near Vienna. There she caught up with the court of Carloman, the eldest son of Louis the German, who had been named king of the Bavarians by his father in 865 and who was traveling in the region with a large number of retainers.[16] In Carloman's presence, Peretkund publicly asked whether anyone wished to contest her right to give the property at Pitten wherever she wished.[17] Count Kundharius responded that the property belonged to him by hereditary right and that Peretkund had no right to give it to any church. Six witnesses were brought forward; they testified in Peretkund's favor. Defeated, Kundharius withdrew his challenge. Peretkund then renewed her original gift to Freising in Carloman's presence. In exchange, she received a benefice, whether of the property in Pitten or of other property is not made clear.

This document, like the one involving Louis the German himself, contains the essential elements of a *placitum*: statement, counterstatement, testimony, surrender. Unlike the earlier record, however, this notice does not describe the royal son Carloman as actually doing anything of substance. What mattered to the unknown scribe who wrote Peretkund's record, and presumably also to Peretkund herself, was Carloman's presence. The scribe went out of his way twice to note that something had taken place *coram Karlmanno*—"in the presence of Carloman"—first when Peretkund raised the dispute and again when she renewed her original gift and received her benefice. In other words, the presence of a Carolingian in the region justi-

15. *TF* 898c. The shared name element *kund* suggest that Kundharius and Peretkund were relatives, but the record does not make their relationship clear. The descriptions of their competing claims to the property do not help matters. Kundharius claimed the property by hereditary right according to the grant of one Ratpod (*iure hereditario per traditionem Ratpodi*). The six witnesses, however, testified that Peretkund's father had given her the property. Störmer, *Adelsgruppen*, 114n. 10, concludes from the phrase *iure hereditario* that Kundharius and Peretkund were relatives; he links them to both the Fagana and the Huosi.

16. Carloman had been assigned Bavaria under the terms of a division of the East Frankish kingdom worked out by Louis the German in 865. The division was not to take place until after Louis's death, but Carloman seems to have begun exercising authority in Bavaria anyway. See *HbG*, 271.

17. The beginning of the charter does not specify which property Peretkund was referring to; we learn from the ending that it was the property at Pitten that was at issue.

fied a lengthy journey to have his stamp placed on the settlement of a property dispute. A king mattered in 869, if he happened to be in the area.

In the foregoing chapters, I have looked at dispute resolution in eighth- and ninth-century Bavaria as a dynamic and constantly evolving process. In other words, I have tried not only to form general conclusions about disputing in the entire period under discussion but also to observe the rhythm, the ebb and flow, of disputing as it reacted over time to political change.

This rhythm emerges clearly from the sources. During the Agilolfing period, there is considerable evidence for conflict within and among the Bavarian aristocratic kindreds. The conflict nevertheless shows up tangentially in the church property records. The memory of a dispute survived in the church archives not because the church itself was a party to it but because the dispute resulted in a property gift to the church or because its settlement somehow involved church property rights. Some of the conflicts appearing in this fashion involved violence between aristocrats. The charters do not tell us what caused the violence. They reveal only that members of the kindreds were fighting with one another over something. A possible explanation comes from Arbeo of Freising's *Life of Saint Emmeram*. In composing this saint's life, Arbeo drew on the ethic of feud as the central device that permitted his hero Emmeram to die a Christ-like death at the hands of an Agilolfing prince. Arbeo's description—and criticism—of an aristocratic culture in Agilolfing Bavaria that embraced violent revenge suggests that culture may also have lain behind some of the violence visible in the charters.

Other disputes during this period were handled peacefully. In these cases, the cause for conflict emerges clearly from the records: competition for property within the landholding kindreds. In the examples that survive in the Freising records, people caught up in this competition turned to kin group councils, to the local bishop, or to the Agilolfing duke for help in resolving their disputes. When a conflict over property erupted within a kindred, a wider circle of relatives advised resort to the bishop. The bishop in turn cooperated by accepting a property gift, either to settle the inheritance arrangements of someone who had been attacked or to defuse conflict by removing disputed property from the sphere of possible competition. Duke Tassilo III, in his single appearance in a Freising dispute record, acted as a mediator.

All the parties involved in the dispute records from the Agilolfing period were tightly linked to one another. The aristocratic landowners, the bishops, and the duke came from the same aristocratic society. Moreover, all, including the bishops and the duke, were connected to one another by kinship, sometimes made explicit, at other times implicit in naming patterns and property holdings. The duke could not separate his public interests from his interests as the head of an extended network of interrelated aristocrats. The stability of the Agilolfing duchy depended on the internal stability of kindreds to which the duke was bound by both politics and blood.

The Bavarian churches too had their own interests. During the Agilolfing period, these interests were intertwined with those of the aristocratic kindreds and the duke. Bavarian bishops cooperated with the kindreds and the duke as they founded and endowed new churches and monasteries. The bishops consecrated churches built by landholders and accepted them as gifts, or participated with the duke in the foundation of kindred monasteries. Nevertheless, they allowed members of the kindreds who had founded the churches or monasteries to continue to control them. These cooperative arrangements honored episcopal rights over churches and monasteries while respecting the needs of the kindreds to settle their spiritual and property affairs, provide for heirs, and find solutions for conflict. At the same time, such arrangements satisfied the dukes' need to have loyal kindreds retain de facto control of the often extensive properties attached to their religious foundations.

Although in the charter collections we find little evidence of conflict that directly involved the church, images from this period of a bishop as a party to dispute appear in Arbeo of Freising's *Life of Saint Corbinian*. This sacred biography of Freising's first bishop projects an almost scripted picture of dispute resolution. According to Arbeo, the ideal bishop/saint, when faced with injury to his property rights or moral precepts, did not appeal to any earthly judicial authority. Instead, he responded with measures designed to force the total surrender of his opponent. Only after his opponent had yielded unconditionally did the saint mercifully allow an end to the conflict. In one case, Arbeo added a supplicating group to this "act of mercy" script. By appealing to his Christian duty to be merciful, the group allowed the saint to make peace without sacrificing his principles.

The first signs of change come in 791, three years after Charlemagne sent Duke Tassilo into monastic exile. In the Freising charter recording the settlement of the dispute among the Huosi over the church at Haushausen, uncertainty and fluidity suddenly appear in the disputing process. At first, the record matches the charters that precede it; a dispute within a kindred over property led to a gathering of the kindred. The leaders of the kindred council advised resort to the bishop of Freising, just as the preceding evidence suggests they would have. The process took a new turn, however, when Bishop Atto of Freising sent the dispute to a new forum: a gathering of the royal *missi*. As this step reveals, a process was under way of grappling with and adjusting to a change both in the power structure in Bavaria and in the sources of authority available for settling disputes.

Bishop Atto's decision to refer the Huosi to *missi* to resolve their dispute makes sense in light of the dispute records that follow. These records show that the Carolingian conquest transformed the playing field for property disputes. Officeholding representatives of the new regime with an interest in introducing Frankish judicial practice into Bavaria upheld the literal terms of property gifts, as well as the letter of church rights over donated property, at the expense of the customary arrangements that had pertained under the Agilolfings. The officials and their judicial assemblies thus provided the Bavarian bishops with a new resource they could exploit in their own interest. To put it more simply, what it meant for the church to "own" property changed. Whereas before the Carolingian takeover a gift of property to a church had left the grantor and his kindred with considerable rights over it, afterward the churches could expect, with the support of the judicial assemblies, to exercise real control over donated property. The preexisting tension between church rights and aristocratic property interests, formerly weighted in favor of the aristocracy, now became weighted on the side of the church. Not that the officeholders heading the judicial assemblies always supported episcopal expansionism; they seem rather to have enforced above all the strict terms of property gifts regardless of which way they cut. Nonetheless, the new atmosphere provided the bishops an opportunity to acquire and control property more aggressively.

The picture does not, however, show a monolithic church pitted against an equally monolithic lay aristocracy. The changes wrought by the Carolingian conquest divided landowning kindreds among themselves or, more likely, redirected the tensions within the kindreds already partially visible under the Agilolfings and moved them more clearly into the light of the church records. The way individual kindred members took sides in property disputes after the conquest illustrates this shift. Some aristocrats allied themselves with the church and against people demonstrably related to them by serving as witnesses at judicial assemblies, by serving as church advocates, or by acting themselves as authority figures overseeing judgments. Others exploited the new normative landscape to defend their property holdings against those with an interest in the same property by working out gift/benefice arrangements with the bishops. Within this divided world, the interests of the bishops interacted symbiotically with the interests of their allies and kin.[18]

These observations help us understand how and why Bavarians responded to Carolingian authority in the first two decades or so following the conquest. Bavarian landholding aristocrats accepted the authority figures representing the new regime and agreed to participate in the judicial assemblies at least in part because they saw it as in their interest to do so. The interest lay in the fact that the church and the Carolingian judicial assemblies could and did serve as resources for landholding aristocrats—whether they held church office or not—to exploit in the competition for property and power. In other words, the fact that the judicial assemblies upheld the literal terms of gifts to churches made both the churches and the assemblies useful for members of landholding kindreds in their disputes with one another. The dispute charters, however, indicate that the acceptance of Carolingian authority and institutions was neither seamless nor uniform and that some people gained from the conquest while others lost.

The Bavarian aristocracy's response to Carolingian authority allowed Charlemagne's allies in the region, especially Archbishop Arn of Salzburg, to import new and centralized-looking dispute-resolution mechanisms into the former duchy. Beginning in 802, the charters contain records of property disputes handled at formal judicial assemblies that followed a set of formal procedures, or that were at least represented as having followed these procedures in formulaic reports mimicking Frankish models. The charters of this type record a great deal of simple adjudication. Regardless of what happened in the world "outside" the records that the formulas do not reveal, the scribes, both those looking to Arn of Salzburg and those from the Bavarian cathedral churches, found it to be in their interest in many cases to record the delivery of a clear verdict in favor of one party or the other. When compromise settlements appear, as they sometimes do at this level, the scribes represent them as acts of power delivered from above. The potent role played by Arn in these settlements emerges not only from the reports written by his scribes but also from rewrites of Arn's records produced by Freising scribes as they tried to restore lost face and preserve future room for maneuver.

Despite their centralized and formal appearance, the judicial assemblies were not uniform and impersonal institutions. Judicial hearings took place in a wide variety of venues. The number and nature of the authority figures running them constantly changed, and the border between secular and ec-

18. See Geary, "Extra-Judicial Means of Conflict Resolution," 573.

clesiastical venues and disputes was extremely fluid. The only stable require-
ments for a formal *placitum* appear to have been publicity and the presence
of a sufficient number of prestigious authority figures. These authority figures exercised a highly personal kind of power. As best we can determine,
they themselves belonged to the Bavarian aristocracy; the most important of
them enjoyed connections to Charlemagne. Archbishop Arn of Salzburg,
the most visible authority figure in the records, drove the whole system. Arn
not only personally introduced the centralizing features that appear in
Bavaria after the Carolingian takeover; he had the ability to influence individual disputes to such a degree that scribes bent the *placitum* formulas to
accommodate him.

Moreover, the formal judicial assemblies did not dominate the disputing
stage. They coexisted with a vibrant and colorful culture of extrajudicial dispute resolution that shows signs of continuity with the Agilolfing past. At
this level, the two parties involved in a dispute worked out a settlement directly with each other, without any meaningful intervention by a third-party
authority figure. Such settlements were dominated by compromises that negotiated rights and face as well as material substance and used ritual to display relative power relationships. These compromises thus hark back to the
images of dispute resolution in the Agilolfing period projected by Arbeo of
Freising's *Life of Saint Corbinian*. In a few cases, they even follow in perfect
detail the "act of mercy" script we saw in the *Life*: a total surrender by one
party prompted a concession from the other couched as a voluntary act of
Christian charity. This narrative pattern allowed one party to a property
dispute to uphold its rights and its prestige while making the concession
necessary to achieve a settlement.

As the third and fourth decades of Carolingian rule in Bavaria pro-
gressed, the imprint of Carolingian authority on Bavarian disputing processes
remained strong. The use of the *placitum* formulas and procedures expanded;
rather than employ the form only in cases involving Arn of Salzburg, scribes
now used it to record cases headed both by other *missi* and by Bavarian
bishops and/or counts. Furthermore, Bavarian aristocrats remained very
much aware of the opportunities presented by shifts in imperial policy.
When Charlemagne's heir Louis the Pious made clear his intent to curb
abuses of property rights by the imperial fisc, his reforming policy triggered
an opportunistic response by Bishop Hitto of Freising that in turn touched
off a battery of disputes between the see of Freising and Bavarians claiming
to hold fiscal benefices.

Nevertheless, there are subtle signs that during the reign of Louis the
Pious the Carolingian impact on Bavaria was becoming more diffuse and
the locus of authority was beginning to revert to the regional level. To

begin with, the character of the imperial *missi* changes. The *missi* no longer crop up in the charter collections with anything like the frequency they showed under Arn's regime; no longer did they exercise a blanket jurisdiction. Instead, they appear sporadically, in a demonstrably ad hoc fashion tied to Freising's disputes with the fisc. Moreover, in one case a pair of special *missi* sent out by the emperor was unable or unwilling, in contrast to Charlemagne's *missi*, to defend the fisc's holdings against Freising's claims. *Missi* could still issue formal judgments, however; at any rate, scribes still recorded adjudications overseen by the *missi* in notices following the *placitum* form.

At the same time, the evidence for extrajudicial settlements increases and becomes more consistent. Such settlements were still characterized by efforts to balance rights and face against material concessions. According to the charter scribes, however, these efforts were becoming more standardized; the "act of mercy" narrative of bilateral compromise occurs much more regularly and predictably. More important, the charters indicate that the extrajudicial world had begun to stray into the judicial one. Church scribes were increasingly interested in recording, in the course of single narratives, dispute processes that started at formal venues but continued and reached their eventual conclusion outside them. This trend includes one record in which a scribe tacked a tiny "act of mercy" compromise onto the end of an otherwise perfectly normal *placitum* report. In short, the center of gravity of scribal attention had begun to shift ever so slightly, even in formally handled cases, toward extrajudicial disputing processes. As a consequence, it becomes easier to see how conflict could form part of ongoing relationships between the churches and their landowning neighbors, relationships the *placitum* formulas tended to mask.

By the late 830s, these changes become impossible to ignore. Extrajudicial and bilateral settlement has wholly captured scribal attention. Not that judicial assemblies headed by counts or bishops ceased to function; they still convened, as references to them in the records show. In this period, however, they had little impact on narratives of dispute. The scribes instead focused their attention entirely on the substance of negotiations and settlements worked out directly between the bishop and his opponent. The Freising dispute notices after 836 all record lengthy bilateral processes that involved a sequence of events stretched out over time and place. Most of these processes followed the "act of mercy" narrative, which by this point has become so predictable as to be itself formulaic. Only in dispute settlements directly overseen by a king do the records report adjudication or reveal any traces of the old *placitum* form. In disputes settled without direct royal involvement, the "act of mercy" script, not the *placitum* narrative, captured the information that scribes most wanted to preserve.

Most of the disputes from this period acted to regulate or adjust preexisting and ongoing relationships. It seems that by this point the landowners who did not want to ally themselves with the bishops had gone their own ways. In other words, as a result of decades of triage, the people appearing in the charters comprised only those who had chosen to continue in relationships with the cathedral churches.[19] Perhaps as a consequence, it appears that the bishops and the landholders associated with them were once again constructing their relationships as they had before the Carolingian conquest. Although bishops and landholders still clashed, in almost every dispute after 836 the parties created or restated their ties in such a way that, as in the arrangements surrounding churches and monasteries under the Agilolfings, they honored the rights of the bishops yet respected the de facto expectations of the bishops' allies.

Seen as a whole, these observations indicate that the authority of the Carolingian kings mattered in Bavaria but that their ability to influence people's behavior indirectly, through a set of statelike institutions, was relatively short-lived. Charlemagne's authority had an impact, and the institutions through which it was expressed worked, because Charlemagne and his allies in Bavaria rearranged the normative playing field on which Bavarian aristocrats competed for property in ways that made Carolingian authority an attractive resource. The initial success of the Carolingian regime in Bavaria depended on engaging local and regional self-interest; people appear to have accepted or even furthered the interests of the "new sheriff in town" because they could use those interests for their own purposes. As a result, Charlemagne and the Bavarian aristocrats who worked with him were able to introduce dispute-resolution mechanisms into Bavaria that affected people's behavior even when the king himself was not present.

Louis the Pious also made an impression on Bavaria. At least some of the players on the Bavarian stage were very aware of what he did and said and were quite prepared to exploit the opportunities created by his actions and policy statements. And yet over the long haul, it seems that the Carolingian impact changed in connection with transformation of the Carolingian Empire itself. The centralized-looking mechanisms visible in the charters sur-

---

19. Fichtenau sees in the charters from this period evidence for a "peaceful symbiosis" between church and nobility (*Urkundenwesen*, 100). If this suggestion is correct, however, we may be seeing only the activity of the aristocrats who had allied themselves with the church and missing the wider behavior of those who had not.

vived for perhaps the first generation after the conquest. The *missi* system never appeared again as so pervasive a part of the Bavarian disputing landscape after Arn of Salzburg's departure from the scene. Episcopal scribes continued to write formal reports; according to these reports, bishops and counts continued to use the formal *placitum* procedure. But this procedure had to compete more and more for scribal attention with extrajudicial methods of disputing until by the beginning of Louis the German's reign it appears to have lost altogether.

Not that things went back entirely to the way they had been under the Agilolfings: the Carolingian conquest permanently changed the landscape of dispute in Bavaria. Church rights remained part of the tactical repertoire of conflict. As a result, conflicts remained central rather than tangential to the records; landowners and church rubbed against each other as potential or active competitors throughout the ninth century. Branches of kindreds continued to make long-term property arrangements with the church that shut out other claimants. In other words, the normative framework within which the church and the landowning aristocracy operated had been altered forever by the fall of Duke Tassilo.

Nevertheless, things worked differently under Louis the German. With Louis and his successors, Bavaria had kings who were themselves regularly on the scene. The king himself, therefore, became the conduit for royal authority in the region.[20] One might argue that Louis the German replaced Arn of Salzburg.[21] Through Arn and other aristocratic allies in Bavaria, Charlemagne had been able to influence Bavarian disputing practices indirectly. What Charlemagne, and to a degree also Louis the Pious, did indirectly, Louis the German did directly by intervening personally in disputes—or, perhaps better, by making himself available as a source of authority to whom disputants could appeal. In this sense, Louis the German pointed not back to his grandfather but rather forward to the personal kind of kingship that would be more typical of the East in the centuries that followed.[22]

It must be stressed that this argument for the diminishing impact of Car-

20. See Goldberg, "Creating a Medieval Kingdom."

21. Eric Goldberg suggested this possibility to me in private conversation in the spring of 1999.

22. See the literature cited in the Introduction, n. 24, as well as Gerd Althoff and Hagen Keller, *Heinrich I. und Otto der Große: Neubeginn auf karolingischem Erbe* (Göttingen, 1985), and Reuter, *Germany in the Early Middle Ages*. Goldberg, "More Devoted," suggests that Louis the German forged a distinct East Frankish court culture that likewise points forward to that of the Ottonians.

olingian institutions in Bavaria does not aim to move the date of any "feudal revolution" forward to the 830s. It simply argues that the Carolingian "state," in a far-flung and newly absorbed corner of its empire, had an immediate and serious impact, but an impact whose success depended on engaging local self-interest and on raising prestigious members of regional aristocracy to positions of authority. This institutional state did not last very long in terms of its effectiveness on the ground; statelike institutions functioning without direct royal participation ceased to have any real meaning for the resolution of property disputes in Bavaria, or at least those involving the cathedral churches and monasteries, after the death of Louis the Pious. One can hardly, however, speak of a general "revolution." Circumstances of royal power and prestige, of aristocratic and ecclesiastical interests, or of scribal tradition obviously changed at different rates in different parts of Europe. The *missatica*, for example, continued to function deep into the ninth century in the western part of the Frankish world. In Wickham's Carolingian Lombardy, the formulaic *placitum* report continued in use, indeed became more formulaic, into the tenth century.[23]

Davies and Fouracre have pointed out that historians often see the effectiveness of a state in terms of adjudication versus compromise. According to this view, the number of uncompromising judgments in the records reflects the relative strength of the state. Davies and Fouracre find this contrast misleading, since state mechanisms could also generate compromise settlements. They argue instead that historians should look not at the varying impact of state intervention, or even at the varying acceptance of judgment over compromise, but rather at the extent to which people opted to use public institutions rather than negotiate privately.[24] The Bavarian evidence adds another dimension to their suggestion. The Freising charters in particular have produced lively evidence both for compromise in the context of state-sponsored institutions and for a level of compromise that took place outside them. I have measured the impact of state institutions in terms of their power to draw the attention of the scribes keeping the records. The fact that scribes chose over time to shift their attention from institutions and formal procedures to often lengthy processes of settlement, even though formal assemblies were still being held, is convincing evidence that they saw the institutions as less and less relevant to their affairs.

This argument also has some general methodological implications. It is

23. McKitterick, *Kingdoms*, 192; Nelson, *Charles the Bald*, 53–54, 260; Wickham, "Land Disputes," in *Settlement of Disputes*, ed. Davies and Fouracre, 106–7, 112.

24. Davies and Fouracre, "Conclusion: Dispute Processes," in *Settlement of Disputes*, 236–40.

based to a large degree on changes in representation, that is, on changes in what scribes chose to record and how they chose to record it. Indeed, as we have seen, the control of representation itself formed part of the game of power. It appears, therefore, that whether the texts studied here provide a window into the past or obscure it, the constructions of the texts themselves, how they changed over time, and to what purposes writers put them provide ways to understand what was going on in the world beyond the records.

BAVARIA BETWEEN WEST AND EAST

The picture of disputing in late-eighth- and ninth-century Bavaria developed in this book looks a great deal like that emerging from the scholarship on the early medieval West. In some respects, however, it also looks different. The similarities and the differences between the two help deepen our understanding of how authority might have functioned in an early medieval society and add substance to possibilities raised by previous research.

To begin with, Bavarian disputing in the period before the Carolingian takeover has some features in common with disputing in France after the Carolingian decline. Although Agilolfing Duke Tassilo III at his height represented a strong, quasi-royal ducal authority, that authority functioned in ways profoundly different from those assumed by a model that looks for effective impersonal institutions. The charters from Agilolfing Bavaria do not reveal any institutional structures for handling dispute.[25] Moreover, they show Bavarian aristocrats resorting to personal violence. Nonetheless, as in "stateless" France around the turn of the first millennium, there were clearly mechanisms that promoted stability. Kindred councils acted both as forums for airing grievances and as a source of advice about what course to pursue. Duke Tassilo himself, acting as the head of an interrelated network of aristocrats, brought authority to bear to resolve individual conflicts in line with his own interests in a way that renders meaningless a distinction between public and private relationships.

Where Agilolfing Bavaria differs from the early medieval West is in the role played in conflict by the Bavarian church. The Agilolfing-era charters do not show the Bavarian bishops as parties to property disputes. They appear rather as peacemaking figures.[26] Bishops and abbots cooperated will-

---

25. See the Interlude, n. 10, on references to judicial institutions in normative sources from the Agilolfing period and the problems with connecting these references to practice.

26. Geary, "Extra-Judicial Means of Conflict Resolution," 596, notes that since bishops in other areas mostly acted in a formal judicial capacity or appeared as par-

ingly (or, in the case of Bishop Virgil of Salzburg, unwillingly) with the dukes and landowning aristocrats not only to contain conflict but also to make property-holding arrangements that formed an important part of the Agilolfing duchy's constitutional structure.

After the Carolingian takeover of Bavaria, a world of disputing leaps into view that looks very much like that visible in the Carolingian West. Churches move into their more familiar role as parties to property disputes. The charters, like those from the West, reveal the undeniable existence of formal courts applying impersonal norms. Written documents, courts, laws, and offices all formed an important part of the tactical repertoire of conflict in Carolingian Bavaria; Bavarian disputants were very much aware of them and used them. But formal institutions, procedures, and officeholders made up only part of the picture. As Nelson and Wickham have pointed out for ninth-century Francia and Italy, the evidence for Bavaria likewise shows courts to have been thoroughly connected to the social and political networks around them and perfectly able to produce compromises as well as judgments.[27]

The importance of formal institutions lay not so much in their ability to dictate behavior as in the factors that prompted people to resort to them and the ways people used them. In exploring courts and how they enforced their decisions, scholars working on the West have focused their attention on

---

ties to disputes, it is hard to find archival evidence that they acted as arbiters or peacemakers. Evidence for the playing of such roles by early medieval bishops comes mainly from hagiography and from Gregory of Tours; see James, "*Beati pacifici*," in *Disputes and Settlements*, ed. Bossy, 25–46.

27. Nelson, "Dispute Settlement," in *Settlement of Disputes*, ed. Davies and Fouracre, argues that despite a seemingly smooth-running court procedure, Carolingian courts were at the mercy of local interest groups that could and did manipulate them for their own purposes. As a result, royal control over the courts was no better in the ninth century than it was in the tenth. Wickham, "Land Disputes," in *Settlement of Disputes*, ed. Davies and Fouracre, 123, similarly concludes that the formal and informal were always inextricably mixed; even in the ninth century, disputes often ended as a result of informal negotiation outside the theoretical frame of reference of the court. According to White, "*Pactum*," 292–99, the same held true for courts in late-eleventh-century western France. Although on the surface his evidence shows formal courts applying impersonal norms, on closer examination plenty of arbitration and compromise emerges in the context of courts that were stocked by people connected with the case. Thus, White concludes that the courts were simply venues for the public recognition of previously worked out arrangements; formal *placitum* reports represented scribes' efforts to summarize lengthy and complicated processes.

both publicity and self-interest. In the conclusion to their collection on early medieval dispute, for example, Davies and Fouracre comment about the publicity of formal proceedings, the public witnessing of the results, and the collective nature of judgment as factors that both encouraged people to come to courts and provided pressure to accept the results. They speculate that some interest must have been involved, as most people in the early Middle Ages, as at other times, did not love the law for its own sake. They suggest, however, that much of that interest lay in the nature of courts as public venues where disputants could bring publicity and peer pressure to bear on each other.[28] Davies and Fouracre have also made the important general point that a king had no hope of getting law accepted unless the men who controlled the courts accepted it—that is, unless those men felt it was in their interest to accept it. Nelson and Wickham likewise note that it was necessary for the Carolingian kings to cooperate with local power and interests if they wanted to influence dispute processing at a local level.[29]

In Bavaria, we have seen that publicity and public witness played an important role not only in formal judicial assemblies but also in extrajudicial dispute settlement. Bavarians clearly viewed publicity as critical to any settlement, not just those reached in the context of a court. According to the Bavarian evidence, people chose to go to judicial assemblies out of material self-interest. Bavarians went to the assemblies and participated in their decisions because they could use the assemblies and the normative systems they represented to acquire or protect property. Bavarian landholders, both clerical and lay, opportunistically exploited the institutional and normative resources available to them in the pursuit or defense of land, churches, or unfree dependents. Courts, in other words, engaged people's interest because they were resources that could produce valuable payoffs.

The scholarship on the West has repeatedly emphasized that formal judicial assemblies functioned as parts of longer dispute processes that ended in settlements outside courts and alongside settlement processes that never made it into a court. The evidence for this level of extrajudicial dispute pro-

28. Davies and Fouracre, "Conclusion: Procedure and Practice," 216, 218, and "Conclusion: Dispute Processes," 234, both in *Settlement of Disputes*. See also Patrick J. Geary, "Moral Obligations and Peer Pressure: Conflict Resolution in the Medieval Aristocracy," in *Georges Duby: L'écriture de l'histoire*, ed. Claudie Duhamel-Amado and Guy Lobrichon (Brussels, 1996), 217–22.

29. Davies and Fouracre, "Conclusion: Dispute Processes," 231; Nelson, "Dispute Settlement," 61–62; Wickham, "Land Disputes," 119–20, all in *Settlement of Disputes*, ed. Davies and Fouracre. See also Fouracre, "Placita," in the same collection, 38–39, 42–43.

cessing in the West has in many cases been fragmentary or subtle, however. In her discussion of dispute settlement in Carolingian West Francia, for example, Nelson ends with the speculative statement that agreement, mediation, or arbitration must have resolved many ninth-century disputes but that these processes were never recorded or the records were lost, possibly because churches were more interested in victory than compromise.[30] Wickham has been able to find more direct evidence for the symbiotic relationship between courts and extrajudicial settlement in his *placita* from Carolingian Lombardy.[31]

The outstanding depth of the Bavarian charter collections has allowed us to get a close look at this phenomenon. Complete records of extrajudicial dispute settlements have survived because they too dealt with church property rights and because they often as not recorded elements of ongoing relationships between the church and other landholders. Some settlements began in courts but ended outside them; many never went to a court at all. To a greater or lesser degree, all these settlements involved negotiation (in the case of Hermperht's theft of animals from Cella, almost literally "horse-trading"). Some of this negotiation involved violence. The destruction carried out by Bishop Atto of Freising's men in the course of the dispute with

30. Nelson, "Dispute Settlement," in *Settlement of Disputes*, ed. Davies and Fouracre, 63. Nelson's conclusion stems to a large degree from her reliance on Hübner's *Gerichtsurkunden der Fränkischen Zeit*. As far as I can tell from a comparison of Hübner's register with the Bavarian evidence, Hübner did not include conflict reports that did not fit his model of what a judicial charter was (for example, *TF* 275, Kyppo and his pig). I suspect this holds for Hübner's western material as well.

31. Wickham, "Land Disputes," in *Settlement of Disputes*, ed. Davies and Fouracre, 118–24, esp. 118, 120, 122–24. Wickham's evidence for compromise and negotiation outside the theoretical frame of reference of the courts consists of such things as remitted fines, later precarial leases of property lost in *placita*, references to attempted compromises that preceded *placita*, and compromises arranged in the course of *placita* with the help of judges themselves. Geary, "Extra-Judicial Means of Conflict Resolution," in a much broader discussion of *convenientiae* in late antiquity and the early Middle Ages, gets at the world of informal dispute processing through formulary books and through the negative view of agreements in law codes and Carolingian capitularies (including *Lex B* C. IX/17, which forbids anyone to accept compensation from a thief unless the thief had been brought before a judge). Geary also opens the door to a discussion of the rich evidence for informal dispute settlement in the charter material from Saint Gall. See also Stephen D. White, "Proposing the Ordeal and Avoiding It: Strategy and Power in Western French Litigation, 1050–1110," in *Cultures of Power: Lordship, Status, and Process in Twelfth-Century Europe*, ed. Thomas N. Bisson (Philadelphia, 1995), 89–123.

Kyppo, like violence in Stephen White's eleventh-century France, appears to have formed part of a lengthy process of pressure and negotiation that led ultimately to a peaceful settlement.[32]

The balancing of rights and face against material concessions that characterizes Bavarian accounts of extrajudicial settlements echoed a broader culture of dispute settlement visible in the West throughout the early Middle Ages. Wickham, for example, has pointed out that written compromise formulas in Carolingian Lombardy often encompass the apparent defeat of the losing party and the surrender of all his property.[33] Geary, in his study of disputing in eleventh- and twelfth-century France, has noted that there too compromises frequently took the form of an act of charity. One could not have a neutral relationship; disputes had to end by replacing a negative relationship with a positive one. Hence, people frequently urged a church to return disputed property to an opponent as a fief. Such compromises, as in Bavaria, served as a face-saving way for the church to make a concession.[34]

As in the West, so too in Bavaria: both land and conflict over land served to forge or adjust connections among people and institutions. As Davies and Fouracre, Geary, and Rosenwein have all pointed out in different contexts, conflict flared up in Bavaria when relationships changed—that is, when a grantor or previous benefice holder died or remarried or when a new bishop took up the reins of his diocese.[35] Conflict could thus serve to rearrange relationships between landowners and the church, or to have them publicly restated and recorded in writing, at any point they appeared uncertain.

Most important, this book contributes to the ongoing debates over conflict and the exercise of power in the early Middle ages by documenting changes over time in all the phenomena discussed above. Studying the development of disputing case by case over a particular century and a half has shown that the dialectic between judicial institutions and social processes, between central authority and local interest, and between different ways of narrating disputes was itself dynamic, not static: it could change relatively quickly in response to macrolevel political developments. Conflict could appear when political change put preexisting relationships in a new light or

32. White, "Feuding and Peace-Making."

33. Wickham, "Land Disputes," in *Settlement of Disputes*, ed. Davies and Fouracre, 123.

34. Geary, "Living with Conflicts," in *Living with the Dead*, 154–56 and nn. 84, 87. See also Koziol, *Begging Pardon and Favor*.

35. Davies and Fouracre, "Conclusion: Dispute Processes," 233, in *Settlement of Disputes*; Geary "Living with Conflicts," in *Living with the Dead*, 139, 141; Rosenwein, *To Be the Neighbor*, 58–59, 203.

provided someone with a new opportunity. The locus of episcopal interests could gradually shift in response to political developments, from cooperation to competition and from formal courts to extrajudicial processes.

The Bavarian evidence naturally also has something to say to the scholarship on the East Frankish world: a great deal of what Anglo-American scholars have learned about conflict and authority in the early medieval West applies equally well east of the Rhine. Dispute-resolution mechanisms in Carolingian Bavaria did not always function in a systematic, impersonal way. Although Bavarians used institutions such as courts, law codes, formal procedures, and charter formulas, these institutions were malleable and flexible instruments that interacted symbiotically with a variable and creative world of negotiation and compromise. The institutions depended for their success both on the prestige of the authority behind them and on the interests, abilities, and resources of the people using them. These people—whose relationships to one another the prosopographers have done so much to uncover—did not form themselves into unified interest blocs based on kinship. The Bavarian kin groups were instead hotbeds of competition; individuals or subgroups allied themselves (or not) with institutions, norms, and authority figures as their needs dictated.[36]

Extrajudicial conflict resolution in Bavaria, with its narratives dealing as much with saving face as with material substance, also looks a great deal like the public, ritual communication of dispute settlement characteristic of East Frankish and German noble society from the tenth century onward. Indeed, the "act of mercy" compromise script fundamentally resembles one of the centerpieces of medieval ritual described by Althoff: the *deditio*. In this ritual, which appears as a peacemaking mechanism from the reign of Otto I to that of Frederick Barbarossa and beyond, an opponent of the king, whether individual (such as a noble rebel) or collective (such as the citizens of a town) had to undergo a public humiliation and surrender and often endure a short-lived punishment. In the end, however, the rules of the game obligated the king to show mercy to his opponent and to restore him (or them) to his grace.[37]

The fact that such peacemaking narratives appear in disputes between bishops and regional landowners in Carolingian Bavaria, and in a Bavarian saint's life produced under the Agilolfings, indicates that they formed a fundamental part of aristocratic culture in the early medieval East from at least

36. See the Introduction, n. 74.

37. See Althoff, "Privileg der *deditio*," and "Königsherrschaft und Konfliktbewältigung," both in *Spielregeln*.

the eighth century on. This observation raises another question, however. Dispute resolution at the highest levels of eighth- and ninth-century society did not have to follow the rules of the *deditio*—far from it. We saw in the case involving Charlemagne and Count Helmoin that Charlemagne could operate within the "act of mercy" structure when he chose, or at least that a Freising scribe could on occasion so represent him. The case pitting Otker against Count Cotehram, however, indicates that the king did not have to be merciful. Charlemagne could, and in that case did, act with autocratic force against a willful subordinate.[38] The same held for the greatest dispute between Charlemagne and a Bavarian aristocrat—that with Duke Tassilo himself. At the great assembly held in Frankfurt in 794, the Frankish king showed his mercy by allowing the deposed Agilolfing duke to renounce all Agilolfing property on behalf of himself and his children and to retire permanently to a monastery. One or two centuries later, according to Althoff's work, one could imagine Tassilo being ultimately restored to his lands and office after making such a surrender. A more general and thorough study of the ways the Carolingian kings themselves appear in dispute narratives, and how that changed over time, would shed light on whether Charlemagne was in this regard also atypical—that is, whether or not he was the last European king of the early Middle Ages to rule successfully outside the bounds of a shared aristocratic culture.[39]

COUNT TIMO REVISITED

How far have we come from our starting point in 834 at Count Timo's court on the heights at Weihenstephan?[40] In many respects, not very far. The picture of dispute resolution in early medieval Bavaria that has emerged from the charters and the hagiography does not look at all like the image presented by *The Song of Count Timo*. The *Song* describes the count and royal *missus* Timo holding a formal court, but things take place at his court that we have not seen elsewhere. Timo orders that thieves be hanged, robbers be branded, and other criminals be mutilated. He oversees the settlement of disputes by ordeal or by the controlled violence of judicial combat. These methods of resolving conflict do not appear in the sources we have been able to exploit.

38. See the discussions of *TF* 166a and *TF* 232ab (Chap. 4).

39. See Althoff, "Privileg der *deditio*," 114–16, and "Königsherrschaft und Konfliktbewältigung," 53–54, both in *Spielregeln*.

40. See the discussion of the *Carmen de Timone comite* in the Introduction.

The differences need not surprise us. To begin with, the charters have had little or nothing to say about punishment. Most of the surviving records deal not with crime but with land disputes among aristocratic landowners. When crime does come up in the charters, it mostly appears indirectly, such as when property changed hands to pay wergeld. In the most explicit description of murder, that of Engilperht's daughter by Freising's maidservant in 853, the record deals only with the compensation given Engilperht by the maidservant's master, Bishop Erchanbert.[41] One would dearly love to know (or perhaps not) what happened to the maidservant herself. From this perspective, at least, the *Song* describes a world mostly outside the one captured by the charters. It is only when we push outward from the church archives into hagiography that a trace of this punitive world emerges: in Arbeo of Freising's *Life of Saint Corbinian*, the saint occasionally physically punishes adversaries, particularly those of lower status.[42]

Ordeals and judicial duels, in contrast, were used to decide issues of truth or falsehood and to settle competing claims—precisely the sort of thing one would expect in property disputes. The Bavarian Law frequently refers to the judicial duel as a means for resolving disputes over property rights, most often as an alternative to swearing an oath.[43] Yet no case of judicial combat appears in the Bavarian charters from the eighth and ninth centuries. One explanation might be that churches did not get involved in judicial combat, a suggestion bolstered by the diatribe against the practice in *The Song of Count Timo*.[44] The Bavarian Law, however, recognizes the possibility that a church could defend its rights through combat. As we saw earlier, if a freeman stole a tame ox or a milk cow from a church and wished to deny it, he

41. *TF* 738 (Chapter 6).

42. As in the incident in which Corbinian has the fishermen lashed to a stake and whipped; see Chapter 1. See also the "gallows miracle" in the *Life of Saint Emmeram* referred to in Chapter 1, n. 90.

43. The clauses referring specifically to combat as a means for settling property disputes include *Lex B* C. IX/2–3 (theft from church, ducal courtyard, workshop, or mill); C. XII/8 (disputed boundary markers); C. XIII/9 (alleged theft of a slave); C. XVI/11, XVI/17 (disputed ownership of sold property); C. XVII/2 (disputed veracity of witness in case of disputed landownership). References to judicial combat in other contexts in the code include C. II/1 and II/11, C. X/4, C. XIII/8, C. XVII/3–4 and XVII/6, C. XVIII/1–2.

44. See Bartlett, *Trial by Fire and Water*, 117–19, for the suggestion that clerical opinion and canon law were more firmly opposed to judicial combat than to the ordeal and that only the degree to which the duel permeated early medieval society forced prelates and ecclesiastical corporations to preside over or participate in it.

had the option of either swearing an oath with six oath-takers or defending his innocence in a duel between two champions.[45]

Nonetheless, when Hermperht stole livestock from Cella in 807, the parties chose not to follow this provision or similar ones in the Bavarian Law that specified punishments for proven guilt or procedures to use in the case of asserted innocence. Instead, the disputants worked out a mutually acceptable agreement. Thus, although to a certain extent *The Song of Count Timo* describes a world of disputing that we cannot get at, it leaves out a great deal about the world we have been able to see. The *Song* describes royal authority working through its local representative to keep the peace, either by administering punishments or by overseeing procedures designed to separate truth from falsehood. The *Song* does not address the ways conflict could be worked out without resort to central authority and its representatives. This latter kind of dispute processing depended more on personal and political relationships and imperatives, as well as on the negotiation of image and concrete compensation. Extrajudicial processes could intersect with central authority, but they did not have to. Royal authority and its institutions were simply one resource among many on which disputing parties could draw, in a variety of ways and at various stages in a dispute. The degree to which central authority compelled or attracted the attention of disputing parties depended on several factors: the interest of disputants in exploiting central authority's goals and aims for their own purposes, their interest in associating themselves with its prestige, the interest of central authority's own representatives in furthering its goals and aims, and the ability of those representatives to do what disputants needed them to. Here the unknown author of *The Song of Count Timo* had it right. If the king were not himself present, his ability to carry out the royal work of keeping the peace depended on both the ability and the goodwill of his delegates. The poet's praise of Timo as a good count and *missus* implies that others may not have been as good.

It is when we look at the *The Song of Count Timo* not as description but rather as representation that it fits with the other sources. The *Timo* poet first set out to praise King Louis. He therefore described the king's peace-securing authority, as visible in Count Timo's actions, as strong and effective. The *placitum* reports described formal judicial assemblies in the decades immediately after the Carolingian conquest similarly—as following a clear set of procedures that brought about a firm and effective judgment. The poet had another set of purposes, however. He was not interested in the wider world of Bavarian dispute processing; he wanted to criticize the ordeal and the judicial duel. The depictions of the ordeal and the duel at

45. *Lex B* C. IX/2.

Timo's court, therefore, were included in order to be censured. More important, the poet had a particular point to convey in the tale of Count Timo's dog. The message implicit in the story of the dog that died after the count allowed it to drink from Saint Corbinian's spring was simple: a royal representative dishonored God, and by extension his saint and his church, at his peril. This is the same message communicated not only by repeated conflict narratives in Arbeo's *Life of Saint Corbinian*—such as the one in which Duke Theodo provoked Corbinian's wrath by allowing his dog to eat sanctified bread[46]—but also by the way episcopal scribes increasingly described disputes in the charters as the ninth century advanced. The *Song* is thus part and parcel of a world in which the control of representation was a crucial element in the struggle for power and in the negotiation or renegotiation of relationships. How church scribes constructed their narratives of conflict reflected where they thought their church's interests lay and therefore represented the version of events that would most likely serve those interests. In the course of the ninth century, the scribes' attention migrated from the actions of formal courts to the maintenance and preservation in writing of episcopal rights and prestige. This progression is coincidentally captured in miniature by the *The Song of Count Timo*. The poem begins with Timo, "your count and legate, glorious king, rendering justice to the good and rightly punishing the evil," but it ends by focusing on the fate of the dog that the count allowed to desecrate the life-giving waters called forth by a bishop.

46. See Chapter 1.

BIBLIOGRAPHY

PRIMARY SOURCES

Manuscript Source
Munich:
Bayerisches Hauptstaatsarchiv
Hochstift Freising Lit. 3a. Cozroh's *Codex traditionum.*
Published Sources
Das älteste Traditionsbuch des Klosters Mondsee. Edited by Gebhard Rath and Erich Re-
iter. Forschungen zur Geschichte Oberösterreichs 16. Linz: Oberösterreichis-
ches Landesarchiv, 1989.
Annales Regni Francorum. Edited by Reinhold Rau. *Quellen zur karolingischen Reichs-
geschichte I. AQ* V, 1–155. Darmstadt: Wissenschaftliche Buchgesellschaft, 1987.
Anonymi Vita Hludovici Imperatoris. Edited by Reinhold Rau. *Quellen zur karolingis-
chen Reichsgeschichte* I. *AQ* V, 255–381. Darmstadt: Wissenschaftliche Buchge-
sellschaft, 1987.
Arbeo of Freising. *Vita Corbiniani: Bischof Arbeo von Freising und die Lebensgeschichte
des hl. Korbinian.* Edited by Hubert Glaser, Franz Brunhölzl, and Sigmund
Benker. Munich: Schnell & Steiner, 1983.
———. *Vita et passio Sancti Haimhrammi Martyris.* Edited by Bernhard Bischoff.
Munich: Ernst Heimeran, 1953.
Capitularia regum Francorum. Edited by Alfred Boretius. *MGH Capit* I. Hannover:
Hahn, 1883.
Carmen de Timone comite. Edited by E. Dümmler. *MGH Poet* I, 2, 120–24. Berlin:
Weidmann, 1884.
Concilia aevi Karolini. Edited by Albert Werminghoff. *MGH Conc* I. Hannover:
Hahn, 1906.
*Conversio Bagoariorum et Carantanorum. Das Weißbuch der Salzburger Kirche über die
erfolgreiche Mission in Karantanien und Pannonien.* Edited by Herwig Wolfram. Vi-
enna: Böhlau, 1979.
Formulae Merowingici et Karolini aevi. Edited by Karl Zeumer. *MGH Legum* Section
5. Hannover: Hahn, 1886.
Gerichtsurkunden der fränkischen Zeit. Edited by Rudolf Hübner. 1891–93. Reprint (2
vols. in 1). Aalen: Scientia, 1971.
Die Gesetze des Karolingerreiches, 714–911. Vol. 2, *Alemannen und Bayern.* Edited by
Karl August Eckhardt. Weimar: Hermann Böhlaus Nachfolger, 1934.

Gesta sancti Hrodberti confessoris. Edited by Wilhelm Levison. *MGH SSrerMerov* VI, 140–62. Hannover: Hahn, 1913.

Das Hildebrandlied. Edited and translated by Georg Baesecke. Halle: Max Niemeyer, 1945.

Ionae Vitae Columbani Liber Primus. Edited and translated by Herbert Haupt. *Quellen zur Geschichte des 7. und 8. Jahrhunderts.* AQ IVa, 395–497. Darmstadt: Wissenschaftliche Buchgesellschaft, 1982.

Laws of the Alamans and Bavarians. Translated by Theodore John Rivers. Philadelphia: University of Pennsylvania Press, 1977.

The Laws of the Salian Franks. Translated by Katherine Fischer Drew. Philadelphia: University of Pennyslvania Press, 1991.

Lex Baiwariorum. Edited by Ernst von Schwind. *MGH LL* V, 2. Hannover: Hahn, 1926.

Notitia Arnonis und Breves Notitiae: Die Salzburger Güterverzeichnisse aus der Zeit um 800: Sprach-historische Einleitung, Text und Übersetzung. Edited and translated by Fritz Lošek. *MGSL* 130 (1990): 5–193.

Passiones Leudegarii Episcopi et Martyris Augustodunensis. Edited by B. Krusch. *MGH SSrerMerov* V, 282–322. Hannover: Hahn, 1910.

Thegani Vita Hludowici Imperatoris. Edited by Reinhold Rau. *Quellen zur karolingischen Reichsgeschichte* 1. *AQ* V, 213–53. Darmstadt: Wissenschaftliche Buchgesellschaft, 1987.

Die Traditionen des Hochstifts Freising. Edited by Theodor Bitterauf. 2 vols. Quellen und Erörterungen zur bayerischen und deutschen Geschichte n. f. 4, 5. Munich: Rieger, 1905.

Die Traditionen des Hochstifts Passau. Edited by Max Heuwieser. Quellen und Erörterungen zur bayerischen Geschichte n. f. 6. Munich: Rieger, 1930.

Die Traditionen des Hochstifts Regensburg und des Klosters S. Emmeram. Edited by Josef Widemann. Quellen und Erörterungen zur bayerischen Geschichte n. f. 8. Munich: C. H. Beck, 1943.

Die Urkunden Arnolfs. Edited by P. Kehr. *MGH DrG Karol* III. Berlin: Weidmann, 1940.

Urkundenbuch der Abtei Sanct Gallen. Edited by Hermann Wartmann. 4 vols. Zürich: S. Höhr, 1863–1931.

Die Urkunden Ludwigs des Deutschen, Karlmanns und Ludwigs des Jüngeren. Edited by P. Kehr. *MGH DrG Karol* I. Berlin: Weidmann, 1934.

Die Urkunden Pippins, Karlmanns und Karls des Grossen. Edited by Engelbert Mühlbacher. *MGH D Karol* I. Hannover: Hahn, 1906.

Vita Goaris confessoris. Edited by B. Krusch. *MGH SSreMerov* IV, 402–23. Hannover: Hahn, 1902.

SECONDARY WORKS

Where I have used several articles or chapters from a collection, I have cited the individual pieces in the notes and cited the collection itself here.

Abel, Richard L. "A Comparative Theory of Dispute Institutions in Society." *Law and Society Review* 8 (winter 1973): 217–347.

Althoff, Gerd. *"Amicitiae* as Relationships between States and People." *In Debating the Middle Ages: Issues and Readings,* edited by Lester K. Little and Barbara H. Rosenwein, 191–210. London: Blackwell, 1998.

————. "*Ira regis*: Prolegomena to a History of Royal Anger." Translated by Warren Brown. In *Anger's Past: The Social Uses of an Emotion in the Middle Ages*, edited by Barbara H. Rosenwein, 59–74. Ithaca: Cornell University Press, 1998.

————. *Spielregeln in der Politik im Mittelalter*. Darmstadt: Wissenschaftliche Buchgesellschaft, 1997.

Althoff, Gerd, and Hagen Keller. *Heinrich I. und Otto der Große: Neubeginn auf karolingischem Erbe*. 2 vols. Göttingen: Muster-Schmidt, 1985.

Barthélemy, Dominique, and Stephen D. White. "Debate: The 'Feudal Revolution.' Comment 1, Comment 2." *Past and Present* 152 (1996): 196–223.

Bartlett, Robert. *The Making of Europe: Conquest, Colonization, and Cultural Change, 950–1350*. Princeton: Princeton University Press, 1993.

————. *Trial by Fire and Water: The Medieval Judicial Ordeal*. Oxford: Clarendon Press, 1986.

Bates, Robert H. *Essays on the Political Economy of Rural Africa*. Berkeley: University of California Press, 1987.

Bischoff, Bernhard. "Salzburger Formelbücher und Briefe aus Tassilonischer und Karolingischer Zeit." In *Sitzungsberichte der bayerischen Akademie der Wissenschaften: Philosophisch-Historische Klasse*, 1973, no. 4. Munich: C. H. Beck, 1973.

————. *Die südostdeutschen Schreibschulen und Bibliotheken in der Karolingerzeit*. Vol. 1, *Die bayerischen Diözesen*. Wiesbaden: Otto Harrassowitz, 1974.

————. *Die südostdeutschen Schreibschulen und Bibliotheken in der Karolingerzeit*. Vol. 2, *Die vorwiegend österreichischen Diözesen*. Wiesbaden: Otto Harrassowitz, 1980.

Bisson, Thomas N. "The 'Feudal Revolution.'" *Past and Present* 142 (1994): 6–42.

Black-Michaud, Jacob. *Cohesive Force: Feud in the Mediterranean and the Middle East*. Oxford: Oxford University Press, 1975.

Borgolte, Michael. *Geschichte der Grafschaften Alemanniens in Fränkischer Zeit. Vorträge und Forschungen*, Sonderband 16. Sigmaringen: Thorbecke, 1984.

Bosl, Karl. "Der 'Adelsheilige': Idealtypus und Wirklichkeit, Gesellschaft und Kultur im merowingerzeitlichen Bayern des 7. und 8. Jahrhunderts: Gesellschaftliche Beiträge zu den Viten der bayerischen Stammesheiligen Emmeram, Rupert, und Korbinian." In *Speculum Historiale: Geschichte im Spiegel von Geschichtsschreibung und Geschichtsdeutung*, edited by Clemens Bauer, Laetitia Boehm, and Max Müller, 167–87. Munich: Karl Alber, 1965.

Bossy, John, ed. *Disputes and Settlements: Law and Human Relations in the West*. Cambridge: Cambridge University Press, 1983.

Brown, Warren. "The Use of Norms in Disputes in Early Medieval Bavaria." *Viator* 30 (1999): 15–40.

Brummer, Jakob. "Das Carmen de Timone comite." *Historische Vierteljahrschrift* 18 (1916–18): 102–7.

Brunner, Heinrich. *Deutsche Rechtsgeschichte*. Vol. 1. Leipzig: Von Dunker & Humblot, 1887.

————. *Deutsche Rechtsgeschichte*. 2d ed. Vol. 2. Edited by Claudius Freiherr von Schweren. Berlin: Von Duncker & Humblot, 1928.

Buc, Philippe. *The Dangers of Ritual: The Politics of Medieval Anthropology*. Princeton: Princeton University Press. Forthcoming.

————. "Martyre et ritualité dans l'Antiquité tardive: Horizons de l'écriture médiévale des rituels." *Annales ESC* 48, no. 1 (1997): 63–92.

Bührer-Thierry, Geneviève. "Formes des donations aux églises et stratégies des familles en Bavière du VIIIe siècle aux Xe siècle." *Mélanges de l'École Française de Rome* 111, no. 2 (1999): 675–99.

Classen, Peter, ed. *Recht und Schrift im Mittelalter.* Sigmaringen: Thorbecke, 1977.

Collins, Roger. *Charlemagne.* Toronto: University of Toronto Press, 1998.

———. *Early Medieval Europe, 300–1000.* New York: St. Martin's Press, 1991.

Comaroff, John L., and Simon Roberts. *Rules and Processes: The Cultural Logic of Dispute in an African Context.* Chicago: University of Chicago Press, 1981.

Conrad, Hermann. *Deutsche Rechtsgeschichte.* 2d ed. Vol. 1, *Frühzeit und Mittelalter.* Karlsruhe: C. F. Müller, 1962.

Dannheimer, Hermann, and Heinz Dopsch, eds. *Die Bajuwaren von Severin bis Tassilo, 488–788: Gemeinsame Landesausstellung des Freistaates Bayern und des Landes Salzburg 1988.* Munich: Prähistorische Staatssammlung, 1988.

Davies, Wendy, and Paul Fouracre, eds. *Property and Power in the Early Middle Ages.* Cambridge: Cambridge University Press, 1995.

———. *The Settlement of Disputes in Early Medieval Europe.* Cambridge: Cambridge University Press, 1986.

Diepolder, Gertrud, ed. *Bayerischer Geschichtsatlas.* Munich: Bayerischer Schulbuch-Verlag, 1969.

"Dispute Resolution: Civil Justice and Its Alternatives" (special issue). *Modern Law Review* 56 (May 1993).

Dollinger, Philippe. *L'évolution des classes rurales en Bavière depuis la fin de l'époque carolingienne jusqu'au milieu du XIIIe siècle.* Paris: Belles Lettres, 1949.

Dopsch, Heinz, ed. *Geschichte Salzburgs: Stadt und Land.* Vol. 1, part 1, *Vorgeschichte, Altertum, Mittelalter.* Salzburg: Universitätsverlag Anton Pustet, 1981.

Duby, Georges. *The Chivalrous Society.* Translated by Cynthia Postan. Berkeley: University of California Press, 1980.

———. *La société aux XIe et XIIe siècles dans la région mâconnaise.* Paris: A. Colin, 1953.

Erler, A., and E. Kaufmann, eds. *Handwörterbuch zur deutschen Rechtsgeschichte.* 5 vols. Berlin: E. Schmidt, 1964–98.

Fichtenau, Heinrich. *The Carolingian Empire.* Translated by Peter Munz. Toronto: University of Toronto Press, 1978.

———. *Das Urkundenwesen in Österreich vom 8. bis zum frühen 13. Jahrhundert.* Vienna: Hermann Böhlaus Nachfolger, 1971.

Firmin-Sellers, Kathryn. "Institutions, Context, and Outcomes: Explaining French and British Rule in West Africa." *Comparative Politics* 32, no. 3 (2000): 253–72.

Galanter, Marc. "Reading the Landscape of Disputes: What We Know and Don't Know (and Think We Know) about Our Allegedly Contentious and Litigious Society." *UCLA Law Review* 31, no. 4 (1983): 4–71.

Ganshof, François Louis. *Frankish Institutions under Charlemagne.* Translated by Bryce and Mary Lyon. Providence: Brown University Press, 1968.

Gates, Paul W. *Land and Law in California: Essays on Land Policies.* Ames: Iowa State University Press, 1991.

Geary, Patrick J. *Before France and Germany: The Creation and Transformation of the Merovingian World.* New York: Oxford University Press, 1988.

———. "Extra-Judicial Means of Conflict Resolution." In *La giustizia nell'alto medioevo (secoli V–VIII).* Vol. 1, 569–601. Spoleto: Presso la Sede del Centro Italiano di Studi sull'Alto Medioevo, 1995.

————. *Living with the Dead in the Middle Ages*. Ithaca: Cornell University Press, 1994.

————. "Moral Obligations and Peer Pressure: Conflict Resolution in the Medieval Aristocracy." In *Georges Duby: L'écriture de l'histoire*, edited by Claudie Duhamel-Amado and Guy Lobrichon, 217–22. Brussels: De Boeck, 1996.

————. *Phantoms of Remembrance: Memory and Oblivion at the End of the First Millennium*. Princeton: Princeton University Press, 1994.

————., ed. *Readings in Medieval History*. 2d ed. Peterborough, Ontario: Broadview, 1997.

Geuenich, Dieter. "Zur althochdeutschen Literatur aus Fulda." In *Von der Klosterbibliothek zur Landesbibliothek: Beiträge zum zweihundertjährigen Bestehen der hessischen Landesbibliothek Fulda*, 99–124. Stuttgart: Anton Hiersemann, 1978.

Glaser, Hubert, Franz Brunhölzl, and Sigmund Benker, eds. *Vita Corbiniani: Bischof Arbeo von Freising und die Lebensgeschichte des hl. Korbinian*. Munich: Schnell & Steiner, 1983.

Gluckman, Max. *Custom and Conflict in Africa*. Oxford: Blackwell, 1959.

————. "The Peace in the Feud." *Past and Present* 7 (1955): 1–14.

Godman, Peter, and Roger Collins, eds. *Charlemagne's Heir: New Perspectives on the Reign of Louis the Pious*. Oxford: Clarendon Press, 1990.

Goldberg, Eric J. "Creating a Medieval Kingdom: Carolingian Kingship, Court Culture, and East Frankish Nobility under Louis the German (840–876)." Ph.D. diss., University of Virginia, 1998.

————. "'Dilectissimus Pater Aquila Transalpinus': Archbishop Arn of Salzburg and Charlemagne's 802 Administrative Reforms." Master's thesis, University of Virginia, 1994.

————. "'More Devoted to the Equipment of Battle than the Splendor of Banquets': Frontier Kingship, Military Ritual, and Early Knighthood at the Court of Louis the German." *Viator* 30 (1999): 41–78.

Graus, František. "Die Gewalt bei den Anfängen des Feudalismus und die 'Gefangenenbefreiung' der merowingischen Hagiographie." *Jahrbuch für Wirtschaftsgeschichte* (1961): 61–156.

————. *Volk, Herrscher und Heiliger im Reich der Merowinger: Studien zur Hagiographie der Merowingerzeit*. Prague: Nakladatelstv' Ceskoslovenské akademie ved, 1965.

Grimm, Jacob. *Deutsche Rechtsaltertümer*. 4th ed. Edited by A. Heusler and R. Hübner. 2 vols. Leipzig: Dieterich, 1899.

Gruen, Erich. *The Hellenistic World and the Coming of Rome*. 2 vols. Berkeley: University of California Press, 1988.

Hammer, Carl I. "Family and Familia in Early Medieval Bavaria." In *Family Forms in Historic Europe*, edited by Richard Wall, 217–48. Cambridge: Cambridge University Press, 1983.

————. "The Handmaid's Tale: Morganatic Relationships in Early-Mediaeval Bavaria." *Continuity and Change* 10, no. 3 (1995): 345–68.

————. "Land Sales in Eighth- and Ninth-Century Bavaria: Legal, Economic, and Social Aspects." *Early Medieval Europe* 6, no. 3 (1997): 47–76.

Hartmann, Wilfried. "Der Bischof als Richter nach den Kirchenrechtlichen Quellen des 4. bis 7. Jahrhunderts." In *La giustizia nell'alto medioevo (secoli V–VIII)*. Vol. 2, 805–37. Spoleto: Presso la Sede del Centro Italiano di Studi sull'Alto Medioevo, 1995.

———. "Der rechtliche Zustand der Kirchen auf dem Lande: Die Eigenkirche in der fränkischen Gesetzgebung des 7. bis 9. Jahrhunderts." In *Cristianizzazione ed organizzazione ecclesiastica delle campagne nell'alto medioevo: espansione e resistenze,* 397–441. Settimane di Studio del Centro Italiano di Studi sull'Alto Medioevo XXVIII. Spoleto: Presso la Sede del Centro, 1982.

Hartung, Wolfgang. "Bertolde in Baiern: Alamannisch-baierische Adelsverflechtungen im 8. und 9. Jahrhundert." *Regio* 1 (1988): 115–60.

———. "Tradition und Namengebung im frühen Mittelalter." *Regio* 1 (1988): 23–79.

Head, Thomas. *Hagiography and the Cult of Saints: The Diocese of Orléans, 800–1200.* Cambridge: Cambridge University Press, 1990.

Jahn, Joachim. *Ducatus Baiuvariorum: Das bairische Herzogtum der Agilolfinger.* Monographien zur Geschichte des Mittelalters 35. Stuttgart: Anton Hiersemann, 1991.

———. "Urkunde und Chronik: Ein Beitrag zur historischen Glaubwürdigkeit der Benediktbeurer Überlieferung und zur Geschichte des agilolfingischen Bayerns." *MIÖG* 95 (1987): 1–51.

———. "Virgil, Arbeo und Cozroh: Verfassungsgeschichtliche Beobachtungen an bairischen Quellen des 8. und 9. Jahrhunderts." *MGSL* 130 (1990): 201–91.

Jänichen, Hans. "Warin, Rudhard, and Scrot: Besitzgeschichtliche Betrachtungen zur Frühgeschichte des Stiftes Buchau." *Zeitschrift für württembergische Landesgeschichte* 14 (1955): 372–84.

Jarnut, Jörg. *Agilolfingerstudien: Untersuchungen zur Geschichte einer adligen Familie im 6. und 7. Jahrhundert.* Stuttgart: Hiersemann, 1986.

Köbler, Gerhard. "Die Begründungen der Lex Baiwariorum." In *Studien zu den germanischen Volksrechten: Gedächtnisschrift für Wilhelm Ebel,* edited by Götz Landwehr, 69–85. Frankfurt: Lang, 1982.

Kolmer, Lothar. "Zur Kommendation und Absetzung Tassilos III." *Zeitschrift für bayerische Landesgeschichte* 43 (1980): 291–327.

Koziol, Geoffrey. *Begging Pardon and Favor: Ritual and Political Order in Early Medieval France.* Ithaca, Cornell University Press, 1992.

———. "Monks, Feuds, and the Making of Peace in Eleventh-Century Flanders." In *The Peace of God: Social Violence and Religious Response in France around the Year 1000,* edited by Thomas Head and Richard Landes, 239–58. Ithaca: Cornell University Press, 1992.

Kraus, Andreas. "Zweiteilung des Herzogtums der Agilolfinger? Die Probe aufs Exempel." *Blätter für deutsche Landesgeschichte* 112 (1976): 16–29.

Langum, David J. *Law and Community on the Mexican California Frontier: Anglo-American Expatriates and the Clash of Legal Traditions, 1821–1846.* Norman: University of Oklahoma Press, 1987.

Le Jan, Régine. *Famille et pouvoir dans le monde franc (VIIe–Xe siècle): Essai d'anthropologie sociale.* Paris: Publications de la Sorbonne, 1995.

Leyser, Karl. *Rule and Conflict in an Early Medieval Society: Ottonian Saxony.* London: Edward Arnold, 1979.

Manitius, Max. *Geschichte der lateinischen Literatur des Mittelalters.* Vol. 1, *Von Justinian bis zur Mitte des 10. Jahrhunderts.* Munich: C. H. Beck, 1911.

Maß, Josef. *Das Bistum Freising im Mittelalter.* Munich: Erich Wewel, 1986.

McKitterick, Rosamond. *The Carolingians and the Written Word.* Cambridge: Cambridge University Press, 1989.

———. *The Frankish Kingdoms under the Carolingians, 751–987*. London: Longman, 1983.

———, ed. *The New Cambridge Medieval History*. Vol. 2, *c. 700–c. 900*. Cambridge: Cambridge University Press, 1995.

Miles, William F. S. *Hausaland Divided: Colonialism and Independence in Nigeria and Niger*. Ithaca: Cornell University Press, 1994.

Mitterauer, Michael. *Karolingische Markgrafen im Südosten: Fränkische Reichsaristokratie und bayerischer Stammesadel im österreichischen Raum*. Archiv für österreichische Geschichte 123. Vienna: Rohrer, 1963.

Murray, Alexander C. *Germanic Kinship Structure: Studies in Law and Society in Antiquity and in the Early Middle Ages*. Toronto: Pontifical Institute of Medieval Studies, 1983.

Nelson, Janet L. *Charles the Bald*. London: Longman, 1992.

Pohl, Walter. *Die Awaren: Ein Steppenvolk in Mitteleuropa, 567–822 n. Chr.* Munich: C. H. Beck, 1988.

Poly, Jean-Pierre, and Eric Bournazel. *La mutation féodale, Xe–XIIe siècles*. 2d ed. Paris: Presses Universitaires de France, 1991.

Price, S. R. F. *Rituals and Power: The Roman Imperial Cult in Asia Minor*. Cambridge: Cambridge University Press, 1984.

Prinz, Friedrich. "Arbeo von Freising und die Agilulfinger." *Zeitschrift für bayerische Landesgeschichte* 29 (1966): 581.

———. *Frühes Mönchtum im Frankenreich: Kultur und Gesellschaft in Gallien, den Rheinlanden und Bayern am Beispiel der monastischen Entwicklung (4. bis 8. Jahrhundert)*. 2d ed. Darmstadt: Wissenschaftliche Buchgesellschaft, 1988.

———. "Herzog und Adel im Agilulfingischen Bayern: Herzogsgut und Konsensschenkungen vor 788." *Zeitschrift für bayerische Landesgeschichte* 25 (1962): 283–311.

Reid, John P. *Law for the Elephant: Property and Social Behavior on the Overland Trail*. San Marino, Calif.: Huntington Library, 1980.

———. *Policing the Elephant: Crime, Punishment, and Social Behavior on the Overland Trail*. San Marino, Calif.: Huntington Library, 1997.

Reitzenstein, Alexander Freiherr von. *Frühe Geschichte rund um München*. Munich: Prestel, 1956.

Remensnyder, Amy G. *Remembering Kings Past: Monastic Foundation Legends in Medieval Southern France*. Ithaca: Cornell University Press, 1995.

Reuter, Timothy. *Germany in the Early Middle Ages, 800–1056*. London: Longman, 1991.

———, ed. *The Medieval Nobility: Studies on the Ruling Classes of France and Germany from the Sixth to the Twelfth Century*. Amsterdam: North-Holland, 1979.

Reuter, Timothy, Chris Wickham, and Thomas N. Bisson. "Debate: The Feudal Revolution. Comment 3, Comment 4, Reply." *Past and Present* 155 (1997): 177–225.

Riché, Pierre. *The Carolingians: A Family Who Forged Europe*. Translated by Michael Idomir Allen. Philadelphia: University of Pennsylvania Press, 1993.

Roberts, Simon. *Order and Dispute: An Introduction to Legal Anthropology*. London: Penguin Books, 1979.

Rosenwein, Barbara H. *Negotiating Space: Power, Restraint, and Privileges of Immunity in Early Medieval Europe*. Ithaca: Cornell University Press, 1999.

———. *To Be the Neighbor of Saint Peter: The Social Meaning of Cluny's Property, 909–1049*. Ithaca: Cornell University Press, 1989.

Schmid, Karl. *Gebetsdenken und adeliges Selbstverständnis im Mittelalter: Ausgewählte Beiträge: Festgabe zu seinem sechzigsten Geburtstag.* Sigmaringen: Jan Thorbecke, 1983.

Schneider, Jane, and Rayna Rapp, eds. *Articulating Hidden Histories: Exploring the Influence of Eric R. Wolf.* Berkeley: University of California Press, 1995.

Schulze, Hans K. *Die Graftschaftsverfassung der Karolingerzeit in den Gebieten östlich des Rheins.* Schriften zur Verfassungsgeschichte 19. Berlin: Duncker & Homblot, 1973.

Searle, Eleanor. *Predatory Kinship and the Creation of Norman Power, 840–1066.* Berkeley: University of California Press, 1988.

Seibt, Ferdinand, ed. *Gesellschaftsgeschichte: Festschrift für Karl Bosl zum 80. Geburtstag.* 2 vols. Munich: R. Oldenbourg, 1988.

794–Karl der Große in Frankfurt am Main: Ein König bei der Arbeit. Sigmaringen: Thorbecke, 1994.

Spindler, Max, ed. *Handbuch der bayerischen Geschichte.* 2d ed. Vol. 1. Munich: C. H. Beck, 1981.

Stahleder, Helmut. "Bischöfliche und adelige Eigenkirchen des Bistums Freising im frühen Mittelalter und die Kirchenorganisation im Jahre 1315." *Oberbayerisches Archiv* 104 (1979): 117–88.

Störmer, Wilhelm. *Adelsgruppen im früh- und hochmittelalterlichen Bayern.* Studien zur bayerischen Verfassungs- und Sozialgeschichte 4. Munich: Kommission für bayerische Landesgeschichte, 1972.

Führungsschicht. *Früher Adel: Studien zur politischen Führungsschicht im fränkisch-deutschen Reich vom 8. bis 11. Jahrhundert.* 2 vols. Monographien zur Geschichte des Mittelalters 6. Stuttgart: Anton Hiersemann, 1973.

———. "Eine frühmittelalterliche Adelsfamilie im Dachauer Umland." *Amperland* 3, no. 4 (1967): 80–81.

———. "Ein Gerichtstag an der Pfettrach im Jahre 818." *Amperland* 4, no. 3 (1968): 65–69.

———. "Mammendorf an der Maisach und seine adeligen Besitzer im frühen Mittelalter." *Amperland* 3, no. 2 (1967): 38–40.

Strzewitzek, Hubert. *Die Sippenbeziehungen der Freisinger Bischöfe im Mittelalter.* Munich: Lentner'sche Buchhandlung, 1938.

Sturm, Josef. *Die Anfänge des Hauses Preysing.* Schriftenreihe zur bayerischen Landesgeschichte 8. Munich: Kommission für bayerische Landesgeschichte, 1931.

———. "Bischof Arbeos von Freising bayerische Verwandte." *Zeitschrift für bayerische Landesgeschichte* 19 (1956): 568–72.

Tabuteau, Emily Zack. *Transfers of Property in Eleventh-Century Norman Law.* Chapel Hill: University of North Carolina Press, 1988.

Wanderwitz, Heinrich. "Quellenkritische Studien zu den bayerischen Besitzlisten des 8. Jahrhunderts." *Deutsches Archiv* 39, no. 1 (1983): 27–84.

Wattenbach, Wilhelm, and Wilhelm Levison. *Deutschlands Geschichtsquellen im Mittelalter: Vorzeit und Karolinger.* Edited by Wilhelm Levison. Vol. 1, *Die Vorzeit von den Anfängen bis zur Herrschaft der Karolinger.* Weimar: Hermann Böhlaus Nachfolger, 1952.

Weinfurter, Stefan, ed. *Die Salier und das Reich.* Vol. 3. Sigmaringen: Jan Thorbecke, 1991.

Weitzel, Jürgen. *Dinggenossenschaft und Recht: Untersuchungen zum Rechtsverständnis im fränkisch-deutschen Mittelalter.* 2 vols. Cologne: Böhlau, 1985.

Werner, Karl Ferdinand. *"Missus-marchio-comes:* Entre l'administration centrale et l'administration locale de l'empire carolingien." In *Histoire comparée de l'administration,* edited by W. Paravicini and K. F. Werner, 191–239. Beiheft der Francia 9. Munich: Artemis, 1980.

White, Stephen D. "Feuding and Peace-Making in the Touraine around the Year 1000." *Traditio* 42 (1986): 195–263.

———. *"Pactum . . . legem vincit et amor judicium:* The Settlement of Disputes by Compromise in Eleventh-Century Western France." *American Journal of Legal History* 22 (1978): 281–308.

———. "Proposing the Ordeal and Avoiding It: Strategy and Power in Western French Litigation." In *Cultures of Power: Lordship, Status, and Process in Twelfth-Century Europe,* edited by Thomas N. Bisson, 89–123. Philadelphia: University of Pennsylvania Press, 1995.

Wickham, Chris. *Early Medieval Italy: Central Power and Local Society, 400–1000.* Ann Arbor: University of Michigan Press, 1989.

Wilson, Stephen, ed. *Saints and Their Cults: Studies in Religious Sociology, Folklore, and History.* Cambridge: Cambridge University Press, 1983.

Wolf, Eric R. "Distinguished Lecture: Facing Power—Old Insights, New Questions." *American Anthropologist* 92, no. 3 (1990): 586–96.

———. *Europe and the People without History.* Berkeley: University of California Press, 1997.

Wolfram, Herwig. "Arn von Salzburg und Karl der Grosse." In *1200 Jahre Erzbistum Salzburg: Die älteste Metropole im deutschen Sprachraum: Beiträge des Internationalen Kongresses in Salzburg vom 11. bis 13. Juni 1998, MGSL* Ergänzungsband 18, 21–32. Salzburg: Gesellschaft für Salzburger Landeskunde, 1999.

———. *Die Geburt Mitteleuropas: Geschichte Österreichs vor seiner Entstehung, 378–907.* Vienna: Siedler, 1987.

———. *Intitulatio.* Vol. 1, *Lateinische Königs- und Fürstentitel bis zum Ende des 8. Jahrhunderts.* Vienna: Hermann Böhlaus Nachfolger, 1967.

———. "Libellus Virgilii: Ein quellenkritisches Problem der ältesten Salzburger Güterverzeichnisse." In *Mönchtum, Episkopat und Adel zur Gründungszeit des Klosters Reichenau,* ed. Arno Borst, 177–214. Sigmaringen: Thorbecke, 1974.

———. *Salzburg, Bayern, Österreich: Die Conversio Bagoariorum et Carantanorum und die Quellen ihrer Zeit.* Vienna: R. Oldenbourg, 1995.

INDEX

"Act of mercy" script. *See* Corbinian: *Life of*; *Deditio*; Settlement: narratives of
Adalram (archbishop of Salzburg), 121
Adalschalks, 13–14, 48n. 49, 180n. 50. *See also* Barschalks
Adalwin (bishop of Regensburg), 76, 88, 105, 106n. 22, 107n. 24, 119, 126
Adjudication, 5, 122n. 87, 164, 182, 194, 196, 199. *See also* Arn; Judicial assemblies; *Missi*; *Placita*; Settlement: and judicial assemblies
Advocates, 75–78, 86, 127–28, 193
Agilolfings, 12–14, 93–94. *See also individual dukes*
Albin. *See* Oberalm
Alemannia, 12, 16n. 36, 46n. 38, 54n. 77, 74n. 3, 133n. 20, 166n. 1, 176n. 31
Anno (bishop of Freising), 188–90
Anthropology: and conquest and colonization, 6–7; and disputing, 5–6; and early medieval history, 7–11
Arbeo (bishop of Freising), 20, 42–43, 52–54, 66, 76; and the Agilolfings, 63–64, 114; kinship of, 43. *See also* Corbinian: *Life of*; Emmeram: *Life of*
Aristocracy, Bavarian: and the Carolingians, 16, 71–72, 101–3, 150, 167, 194–95, 199; and the church, 72, 66, 74–75, 184–87, 197; defined, 13–14, 25–26; interests of, 45–46, 98–100, 187, 192, 193–94, 202; naming patterns and property holdings of, 26–29, 96, 192; and settlement, 65, 125, 134, 139, 191; and Tassilo III, 15, 65; and violence, 32, 35, 65, 191. *See also* Kindreds
Arn (archbishop of Salzburg), 69, 73, 76, 79, 88, 96, 144–45; and Charlemagne, 16, 83–85, 102–5, 121, 123, 198; early career of, 33–34, 41; kinship of, 27–28, 103; and Louis the Pious, 141; and *placitum* formulas, 108–13, 122, 142, 152–53, 163–64, 194–95; range of judicial activity

of, 105–8; and settlement, 113–21, 123, 194; and Tassilo III, 104; titles of, 108, 120–22
Arnulf (emperor), 188n. 9
Atto (bishop of Freising), 20, 73, 106, 140, 144, 171, 185; as Abbot of Schlehdorf, 43–44, 86; and the Agilolfings, 74–75, 92, 95; and Arn of Salzburg, 113–20; and the Carolingians, 69–71, 78–79, 94, 100, 193; kinship of, 43, 66; and property gifts, 76–83, 86–88, 92–93, 97–100; and settlement, 127–29, 132–33, 135–38
Audulf (count and prefect of the Bavarians), 96–97, 106n. 22, 107n. 24, 108, 120n. 79, 141
Authority, central: Agilolfing, 46, 54–55, 65–66, 99–100, 200; in anthropology, 5–6; Carolingian, in Bavaria, 17, 69–72, 75, 98–100, 121–23, 182–85, 193–99; and charters, 19; and conquest, 6–7; in the early medieval East, 10–11, 205–6; in the early medieval West, 8–10, 200–202, 204; and *The Song of Count Timo*, 4–5, 208
Authority figures, 74–75, 103, 141, 144, 169–70, 182, 193–95; defined, 105. *See also* Arn; *Missi*
Avars, 37, 69

Barschalks, 14n. 32, 180, 181n. 51
Baturic (bishop of Regensburg), 144, 147, 159
Bavaria: and the early medieval East, 205–6; and the early medieval West, 200–204; in the early Middle Ages, 11–17. *See also* Tassilo III; *individual Carolingian rulers*
Bavarian law. *See* Law of the Bavarians
Bishops: as authority figures, 141–42, 144, 163, 176–79; in disputes, 32, 55, 65–66, 176–79, 191–93, 195–98, 200–201; interests of, 45, 66, 74–75, 99–100, 187, 193–94, 205; power of, 184–85. *See also individual bishops*

Judges, 29, 39n. 21, 54, 71n. 10, 103, 121, 122n. 87, 130n. 12, 203n. 31

Judicial assemblies, 4–5, 71–74, 124, 141–42, 144, 152–55, 194–99, 208; and Arn of Salzburg, 105–8, 194–95; composition of, 95–97, 100, 193; defined, 8; and the "feudal revolution," 9–10; as resources, 75, 92, 100, 102, 193–94. *See also* Courts; Settlement

Judicial combat, 3–4, 130n. 12, 206–9

Kindred councils, 32–34, 52–53, 65, 69–70, 99–100, 191–93, 200

Kindreds: in the Agilolfing period, 30–35, 52–55, 64–65, 98n. 79, 191–92; in the Carolingian period, 68–71, 75, 86–101, 147–48, 156–59, 162–63, 170–71, 176–78, 192–94, 198, 205. *See also* Aristocracy, Bavarian

Kremsmünster monastery, 94–95

Law of the Bavarians, 13, 16, 21, 148n. 28, 160n. 65, 176n. 31; and feud, 40, 179–80; and judicial assemblies, 71n. 10; and judicial combat, 207–8; and modern scholarship, 24–25; and oaths, 118n. 75, 132; and property divisions, 53, 78n. 14; and theft, 130, 207–8. *See also* Norms

Law codes. *See* Law of the Bavarians; Norms

Leo III (pope), 16, 104–5

Libellus Virgilii, 47n. 41, 85, 98n. 79

Liutpoldings, 17

Liutpirg (duchess), 68, 114–15

Lombardy. *See* Italy

Lothar (emperor), 16–17, 141, 166. *See also* Carolingian: judicial institutions of

Louis II (king of the Lombards), 189

Louis the Child (king of the East Franks), 17

Louis the German (king of the East Franks), 1–5, 16–17, 152, 208; and Bavaria, 141, 166–67, 182, 184, 198; in disputes, 188–89. *See also* Carolingians: judicial institutions of

Louis the Pious (emperor), 140–42, 166, 195; and Bavaria, 16–17, 141, 197–99. *See also* Carolingians: judicial institutions of; Fisc

Mallus. See Judicial assemblies

Mediation. *See* Settlement

Merovingians, 12–13

Missi, 69–72, 87–88, 103, 120, 134, 198, 206; defined, 8; identity of, 103; under Louis the German, 168, 170; under Louis the

Pious, 141–42, 144–52, 163, 195–96; and property gifts, 76–81, 92–95, 100, 193

Missatica, 104–5, 122, 199

Mohingara *genealogia*, 28, 81–82, 98. *See also Genealogiae*

Mondsee monastery, 85n. 34. *See also* Charters

Murder, 181, 207

Naming patterns. *See* Aristocracy, Bavarian

Negotiation. *See* Settlement

Norms, 5–10, 98, 160, 201–2, 203n. 31, 205; *Pactus legis Salicae*, 160n. 65; and property, 45–52, 75–76, 80–81, 84, 87, 98, 189, 193, 197–98; Ripuarian Law, 39n. 21. *See also* Canon law; Capitularies; Law of the Bavarians; Property gifts; Synods

Notaries. *See* Scribes

Notitia Arnonis/Breves Notitiae, 24, 32–33, 47–51, 83–85

Oaths, 130n. 12, 132, 188, 207–8

Oberalm, 48; *genealogia* from, 48–50, 84

Odilo (duke of the Bavarians), 14, 46–50, 84, 92, 149

Ordeals, 3–4, 206–7, 209

Otting monastery, 51, 84

Ottonians. *See* Germany

Passau, see of, 14. *See also* Charters; Reginharius

Pigs, 136–38

Pilitrud (duchess), 61–63

Pippin III (king of the Franks), 14–16, 49, 78–79, 147

Placita, 108–12, 122–23, 142, 152–54, 163, 168–69, 184, 188–90, 194–99, 208. *See also* Arn; Judicial assemblies

Property gifts: in the Agilolfing period, 32, 40–46, 50, 66, 191; in the Carolingian period, 74–76, 80–81, 85, 90–92, 97–101, 143, 162, 186–87, 193–94. *See also* Canon law; Norms

Prosopography, 26–29, 35, 205. *See also* Aristocracy, Bavarian

Publicity, 118–19, 136, 138, 154, 195, 202

Regenharius (bishop of Passau), 143–44, 155–56

Regensburg, see of, 14. *See also*, Charters; *individual bishops*

Representation. *See* Settlement: narratives of

Ritual and settlement, 118–19, 124, 135–36, 138, 161, 183–84, 195